D0897837

Autobiographical Quests

Augustine, Montaigne,
Rousseau, and Wordsworth

Autobiographical Quests
Augustine, Montaigne, Rousseau, and Wordsworth

Elizabeth de Mijolla

University Press of Virginia

Charlottesville and London

The University Press of Virginia
Copyright © 1994 by the Rector and Visitors
of the University of Virginia
First published 1994

Library of Congress Cataloging-in-Publication Data
De Mijolla, Elizabeth.
    Autobiographical quests : Augustine, Montaigne,
Rousseau, and Wordsworth / Elizabeth de Mijolla.
        p.   cm.
    Includes bibliographical references (p.   ) and index.
    ISBN 0-8139-1468-X
    1. Authors—Biography—History and criticism.
2. Autobiography.   3. Mimesis in literature.
4. Memory in literature.   5. Augustine, Saint, Bishop of
Hippo.   Confessions.   6. Montaigne, Michel de, 1533–
1592.   Essais.   7. Rousseau, Jean Jacques, 1712–1778.
Confessions.   8. Wordsworth, William, 1770–1850.
Prelude.   I. Title.
    PN452.D38   1994
    909'.93592—dc 20   93-28201
                                                            CIP

Printed in the United States of America

For my

Mother and Father

CONTENTS

ACKNOWLEDGMENTS

SOMEWHERE BETWEEN university studies and journal entries, this book began. And like the autobiographies it analyzes, it invites revision again and again. Given these uncertain beginnings and this retreating end, the thanks I offer will never suffice, yet I wish to start before my debts multiply.

For financial assistance, I am grateful to Columbia University, particularly for the George W. Ellis, Reid Hall, and President's Fellowships it administers. And to the Lurcy Foundation, for the fellowship that brought me to France, I owe special thanks.

To those who have read and responded to parts or all of the manuscript, combining kindness with critical acumen, I offer my heartfelt thanks. Carole Slade has helped with the theory of autobiography, Kay Fleming with the logic of Augustine, Gita May with the resonance of Montaigne and Rousseau, and Karl Kroeber and Carl Woodring with the complexities of Wordsworth. Reading all, generously and discerningly, John D. Rosenberg has fine-tuned many a false chord in my thought and prose. And Kay Fleming, helping in the end as in the beginning, merits more praise for late revision. Given such wise advice, if I persist in infelicities, they are of my own doing.

Toward my family my debt is different and deep. With infinite patience and practical assistance, they have balanced my hours of writing with other ways of living, sustaining me best by never reading this book. To my mother, my father, my brother, and especially my husband, Hubert, goes my unending gratitude for striking the fine equilibrium through the years of writing in Puygarreau and this year of rewriting in Matour.

Autobiographical Quests

Augustine, Montaigne,
Rousseau, and Wordsworth

INTRODUCTION

Mᴏʀᴇ ᴏʀ ʟᴇss consciously, autobiographers compromise between mimesis and memory. Mimesis, traditionally, is orderly, given to the historical and the communicable. Memory is achronological, afigural, and individually disorderly.[1] Metaphor offers the equations, approximations, and substitutions that carry mimesis to representation and memory to expression. For, inevitably, living becomes metaphoric in writing.[2] But how reliably does memory yield a history or self become a story? If memory is alternately clear and cloudy and changing, laced with lacunae and unconscious conflicts, by what linguistic magic does such confusing multiplicity yield mimetic history? Indubitably, metaphor negotiates between mimesis, rigorously communal, and individual memory, relentlessly psychological. But, does, then, the self become conventional in the inherited figures of the communal language, which convincing readers may convince autobiographers? Does the self, creating for others, become other?

Tradition defines and—unless tested "on the pulses"—dulls perception. Even in autobiography, the genre of assumed self-creativity, traditional mimesis dominates individual memory. Vast worldviews (classical, Renaissance, Romantic, modern) vary, and with them vary accepted autobiographical forms and figures that structure the universe and solve the self[3]—passing over in silence what does not suit. Autobiographers may comply, compromise, or speak in challenge to each system by arguing new forms for the amorphous universe, new figures for the ambiguous self. Shunning accepted symbolism for contrary emotion, figural similarities for singular discontinuities, they may revise tradition to individual talent.[4] But never finally. For always mimesis vies with memory, convention with exception, in this genre of tradition and transgression. For time allows little stillness of spirit, though wrestled from history and written on paper, and each autobiographer unless complacent is soon curious. Hence even when life story is completed autobiography, choices between tradition and transgression return, but newly, more individually, between past composition and new revision, between staunch standing by the written identity and questioning self, life, and language again.

Between mimesis and memory, tradition and the individual, compromise often begins with a choice of hero—pilgrim, quester, artist, other—as autobiographical alter ego. The Scriptures offer many admirable figures, most in the tradition of *Imitatio Christi,* or Paul, or every sinner come to see, be cleansed, and called to tell. Unified in the scriptural figural tradition, these become sectarian in autobiographical interpretation. Augustine is the original master of accommodation—scriptural figure to spiritual measure, prodigal son to self, sinner to seer—in confessional become autobiographical examination. Bunyan offers later Protestant versions—allegorical and autobiographical—of the pilgrim in every person seeking God.[5] From the common resource of the Scriptures, Augustine and Bunyan derive their intricate, different, and decisive systems for judging life in this world; even what is irrational, immoral, or evil, which assuredly, if inexplicably, is part of divine design. Although they map the straight and narrow path personally—their figures and forms varying, Augustine's sinner turning with conversion, Bunyan's pilgrim progressing—theirs is ever the same arrival: eternal life is their promise, God's omnipotence their guarantee.

So great is the individual comfort in communal order that autobiographers turn conventional figures to new uses, whether wisely or abusively, often unwittingly. Christian figures and forms, fulfilling to the faithful, are filled at will by those lacking faith. But will may be subject to power or perplexity, as autobiography may present the imposition or the pursuit of self. Ardent in trusting to eternity, autobiographers may discover a self in chosen Christian figures and sanctioned Christian forms, as does Augustine in his *Confessions,* Bunyan in his *Grace Abounding* and *Pilgrim's Progress,* and later Cardinal Newman, following first the Protestant then the Catholic, in his *Apologia pro vita sua.*[6] Dutiful, many others—the writers through centuries of Memoirs of sin, Confessions of saving grace—may easily define a self by conformity.[7] Secular and adaptable, others may compromise convincingly if they trust their sense of honesty, as does Franklin climbing virtuously to prosperity in his *Autobiography,* Carlyle in *Sartor Resartus* rehearsing for historical prophecy, and Tennyson in *In Memoriam* searching the way of self in society. Or—borrowing the figures without the feelings, the forms without the foundations—others may betray only their consummate artistry or biting irony, as Pater, "The Child in the House," relishes aesthetically sacred ceremony, or Gosse, the irreverent Son, debunks Father's religious fundamentalism.

Introduction

Varying motives and methods, all are revelatory, but not all subject to autobiographers' questioning. And even when questioning their feelings, ardent, compromising, or contrary, their figures formed by belief, use, or contrivance, even then autobiographers may—confusing intention with execution—confound their individual wills with their written identities, unsure of which are their "true" selves.

Or eschewing conversions and the ardor of pilgrims, merely defining a life view from autobiographical high ground, an assured present prospect over past experience, even thus secularists may subscribe to Christian constructs. Writing from a perceptive present deemed fit for telling early confusion from later true direction, autobiographers assuming hindsight free from human uncertainty appropriate from Christian mimesis a God-like objectivity, an omniscience to justify temporality and assess life rightly, an omnipresence to render reality rationally and impartially.[8] Merely choosing a profession, working to progress, and writing assured autobiography of intellectual wandering to inevitable wisdom—Gibbon plotting the years of Roman empire to extinction, Mill laboring through tracts of logic to political science, Darwin unraveling creation, beetle by beetle, seed by seed, into evolution—even thus radical thinkers write conventional *Memoirs* and *Autobiography,* their sense of self, calling, and success grounded in Christian assumptions.[9]

What is the legacy of these traditionalists, both the ardent and the inadvertent? Genre expectations and moral imperatives that together demand of life an education; of memory, storehouse breadth; of the passing years, a comprehensive and coherent account.[10] And habitual literary-critical practices that in the dash to identify tradition demand autobiographical design, readily finding the pilgrim in every person, every one on an ineluctable progress, or picking out the convert in every sinner who turns in response to an inaudible, but construable, "take it and read."[11] Never mind the autobiography or its author's individuality; order prevails, formlessness is denied, and a figural pattern for life, time and again, is inscribed.[12] Whether the Bunyan figure of arduous progress or the Augustinian figure of sin and conversion, or the philosopher construing Edenic innocence, the artist cultivating original creativity—for any and all the written chronological line advances the autobiographer either steadily through spiritual traps and riches or circularly from birth to misled maturity to spiritual rebirth. With either form, linear or circular, the traditional autobiographer, spiritual or secular, ends endowed with the wisdom to survey from the high and wise altitude of age all the multifarious past, now gathered readily in the habitual harvest of hindsight, the years ranged like vintages, the vines carefully tended to give again. Thus the heirs to Christian order plot their lives so that conversion embraces tradition or pilgrimage promises moral progress, general wisdom, or simple happiness; thus their harmonious enlightenment coincides with their autobiographic closure.[13]

Yet enlightenment is precipitant, for religious figures adapted to secular purposes have decided temporal and moral limits. The lucid perspective on the past is patterned on God's all-seeing vision from eternity,[14] but, for unbelievers, with what validity? One need merely switch mythologies, Christian to classical, to construe the pseudoeternal autobiographical view as empty of almighty sense. When God's eternal vision is stolen into time, the self in prospect is static, good or evil, blessed or damned, judged once and finally. With God absent and gods in power, the changeless self is shadelike, fated to years of longing. The immortality of the Christian is in eternity, that of the pagan in ahistory (where godly generations strive through ages, where mortals come and go in Hades with a song, a glance, a dream). The lesson for autobiography is in the frame to personal history. Unseating the deities, undoing eternity, thus autobiographers enter fully into history, subject to the secular in Renaissance, Romantic, modern, the many temporal and moral orders. Refusing religious symbols, their original validity with their unaccepted theology, thus autobiographers braving secularism brave the mutability not only in history but also in memory.

What they find is autobiographical meaning in time, each moment potentially altered by another moment, another mood, the individual, young, mature, or old. What they recognize as autobiographical meaning is a judgment given in a context and grounded in conviction, convention, or continuing invention. Yet when sequential links between past moments give way to present separated memories, when the logic of the past creating mind becomes that of the present re-creating mind, perhaps forging false links, perhaps belying past logic, readily, marvels and muddles emerge. Irresistibly, marvels and muddles entice an autobiographer as much to reviving as to recollecting a memory, as much to imagining as to explaining a sequence, as much to creating as to interpreting a life story.[15] Mnemonic and imagined metaphors meld and abound as fact and fiction merge, hardly settling simply or steadily into ruling figures of autobiographical mimesis (prodigal son, pilgrim, original innocent, earnest artist) traditionally held to rigid forms of autobiographical learning (conversion, progression, or exploration come full circle to early individual essence).[16]

Introduction

The original mocker of singular and static autobiographical identity—mocking the private person cut to public pattern, the individual dovetailed into tradition—is Montaigne. The pilgrim? He is a seeker after preconceived verities that he will ratify or justify; either way, the goal hallowed and hardy, why bother? Similarly well-spared are the efforts of the secular quester, unless he relish the chase as intellectual and autobiographical exercise. And the philosopher? Endorsing the slightest system, he is a Socrates wrongheadedly spouting answers instead of questions. The artist? His portrait will never be like unless he paint passing, repeatedly beginning his portrait in the changing present. Any other figure? If he is sure and singular, he is a poseur. If he is strange and protean, he is the self. For solo, steady, and extensively explanatory, a figure turning sequence into artful history seldom is convincing. What of details and digressions, a rush of discoveries that are disorderly or depths that escape admirable clarity? What, simply, of change? A chosen figure may suit the self sublimely one day, soberly the next, the next not at all. The lesson for autobiography? What is static, as truth, is fleeting, for as figures and forms stay in writing, the self slips away

The only valid autobiographical activity is questioning, Montaigne answers in his radically revisionary *Essays*. Without sure identity, without essential integrity, Montaigne knows no stable stance from which to write traditional mimetic history.[17] He merely tries on traditional figures: Christian figures with due humility, classical heros for stature, various historians, philosophers, and poets for diversity in speaking his philosophy. Tested, quoted, and appropriated, all become alternate, conflictual, and expendable identities, each a mask to Montaigne's face stealing the stage where many selves play to pride or the public, their script written in alternate, conflictual, and expendable "essays." Changing selves, Montaigne changes figures; changing figures, he changes forms, histories, philosophies, cosmologies.

Writing while metamorphosing, Montaigne is an autobiographer of the present, mastering multiplicity, but only momentarily. His movement in time is demonstrated, not by literary patterns, but by pages in his manuscripts. His metamorphoses are recorded in his continually written pages that, concentrated, show identity and, contrasted, show history. Examining self, life, and writing in amplitude and minuscule detail, in this moment and metamorphosed in the next, Montaigne's revisionary writings (not journals addressing a day, not letters to a single addressee, but essays at self-discovery) are—when essence rules semantics—autobiography. Only allowing autobiography to be identified by its themes—

the self, its life, its writing—will allow diversity in this genre dedicated to individuality. Only a descriptive, nonprescriptive approach to the genre will allow tradition (the first-person retrospective, far-from-fictive, necessarily narrative autobiography)—and transgression.

But beyond Montaigne, autobiographers of the present are rare who dare the endlessly revisionary endeavor, revelatory of their fervid conviction that the self is myriad, moving in the moment, and alarmingly free. Far more common are autobiographers seeking to evade the unruly present in a past seemingly orderly, distant, and decided where communal mimesis definitively translates individual memory. Yet how does order hold when, as surely as the present becomes the past, metamorphosing moments become metamorphosing memories? And how is distance possible when the autobiographical past is recalled only in the present? Traditional autobiographers may trust to eternity or mimic its certainty, but heirs to Montaigne's willed disorder know the unruly past is kin to the unruly present in all the freedom of always deciding and, freer still, always imagining again. No other autobiographer of Montaigne's stature writes the present, but later revisionary autobiographers explore later variations of his multifaceted moment, which resurfaces in Romantic memory, Victorian fragmentation, modern stream-of-consciousness, contemporary experimentation—not one of which steadies easily into mimesis.

Incessantly questioning, the Romantics are the first to ignite decisively the clash between communal mimesis and idiosyncratic memory. Fascinated by pagan myths and Christian metaphors, they repeatedly test accepted patterns on perpetually unsteady pulses. Autobiographers such as Rousseau, such as Wordsworth and Stendhal and De Quincey, set mimesis and memory at strife in metaphors of opposition. They write against logical sequence, the orderly chronology of mimesis, at most bending in compromise to circular metaphors for their narrative life paths in story, essay, prose and verse history. They mine mimesis with memory by looking back, down, under, in Romantic metaphors of darkness, depth, and deviation for memory indelible within. Doubling and digressing, they split into social and solitary selves, fragmenting further as imagination becomes nostalgia, deviation the depths of the unconscious.[18] Even while they detail their lives in accepted literary designs, they deconstruct their work with inapt or contradictory or revolutionary words. Even while they write of harmony and organicism in metaphors of unity, while they soar in dream visions and imaginative other lands, they write their metaphors in prose fragments and reworkings of verse.

At most they master a tenuous compromise, they in whose works the imagination takes flight and the unconscious goes underground.

Seeking not Divinity but metaphors for individuality, secular Romantics follow scriptural paths to personal ends. In his *Confessions,* Rousseau patterns his individual happiness on paradise, his own restlessness on a fall, yet hardly simply, for he falls repeatedly while protesting his innocence continually. De Quincey, echoing Rousseau's title in his *Confessions of an English Opium Eater,* goes further, finding paradise in opium-induced dreams and exile in the world of men.[19] Seeking in *The Prelude* shrines for past time, Wordsworth dedicates his spirit to more than his own creativity, to God, Nature, his society, his century. And Stendhal, writing his own *Souvenirs d'égotisme,* rues Napoleon and lost love as promises, unheld, of a better life.[20] Thus Romantic autobiographers alter scriptural figures and sanctioned forms to tell secular life stories. Necessarily, their figures suffer some temporal trimming when the turn in conversion is not to God, the goal of pilgrimage not in eternity but history. Necessarily, their forms take some moral manipulating when faith is not in the authoritative Word but in autobiographical words, not in the workings of divine inspiration but in those of human imagination. Thus trimmed, thus managed, tradition newly serves the individual; newly, mimesis is made to suit memory.

Challenging realist mimesis with memory, investing traditional mythology with idiosyncrasy, innovative autobiographers inevitably feel fissures gape between the compelling extremes of living and language. Language, the metaphor maker for memory and mimesis, is ever the autobiographical troublemaker. Serving whichever master in whatever autobiographical pact, language halfheartedly serves the writer, halfheartedly the reader. And often it serves least well autobiographers as their own readers, they who know best where the schism opens between living and language. Language is the mediator in experience shared between individuals: for traditionalists who trust in community and communication, the faithful true to God's Word, poets creating classical beauty, autobiographers unworried by ambiguity, any writer sworn to the unequivocal signifier. Or language is the distorter in life: for doubters of all degrees, those to whom words seem either limited and mean-spirited beside the exuberance of lived experience or dangerously creative of essential beauty, beguiling but "sans Merci."[21]

Distrusting language much, admiring imagination more, skeptical autobiographers question autobiography hard. When the presentness of their living passes into the successiveness of language—their far-ranging spirits submitting to syntax, their multifarious sensual, emotional, intellectual experience squeezing into the narrow written line—does the rush and excess of experience threatening dispersion as each autobiographer scratches hastily along the page . . . disperse? Does the inner *jouissance* of experience and memory succumb to the judgment of ethics and aesthetics? Does experience yield to knowledge, reverie to record? When the oddity of moment, memory, reverie is cut, colored, contoured in the imaginatively crafted tale, does the sincerity of personal truth withstand the cunning artifice or end overwrought in aesthetic truth?

If autobiographers privilege traditional myth over transgressional moments, they risk the rigidity in mimesis. The meaning that a moment, a memory, a reverie gleans, explicitly or allusively, from sensation, emotion, remembered rationalizations or various associations—such meaning, which in life is fleeting, in mimesis is fixed. Firmly in inner logic or outer language—be it faith or folly—autobiographers given to myth lodge a determined meaning for moment, memory, or reverie, there explained, there no longer questioned. There further manipulated. For merely by entering into the plot of story or the plan of history, each experience is colored, interpreted, and completed to meet the demands of the ruling figure in the chosen form. Context grants shading and convention gives meaning as story and history call for continuation, for other memories and other moments, completing them with their plotted and planned complements. What does not fit is imaginatively recontoured or discarded.[22] Autobiographical meanings thus construed may hold firmly in immovable harmony as long as—with whirling circular reasoning— the autobiographical plot or plan is unrepudiated, the language of story or history unrevised.

Yet in a traditional autobiographical tale (of conversion, pilgrimage, any voyage to wisdom) the fit of moment, memory, or reverie may slip, loosing unruliness in the structure of narrative. The exceptional moment may exceed its place in the tale, sadly or strangely, as Rousseau's *Confessions* experience of the worst wins over his touted innocence, or Wordsworth's *Prelude* revelation sputters lighting the language of poetry's praise. Or, simply, the exceptional moment, irrelevant or outrageous, finds no apt place in the chosen tale of pilgrim, artist, eager philosopher, as De Quincey's "Pleasures of Opium" exceed his "Pains," his splendid recounted dreams undermining his *Confessions* tale of freedom from opium. Or, extremely, the moment is wholly ineffable, so profoundly emotional, sensual, personal that the autobiographer stops his tale to tell at length what he cannot show in language—as Stendhal in *Souvenirs d'égotisme* recalls but will not write his greatest passion—his explanation filling in for description, his theory for imaginative re-creation.[23] Thus the truth of the moment disrupts the truth of the tale; thus memory deconstructs mimesis.[24]

Where, then, falls the autobiographical compromise? When a youthful quester (after philosophical innocence or poetic sublimity, or any spiritual riches) falters, when from conversion he falls to hesitations, from progression to digressions, as before him paths splinter, leading not back to youthful paradise but on to worldliness, what, then, of the youthful quester as autobiographical figure? When an autobiographer, become an older dreamer or an aged conservative, no longer has the energy to go out and see, how will the same youthful questing-for-spiritual-riches figure express his disillusion and exhaustion, illuminate the dark as well as the earlier revelation, even as years dim the light of imagination? Will such an autobiographer—as in life, so in language—metamorphose into new autobiographical figures undertaking new autobiographical forms? If not, his early figure persistently questing obscures his mature movements, or hides his manifest digressions, or denies outright his metamorphoses. If he allows change—as in life, so in language—his written metamorphoses will undercut his original mythic figure as his revisionary memory undercuts his mimetic history.

Mimetic history and memory only accord gracefully when both are judged pseudoeternal in the timeless space of figure, form, story, autobiographical history—where generations meet to speak and share, where often the meaning is transmuted Christian, where often the original model is scriptural symbol. Yet secular, skeptic, or simply idiosyncratic autobiographers may to the same timeless story bring rebellious memory. Forcing against the anxiety of influence, against the necessity of compromise, against even the clarity needed for communication, autobiographers vying with traditional mimesis may privilege each memory come again in the moment—alive with sensation, emotion, earlier mixed with later wonder, whatever power will not go glibly into words. Never mind the place in traditional timeless story, never mind the place in history, whether decided by cause and effect, theories of influence, or mere sequence; their endeavor is to give to each memory the meaning of the moment. Their sense of history is secondary, their memory revisionary, for fundamentally their freely mnemonic mode is not measured historic, not once-decided-then-tried-and-true-autobiographic.[25]

As revisionary memory reshapes traditional mimesis, autobiographers

changing in person change on paper. In the days, months, years of autobiographical writing, they deviate from chosen life designs, as details slip,
and images jostle, as figures form askew then newly in alternate designs.
Adaptation telling on every stance, thus they read, remember, and write
differently, repeatedly, between the beginning and the book—or the several books. For when life story is completed autobiography, sometimes
the autobiographer would begin again, questioning again sequence, syntax, and style, seeking still the self slipping from language, newly in
revision, newly in entire new versions of ongoing autobiographies. Montaigne undertakes (*a*), (*b*), and (*c*) editions of his *Essays,* printed in 1580,
1588, and 1595. Rousseau offers generic variations—*Confessions, Dialogues,*
and *Reveries*—of his autobiography of innocence. And Wordsworth creates three versions of his supposed *Prelude*—1799, 1805, and 1850—to his
Excursion of 1814. These are radically revisionary autobiographers, relent-
less in their efforts to write the self right. Others, revisionary kin but less
driven, let extensive efforts give way to omissions and fragments, as Stendhal leaves twenty years autobiographically unwritten between his *Vie de
Henry Brulard* and *Souvenirs d'égotisme,* as De Quincey gathers variously
his autobiographical essays into versions of *Suspiria de Profundis.*

Be it in fragments and autobiographical rearrangements, even so
memory vies well with mimesis when Renaissance, Romantic, whatever-
age autobiographers care deeply about what is reality and what is fiction,
what is personal poetry and what is artistic theory in their written lives.
Yet increasingly during the last and this century, memory and mimesis
contend less to interact more in fruitful ambiguity as ideas of true versus
false, real versus imagined, life versus art—all such absolutes—lose their
polarity to gain their acceptable modern relativity.[26] Ambiguity and
relativity, though, do not promise literary equality. While autobiographers trusting more to revisionary memory tend to written fragmentation, as Ruskin in *Praeterita,* Woolf in *Moments of Being,* and Nabokov in
Speak, Memory; autobiographers trusting more to mimesis tend to complex worlds of fictive autobiography, as throughout their oeuvre Joyce
and Lawrence tame strong memory with ancient myth, and Proust and
Woolf elongate the expressive moment to tell of timeless being. Indeed,
memory bright in fragments is often eclipsed in brilliant artistic patterns,
as mimesis merely rules differently when autobiographers pattern their
lives on harmonious—no longer Augustinian or Bunyanesque, become
mythically modern—models of clarity and finality. Thus the two strands
of autobiography persist, the revisionary and—newly mythic, fictive, or
modern eclectic—the still traditional.

Introduction

The new embraces the old, for no traditional autobiographical figures—not the scriptural, not the classical, not the modern mythic mix—allow the returning and rewriting of personal history. Not the pilgrim's progress, for that is in one direction, forward and fully, if with some difficulty. Not a conversion, for that necessitates a turn, full face to self-knowledge, but only once. And even a Proustian or Woolfian moment chisels the past into literary artifact, as Marcel tasting memory in the madeleine ends consecrating his life to eternal art, and Woolf remembering waves sounding haunts her novels with rhythmic significance. And a modern, for instance, Joycean, epiphany implies something learned definitively, however unconsciously. We are not to understand that Maria will rethink the clay, finding in her spinster's sadness the stuff for later years of gaiety. Or that Stephen will change his chosen vocation, or for that matter Molly hers. No, only autobiography underwriting traditional mimesis with revisionary memory, multiplying singular figures and animating static forms, constructing autobiographical design while deconstructing the pattern in the margins of meandering and the pages of exception—all to escape the finality of the traditional mimetic tale, person, place, and plot fixed, here to there finished—only such revisionary autobiography allows the flux of re-creation in the moment, the mood, the manuscript. Only autobiography such as Montaigne's, Rousseau's late and Wordsworth's early, and De Quincey's, Stendhal's, unintentionally Ruskin's, nonfictively Woolf's, expressly Nabokov's, and surely others to follow—in which each autobiographer, accepting flux, accepting fixity, never imposes autobiographical figures too firmly—allows such interpretive flexibility.

Indeed, tradition does define perception. With a figure comes a philosophy, which only a true iconoclast and sure visionary can recreate, wiping the windows of perception clean of accumulated meanings, sometimes outmoded, often insufficiently investigated. A figural language may offer inspiration, authorization, and confirmation to the active and devoted seeker. Or to the dutiful devotee, simple and unquestioning, the same figural language may offer cast-in-concrete conventions, such as hackneyed conversions to obvious answers and foot-weary pilgrims with out-of-date maps. Autobiographical validity is in the vitality of each autobiography. If tradition is transmuted into individual values, if mimesis is animated by memory, if the creative exchange between past and present "pulses," then the vitality is apparent. The essential autobiographical act is self-creation in the moment; the essential resource is memory, the reward self-realization in metaphor. Even when felt in the rush of the blood, an experience, more than evaluated, must be held creatively, potentially changeably, in memory. Else—the sensation subsiding, the lesson fading—an autobiographer, Christian or secular, may weaken; having seen, may awaken; and forgetting, may unwittingly, with borrowed imagery and secondhand machinery, arrive at others' answers. The human desire for order is universal, but personal memories are hardly transferable, and oddly durable, and no one is archetypically autobiographical. Finding mimesis the surface of others, feeling memory mixing deeply with creative desire, autobiographers must create their selves incessantly with their own metaphorical alchemy.

1

AUGUSTINE
Confessions

I write this book for love of your love

AUTOBIOGRAPHY BEGINS in community, emphasizing less what is singular in a life than what a life holds in common with other lives. At least, what many call the first autobiography, Augustine's *Confessions,* is such an autobiography:[1] the account of one life seen wholly in the light of Christian truth for all lives. What is singular, what is Augustine's, in the *Confessions* is his erring life into which he reads Christian meanings—and the work of this reading. What are common to Augustine and all Christians are the religious and moral principles that shape this reading, and a good many of the figures and phrases that express it. These are derived from the Bible, the Word that governs all of Augustine's words, and serve to liken the life of this one sinner to the lives of other sinners. Augustine's faith permits him to interpret the one register of truth, the personal and the changeable, in terms of the other, the truth "that belongs to us all" (12.25), that is "unchangeable" (1.4).[2] And as Augustine interprets his life by the Scriptures, so he would have others do likewise. Both practicing and preaching Christian self-interpretation, he writes the autobiography of an extraordinary man that he would also have be the biography of more ordinary men. Given such a reading, a reading in which the barriers between private and public are leveled, Augustine's *Confessions* reveal, less Augustine's particularity, than the parallels he portrays between Christian lives.

To questions about why his work is being written, what its plan and purpose are, and who its audience is to be, Augustine seeks answers not only in the Scriptures but also in his sense of a Christian community. To every question he finds answers of two sorts: an answer that reveals him alone before God and an answer that reveals him in relation to his fellow

Christians. Thus the reason for Augustine's writing the *Confessions* is twofold. Christianity teaches both humility and charity: the one virtue compels Augustine to confess to God; the other impels him to confess to all believers and to all who, erring yet seeking truth, might yet become believers.[3] How and to what purpose Augustine confesses is also subject to twofold reasoning. To God the Omniscient, Augustine reveals nothing in his *Confessions* but his ongoing praise for His mercy. It is to men, fallen spirits needing worldly sense, that Augustine reveals all the details of his life, all plotted within time to illustrate God's timeless grace: "I need not tell all this to you, my God, but in your presence I tell it to my own kind, to those other men, however few, who may perhaps pick up this book. And I tell it so that I and all who read my words may realize the depths from which we are to cry to you" (2.3). Intention is a suspect concept these days, but Augustine has little trouble with it. He is insistent, here and elsewhere in the *Confessions,* about the aim of his work. The words of his *Confessions* are addressed to God, but their appeal is addressed to men: "When they hear what I have to tell, all who adore you will exclaim, 'Blessed be the Lord in Heaven and on earth. Great and wonderful is his name'" (8.1).

"All who read [Augustine's] words" and "all who adore [God]" are not identical audiences, but Augustine would have them be. The desire dictates, in large part, the form his *Confessions* take. It is a form known to all his readers and practiced by many, a form that at once expresses his personal devotion to God and publicly pronounces it. Augustine writes his *Confessions* as a prayer that God is to hear and men are to overhear. To God, Augustine makes his "confession . . . in [his] heart" (10.1), "with the voice of [his] soul and in [his] thoughts which cry aloud to [Him]. [His] ear can hear them" (10.2). This unity of thought and expression, wholehearted and wholly effective, is the essence of Augustine's confession to God. But such sincerity does not preclude sophistication in the writing of this same confession for "the many who will read it" (10.1). Nor is it compromised by the circuitousness of Augustine's efforts to make of his ardent confession a rhetorical prayer that artfully convinces men, without confronting them, to praise the Lord.[4]

Augustine would "fire . . . the hearts of [his] readers with love of [God]" (11.1), but his appeal is never simplistically to the hearts or to the minds of his readers, his methods are never facilely emotional or narrowly intellectual. Augustine's study of his own emotions is too intellectual, his enjoyment of his own intellect too emotional to allow such simplism in an appeal to an audience he respects. Synthesis is instead the course he takes, and a most complex structure it gives to his work.

Quite aside from the not easily evident relationship of books 1–9 to books 10–13 of the *Confessions,* the much-debated relationship of the narrative books to the more overtly dogmatic books, the structure of the narrative section alone is intricate. It is there that Augustine, denouncing with equal ardor the wrongdoing and the wrong thinking of his youth and early manhood, embarks on an exposition of his Christian principles that is not the less dogmatic for being couched in a narrative. For the denunciation of his sinful acts, Augustine composes descriptions of the sins of each of his ages—infancy, boyhood, youth, maturity—which show him little reticent to reveal fully what he has come to loathe fully. Description, vivid and vehement, serves Augustine well as he articulates his abhorrence of his past acts, but his past ideas are not so readily reviled. They are wrong, very wrong according to Augustine at the time of writing, but they are to be respected as the wrong turns of a man sincerely seeking the right path—a path that perhaps some of his readers are still seeking. It is for this reason that Augustine does more than describe and denounce his early philosophizing; he also demonstrates the ways it was wrong. To this end, Augustine tests all the influences on his intellectual life—Virgil, Homer, Terence, Cicero, the Manichees, the astrologers, the Academics, the Platonists, Ambrose, Monica—against his one touchstone for the truth, the Bible. And he demonstrates, in detail, the failings of what misled him in his youth and the excellence of what guides him in his maturity. Analyzing thus the wrong and the right in the evolution of his ideas, always from the present position of his belief, Augustine imposes on his narrative an order that is at once chronological and logical. The first nine books of the *Confessions* are the narrative of a life, but their construction is that of an argument. The point argued is uniformly the same throughout the nine books—the denunciation of untruth and the annunciation of God's truth—but the means used to prove it are alternately the description of Augustine's past and the demonstration of Augustine's principles, the one method complementing the other.

Self and Scriptures, the one subject prompts thinking—and further writing—on the other. In his last books, Augustine's ostensible subjects are, in book 10, an account of his ongoing struggle against sin and, in books 11–13, a commentary on the opening chapter of Genesis. But account and commentary are only other versions of self-interpretation.

The parallels between the narrative and the theoretical books are striking. Augustine draws on his memory to write the narrative account of his finding the Lord. In book 10, his exploration of the "vast field of his memory in search of [the] Lord" (10.24) leads him to theorize about the workings of memory. Augustine assesses in his narrative the time past he spent in search of God's eternal truth. In book 11, he meditates on the opening verse of Genesis and modulates his meditation into a theory of human time, which he contrasts to God's eternity. At length, Augustine writes in his narrative about his learning to rightly interpret the Scriptures, and his life in terms of them. In book 12, continuing his scriptural exegesis, he confronts rival interpretations of Genesis and theorizes about the truth of interpretations, which he gauges more by their sincerity than by their success. And what is the "plot" of the *Confessions* but that of Augustine's escape from ignorant "darkness" into the "daylight" of faith? In book 13, fittingly, then, Augustine's principal text is "Let there be light and the light began," for light metaphorically manifests faith to Augustine, and thus he closes his *Confessions* by silencing his too fallible, too human intellect to "let [his] faith speak for [him]" (13.12). These parallels between Augustine's self-analysis and his scriptural analysis reveal that the issues—memory, time, interpretation, faith—that inform and shape Augustine's narrative books continue consistently into his theoretical books.

But the issues are radically reworked. In his last books, Augustine continues his discovery of self in another register, one no longer concrete and individual, grounded in the day-to-day living of his actual years gone by, but abstract and communal, governed by the desire to understand the passing of years in a lifetime and the pronouncements men make on them. The movement Augustine effects is from a meditation on his memories to a meditation on the human methods of registering, remembering, interpreting, and writing memories. And he makes of it—though he switches form and style abruptly between the narrative and the theoretical books—a logical sequence in the following out of his subject, not the start of a new and separate subject, by once again, as always, using the Scriptures to resolve the relations between the lesser and the greater aspects of his subject.[5] Nearing the end of his narrative, Augustine writes that he "must hurry on to tell of greater things" (9.4). The "greater things" of these last books are the psychological, metaphysical, and hermeneutical theories Augustine forms there and the exegesis of "[God's] law" that governs their formation. In comparison to Augustine's theories on memory, time, interpretation, faith—theories that are drawn from the

Scriptures that speak to all human lives—Augustine's practicing them in his own life narrative is the lesser thing.

Such is Augustine's assessment of the lesser and the greater in his *Confessions,* but he has his doubts about his readers readily accepting his opinion.[6] In one of the rare passages of ill will in the *Confessions,* Augustine touches on just these doubts: "Why, then, does it matter to me whether men should hear what I have to confess, as though it were they who were to cure all the evil that is in me? They are an inquisitive race, always anxious to pry into other men's lives, but never ready to correct their own. Why do they wish to hear from me what sort of man I am, though they will not listen to you when you tell them what they are?" (10.3). To Augustine's mind, men are indeed an inquisitive, prying race if they find his account of his past and present sins the veritable subject of his work and the account of the values by which he judges his sins ill-advised, ill-integrated, or irrelevant. If men are to "listen to [God] when [He tells] them what they are," if they are "to correct their own [lives]," they must listen to and learn from the Scriptures. In the last books of his *Confessions,* Augustine instructs men in how they are to register their lives in time, remember them, and interpret them, all in the light of the Scriptures, and, the lessons well-learned, go on to "ask [truth] of [God], seek it in [Him] . . . knock at [His] door" (13.38). These last books contribute, and extensively, to Augustine's desire to make his readers "realize the depths from which [they] are to cry to [God]" (2.3). They contain so many lessons in self-interpretation derived from the Scriptures in order to direct men back to the Scriptures.

In Augustine's belief, the "plain language and simple style [of the Scriptures] make [them] accessible to everyone, and yet [they absorb] the attention of the learned" (6.5). Such an assertion seems a given after centuries of scriptural readings, simple and abstruse. But it is one of the fundamental and quite early revelations Augustine reached in his long approach to the Christian faith, and one that he takes pains to reiterate: "How wonderful are your Scriptures! How profound! We see their surface and it attracts us like children. And yet, O my God, their depth is stupendous. We shudder to peer deep into them, for they inspire in us both the awe of reverence and the thrill of love" (12.14). Whether the image for the layers of meaning imbedded in the Bible is one of profundity, as here, or one of hidden mysteries requiring penetration, as in an earlier book (11.2), always for Augustine the Scriptures are adaptable and inexhaustible, the repository of all truths.[7]

Augustine's admiration for the mode of accommodation found in the Scriptures argues for his use of this mode in the *Confessions*.[8] His decision to divide his work into different levels of discourse—lesser and "greater things," narrative and theories—argues for his conscious effort to construct multiple levels of truth in the *Confessions*. One sees from his narrative that Augustine never could resist assessing his interlocutors' intellects, and one sees from his repeated declarations of his intention that he was ever attentive to the reception of his *Confessions*. There may well be something of accommodation to different types—Augustine might well say different levels—of readers in the basically bipartite structure of the *Confessions*.

In the context of a passage of praise for the Scriptures, Augustine implies as much: "For my part I declare resolutely and with all my heart that if I were called upon to write a book which was to be vested with the highest authority, I should prefer to write it in such a way that a reader could find re-echoed in my words whatever truths he was able to apprehend. I would rather write in this way than impose a single true meaning so explicitly that it would exclude all others, even though they contained no falsehood that could give me offence" (12.31). Augustine's version of accommodation is quasi-modern in its resemblance to reader-reception theory. The theory of accommodation itself is an elitist theory, one that separates those who are qualified to interpret God's Word from those who are not, but it is also a theory that liberates men to look for themselves, however they are able, in the Word given them. Augustine's version of accommodation is elitist, but not emphatically so, and it is liberal—extremely so. It downplays the author's privileged position as possessor of his truths and sees the text, not as the place for the imposition of these truths on passive readers, but as the meeting ground for inquiring minds.[9] What prevents Augustine's theory from being truly modern—its reservation that, nevertheless, truths exist and have authority and are not lost in the echoes of multiple meanings—is what allows Augustine's adherence to it. But not a word here, or elsewhere in the *Confessions,* suggests that study alone determines truths; rather—and the point is emphasized throughout the *Confessions*—sincerity too is necessary for understanding Christian truths. Accommodation to a range of readers may explain Augustine's division of the *Confessions* into his story of a self and his study of the self; into easier and more erudite matters, lesser and greater things. One or the other section may more readily find echoes in the minds of Augustine's readers. But Augustine would not have his meanings sound without belief in the always greater truths of the Scriptures.

To the Scriptures Augustine refers his readers, not as to a body of law that admits no inquiry, but as to the Book that, indeed, best stimulates inquiry. Hence the readings of the Scriptures that Augustine urges his readers to undertake are to his mind never restrictive readings—nor impersonal readings: "There is only one God, who caused Moses to write the Holy Scriptures in the way best suited to the minds of great numbers of men who would see all truths in them, though not the same truths in each case" (12.31). It is impossible to reconcile Augustine the indefatigable polemicist with such permissiveness, but he is here, and often, silent in the *Confessions,* leaving Augustine the ardent self-analyst free to speak. What better mirror for Christian self-analysis than the surface and the depths of the Scriptures, different for every seeker? They are the mirror God set before Augustine's eyes at the moment he read his way to conversion. They are the mirror to which Augustine refers his readers for self-scrutiny, the requisite for all Christian inquiry.

The closing words of the *Confessions,* those that direct the reader to "ask [truth] of [God], seek it in [Him] . . . knock at [His] door" (13.38), are an explicit invitation to such inquiry. Because it arrives at this closing that is an opening for others' work, the autobiography Augustine writes is the odd hybrid it is: an autobiography that he would have be the biography of every Christian. Neither arrogant pride in his narrative of individualism nor the refusal of others' individualism in his theories of self-interpretation disallows his desires. Augustine's self-readings in the Scriptures are meant to inform, not to force his readers to conform. And his theories are meant to direct, not dominate, his readers' scriptural readings of self. By the parallels in self-interpretation that faith permits and Augustine illustrates, the *Confessions* tell of more than Augustine's life. By these Christian parallels, Augustine would have the *Confessions* inspire still other confessions.

This, certainly, they have done. Nearly sixteen centuries have passed since Augustine closed his *Confessions* with his call to others to find the truth of themselves in the Scriptures. Many autobiographers have responded to Augustine's call. Some have been devoutly Christian, diligent in their imitation of the *Confessions;* some only vaguely Christian, intent on borrowing the form and figures of the *Confessions* without the faith that informs them. But these are the subjects of other studies, which trace autobiographical influence and formal congruence, which legislate the generic tradition. What is important here is how Augustine, in accord with his own theories, structures his own *Confessions*. Because it is from the accord between theory and practice in the *Confessions* that Augustine's influence follows, for thus his Christian logic and love become the auto-biographical paradigm—from which many must depart.

The great storehouse of memory

Unruly memory may undo autobiographical method, but not in Augustine's theory. In book 10, Augustine acknowledges the mystery of memory: "The power of memory is prodigious, my God. It is a vast immeasurable sanctuary. Who can plumb its depths?" (10.8). Nevertheless, Augustine finds memory—in theory—a controlled phenomenon, that is subject, in particular instances, to the requests he makes of it and, in general, to reason, which rules it:

> When I use my memory, I ask it to produce whatever it is that I wish to remember. Some things it produces immediately; some are forthcoming only after a delay, as though they were being brought out from some inner hiding place; others come spilling from the memory, thrusting themselves upon us when what we want is something quite different, as much as to say "Perhaps we are what you want to remember?" These I brush aside from the picture which memory presents to me, allowing my mind to pick what it chooses, until finally that which I wish to see stands out clearly and emerges into sight from its hiding place. (10.8)

Memory and mind are in dialogue here, and in a most amiable dialogue at that, one that illustrates well how in Augustine's theory memory and mind are—strangely—separate, though the one is willingly subservient to the other.[10] To ask of memory "to produce whatever it is [the mind wishes] to remember," to let the mind "brush aside" whatever does not suit, to "pick what it chooses," until a desired recollection "stands out clearly," cooperatively: this is an enviable orderliness in remembering. An orderliness to which a post-Freudian autobiographer would not lay claim. Memory, in Augustine's theory, is a source of sure reference for the mind, not a source of revisionary thinking; it is affirmative of what is known from the past, not disruptive of the present. Given to answers, not to questions, it is most amenable to Augustine's task of writing auto-biographical, derived from scriptural, truth.

The responsiveness of memory to the mind's demands for recall has much to do with how well experiences—sensual, intellectual, and emotional—are ranged in memory from the moment of their apprehension:

In the memory everything is preserved separately, according to its category. Each is admitted through its own special entrance. For example, light, colour, and shape are admitted through the eyes; sound of all kinds through the ears; all sorts of smell through the nostrils; and every kind of taste through the mouth. The sense of touch, which is common to all parts of the body, enables us to distinguish between hard and soft, hot and cold, rough and smooth, heavy and light, and it can be applied to things which are inside the body as well as to those which are outside it. . . . The things which we sense do not enter the memory themselves, but their images are there ready to present themselves to our thoughts when we recall them. (10.8)

Categories receive and re-present experiences of the senses: the principle of order in memory is respected and apparent. For experiences that come from learning, whether from the "liberal sciences" (10.9) or from "the innumerable principles and laws of numbers and dimensions" (10.11), the process of retention and recall is different. Facts of rhetoric, of mathematics, of whatever is acquired through teaching, are in memory even before they are learned, but there they are "muddled and confused . . . lying scattered and unheeded" (10.11) until they are collected, "brought to the fore by [the] teaching" (10.10) of them. Again the principle of order in memory is respected and apparent. Emotional experiences, too—perhaps one way, perhaps another—are subject to the same principle. Either "the ideas of the emotions . . . are committed to the memory by the mind itself, as a result of its own experience of emotion, or else the memory [retains] them even though they were not entrusted to it by the mind" (10.14). Either way, they are more ideas than emotions and as such are consciously ranged in memory:

My memory also contains my feelings, not in the same way as they are present to the mind when it experiences them, but in a quite different way that is in keeping with the special powers of the memory. For even when I am unhappy I can remember times when I was cheerful, and when I am cheerful I can remember past unhappiness. I can recall past fears and yet not feel afraid, and when I remember that I once wanted something, I can do so without wishing to have it now. . . . when I say that the mind can experience four kinds of emotions—desire, joy, fear, and sorrow—I call them to mind from my memory, and if I enlarge upon this by analysing and defining each of these emotions according to the different forms which each can take, I draw upon my memory and produce from it whatever I am going to say. Yet while I remember these feelings by drawing them from my memory, they do not produce any emotional effect on me. (10.14)

The desired memories obey the "call" for them; they "produce" what is wanted and no more. Before the control of the mind the only rebellion memory seems capable of is full forgetfulness.

Thus far in book 10, memory for Augustine is methodical, verging on mechanical, and from this manner of conceiving memory, Augustine's strangest image for memory results: "We might say that the memory is a sort of stomach for the mind, and that joy or sadness are like sweet or bitter food. When this food is committed to the memory, it is as though it had passed into the stomach where it can remain but also loses its taste" (10.14). Augustine hastens to call this image absurd, but he works it all the same. He extends the parallels between memory and a stomach to the extreme of memory bringing up past emotions "as cattle bring up food from the stomach when they chew the cud" (10.14). But then he encounters a decisive difficulty: "why does [a man] not experience the pleasure of joy or the pain of sorrow in his mind, just as the animal tastes the food in its mouth?" (10.14). Rather than acknowledge that past emotions have power over the mind—an alarming proposition rendering the *Confessions* a dangerous enterprise[11]—Augustine abandons his image: "Perhaps the simile is unjustified, because the two processes are not alike in all points" (10.14).

Even in this odd image for the oddly compliant workings of emotional memory, Augustine touches upon the chief characteristics of almost all his images for memory: the characteristics of a container, and of a capaciousness within it. Augustine's other, more usual images for memory, which reveal these same characteristics, are less anatomical, more lyrical: "memory . . . is like a great field or a spacious palace, a storehouse for countless images" (10.8); it is "the vast cache" of the mind (10.8); "the wide plains . . . and . . . innumerable caverns and hollows are full beyond compute of countless things of all kinds" (10.17). Over this last metaphor of plains, caverns, and hollows in a mental landscape, Augustine rises to his highest flight in praise of the mind's power over memory and all the riches within: "My mind has the freedom of them all. I can glide from one to the other. I can probe deep into them and never find the end of them. This is the power of memory! This is the great force of life in living man, mortal though he is!" (10.17).

But there is for Augustine, as there must be for a man confessing, a descent from this soaring praise of his own "great force of life," a descent that takes Augustine down to regions in memory less admirable and more problematical. Moderns would call these regions the unconscious, but Augustine has neither the term, nor the concept, nor the inclination to know their unsettling depths. Yet even so, he confronts what he cannot admire: that down in the caverns and hollows of memory are sensual images that are unwanted by his mind awake, yet sought by his mind asleep; that these combine to make nighttime dreams unacceptable by his daytime standards; that the formation of these dreams may be investigated, even explained, and the responsibility for them disclaimed, and, all the same, he will "still [be] troubled by this kind of evil" (10.30). From Augustine's dismay at these dreams comes a series of questions that receive no answers, in which Augustine goes so far as to wonder whether he is himself in sleep as in waking:

> The power which these illusory images have over my soul and my body is so great that what is no more than a vision can influence me in sleep in a way that the reality cannot do when I am awake. Surely it cannot be that when I am asleep I am not myself, O Lord my God? And yet the moment I pass from wake to sleep, or return again from sleep to wakefulness, marks a great difference in me. During sleep where is my reason which, when I am awake, resists such suggestions and remains firm and undismayed even in face of the realities themselves? Is it sealed off when I close my eyes? Does it fall asleep with the senses of the body? (10.30)

"Surely it cannot be that . . . I am not myself?" "Where is my reason?" In sleep, the control of mind over memory receives its firmest check.

Augustine's defense against what is distressing in his dreams is a theory of dreams, alluded to in the *Confessions* but only elaborated later and elsewhere, in which he consigns dreams that have their origins in men's minds—"phantasiae" he calls them—to the lowest level of a hierarchy that has dreams of divine origin—"ostensiones"—at its height.[12] The dream mechanisms of both "phantasiae" and "ostensiones" interest Augustine, but only the visions seen in the latter sort of dream, according to Augustine, have truth and therefore value. If reason sleeps and a man is not himself in dreams of human origin, his mind and body may be stimulated, even sin simulated, but the significance of the dreams is nil. If reason sleeps and a man is not himself in dreams of divine origin, the images seen in these dreams are given by God's grace, as is their assuredly great significance. In relation to this significance, mind, memory, and all that is of human origin are quite secondary: revelation shines over reflection.

Responsibility is what is at issue in Augustine's theory of dreams— and his whole theory of memory. Christian dogma deciding the issue for Augustine, it also decides the options of his argument. Man has reason, he has free will, and because he has both he can determine the life, sinful or less so, that he leads: these are the Christian presuppositions that direct Augustine's argument. The mind must control memory; it must categorize sensual experiences, collect intellectual experiences, contain emotional experiences in order that recollection be always subject to reason, man's greatest gift from God and his principal path to God. Reason ruling recollection, every man is responsible for what use he makes of his past, in the present and in the future. If in sleep the mind must temporarily cede control over memory, best that it cede completely—not only control, but reason, responsibility, even its very identity. Abdication is better than blame. For reason absent from recollection, habit may be held responsible for insignificant and unacceptable dreams. And man, free in sleep from his free will, will wake to his reason and responsibility again.

If memory were always liberated from the mind's control, all that follows from such an idea would be anathema to Augustine: character formed unconsciously in reaction to early experiences; character formed deterministically in accord with early environments; character formed continually in relation to memories resurfacing and restructuring the mind. These are modern theories—Freudian, behaviorist, Bergsonian— all determined by memory, unreasoned and unruled, bringing emotions, events, experiences to mind, all owing their development to the eighteenth-century discovery and nineteenth-century cult of memory.[13] These are theories, were they known to him, unacceptable to Augustine. Augustine allows that memories may menace a man, habits may hold him, wrong thinking mislead him, but for all the subtlety of his psychological analyses, Augustine never allows that a man, ultimately, is denied conscious choice in determining his character.[14] This Augustine must not allow, because Christianity is a religion of choice, because the concept of choice is central to conversion and continuation in the faith.

To the meanings memories hold, Augustine extends a man's power— to his mind, a man's duty—of choice. The meanings of memories, according to Augustine, are not intrinsic and evident, nor changing and controversial: they are true or false. Memories are not to be judged by when, where, why, or how they occurred; they are not to be judged by one person's or another's assessment: they are to be judged by the truth of the Scriptures. How? Closing his theory of memory with the attempt, unsuccessful, to find God's place in memory, Augustine, addressing God, concludes:

> Whether we approach you or depart from you, you are not confined in
> any place. You are Truth, and you are everywhere present where all seek

counsel of you. You reply to all at once, though the counsel each seeks is different. The answer you give is clear, but not all hear it clearly. All ask you whatever they wish to ask, but the answer they receive is not always what they want to hear. The man who serves you best is the one who is less intent on hearing from you what he wills to hear than on shaping his will according to what he hears from you. (10.26)

This is more laudatory of God's omnipresence and omniscience than explanatory of man's learning from Him, but before the mystery of God speaking to man, Augustine moderates his methodical efforts to explain mind and memory. He contents himself with ascribing the attainment of "true" knowledge to an inner dialogue with God. When a man hears God's "answer" "clearly," and when he shapes "his will according to what he hears from [God]," he discovers the "truth": the "true meaning" of, to speak generally, any experience he would understand in the Christian light; of, to give a narrative example, an uncontrollable obsession for cruelty; of, to give another example, a vision of divine origin.

A remark Augustine makes in book 6 pertaining to Alypius's memories, not his own, to Alypius's later learning from them, not his own, illustrates well what Augustine considers to be "true" knowledge. The context of Augustine's remark is his commentary on the story he tells of how Alypius– falling from confident self-control, to curiosity, to blood-lust—came to be obsessed by the gladiatorial shows. To this story, Augustine appends that God taught Alypius to trust "in [Him], not in himself. But this was much later" (6.8). Then Augustine remarks: "Nevertheless, all this was stored away in [Alypius's] memory so that later he might turn the lesson to good account" (6.9).

In this one sentence is an application of Augustine's theory of memory. "All this" includes the sensual images of Alypius's experiences that were "stored away in the great storehouse of memory" (10.8) "separately, according to their category" (10.8); the emotions attendant on them that "[remained] but also [lost their] taste" (10.14) and whatever intellectual ideas, imperfect at the time, accompanied Alypius's experience. Alypius's "mind [had] freedom of them all" (10.17); it "[could] glide from one to the other" (10.17). "All this," images, emotions, and ideas, remained sequestered, without change, until Alypius's mind drew a "lesson" from them and turned it to "good account." "Later," Alypius may have learned a lesson by "[gathering] together things which, although . . . muddled and confused, [were] already contained in the memory" (10.11): this is what happens when facts are brought "to the fore by [the] teaching . . . of them" (10.10). He may have learned of his own frailty, of human cruelty, of harsh Roman reality. "Much later" (6.8), Alypius learned the lesson he could turn to "good account" (6.9), although how he came to trust in God remains mysterious, venerated and vague, to Alypius remembering and Augustine writing.

The dream of the wooden rule may serve as the example of Augustine's later learning of "truth," not from reflection, but from revelation. The dream is his mother Monica's, not Augustine's, but Augustine appropriates it as a revelation, then a realization of God's will for him, thus making it stand in the *Confessions* in the place of his own dream of revelation that never was. The passage on the dream is well known, but to reveal the intricate interchanges between a memory and its meanings, false then "true," it must be cited at length:

> She dreamed that she was standing on a wooden rule, and coming towards her in a halo of splendour she saw a young man who smiled at her in joy, although she herself was sad and quite consumed with grief. He asked her the reason for her sorrow and her daily tears, not because he did not know, but because he had something to tell her, for this is what happens in visions. When she replied that her tears were for the soul I had lost, he told her to take heart for, if she looked carefully, she would see that where she was, there also was I. And when she looked, she saw me standing beside her on the same rule.
>
> Where could this dream have come from, unless it was that you listened to the prayer of her heart? For your goodness is almighty; you take good care of each of us as if you had no others in your care, and you look after all as you look after each. And surely it was for the same reason that, when she told me of the dream and I tried to interpret it as a message that she need not despair of being one day such as I was then, she said at once and without hesitation "No! He did not say 'Where he is, you are,' but 'Where you are, he is.'"
>
> I have often said before and, to the best of my memory, I now declare to you, Lord, that I was much moved by this answer, which you gave me through my mother. She was not disturbed by my interpretation of her dream, plausible though it was, but quickly saw the true meaning, which I had not seen until she spoke. I was more deeply moved by this than by the dream itself in which the joy for which this devout woman had still so long to wait was foretold so long before to comfort her in the time of her distress. For nearly nine years were yet to come during which I wallowed deep in the mire and darkness of delusion. (3.11)

What is striking in this distant dialogue between Monica, the devout, and Augustine, the not-yet devout, as recounted much later by Augustine the then-devout (the distinctions are awkward, but must be observed) is that the vision of mother and son on the same wooden rule, a vision of divine origin, seems to be of less importance than its human interpretation. How might this be? The answer is in the time frames around the dream, the several stages in Augustine's coming to understand the dream's "true"—and original—meaning.

The dream is invariable, having been revealed once by God. In Monica's mind, the invariable vision of the dream remains, and, in Augustine's mind, a secondhand but similar version of the dream remains: both are preserved in "the great storehouse of memory" (10.8). In memory are also preserved rival versions of the dream's interpretation: one offered by Augustine and refused by Monica; one offered by Monica and accepted by Augustine. All the question is, When does Augustine accept Monica's interpretation of the dream? Augustine himself seems hesitant to make a pronouncement; he calls especially on his memory for verification of his past feelings: "I have often said before and, to the best of my memory, I now declare to you, O lord, that I was much moved by this answer which you gave me through my mother." Monica's interpretation of the dream, this "true" answer, and Augustine's interpretation of the dream, "plausible" but proven false, are at odds, and Augustine admits: "I was more deeply moved by this than by the dream itself." Which is as much as to say that he was more moved by the truthfulness—that is, the correctness—of Monica's interpretation of the dream than he was by the truth in the dream. Early, there is no certainty that God's message reaches Augustine. The doubt is deepened, becomes unmistakable, by the distance Augustine then puts between the "true meaning" of the dream and himself, in the next sentence, in the next nearly nine years of his life "during which [he] wallowed deep in the mire and the darkness of delusion." Truth and delusion, truth in the dream and delusion in the time Augustine spent heedless of it: the contrast is complete. But only Augustine's judgment later of his response to the dream then can reveal the contrast, for it is the final frame that forms around the dream—already framed by Monica's retelling it, Augustine's initial reaction to it, and the interchange between the two in the past. It is Augustine's view over the years, his view from the other side of his conversion, that finally gives him more distance, distance from his delusion, which enables him to see through his hermeneutical evasions of revelation to the "true," the original, meaning of the prophetic dream.

There is nothing notable in this process of discovering for oneself the meaning of a dream, an event, an experience of any kind much later, after the fact; there is even nothing notable about the meaning discovered being emphatically Christian while pertaining to an un-Christian past—except that it is the pattern in all the narrative of the *Confessions* up to and including Augustine's conversion in book 8. There is not a memory of Augustine's preconversion past, nor a memory of his conflict during his conversion, that is untouched by this process of aftersight. And yet the first sight, as it were, of these experiences remains beside each of their re-touched memories. First sight is intertwined with aftersight, as thought with later thought, throughout the narrative of the *Confessions*. This bifurcated narrative method of Augustine's, as he describes his past as felt in the past and his past as judged from the present, has been often noticed by critics. But it is important to do more than notice it and relate it to Augustine's conversion from a past life of sin to a present life of condemning sin.

It is important to see in this bifurcated narrative method the extended practice of Augustine's theory of memory. What permits Augustine's past experiences to serve as action awaiting the commentary of his present writing are, in Augustine's theory, the intricate mechanisms by which these experiences are preserved in "the great storehouse of memory" (10.8) until the mind decides the meanings they are to have. Given this permitted revisionism, Augustine's theory of memory is liberal. But its liberalism is limited by Augustine's inflexible criteria of "truth" to which all meanings for memories must—not may—be subjected. The paradox in Augustine's theory of memory is in its potential for revision of past experiences, yet its absolute restriction of readings—one, by the Scriptures—that it allows of past experiences.

It is in my own mind, then, that I measure time

Just how important Augustine's concept of the "great storehouse of memory" is becomes evident when one reads on from book 10 to book 11 to discover that his entire theory of time depends on it. For only this concept of memory allows Augustine to answer the question "How do we measure time?" which, once answered, allows him the development of his psychological theory of time. Advancing a number of hypotheses about past, present, and future time to reject them and a number of arguments against his own hypotheses to refute them, Augustine is meticulous, and long, in developing his theory. At the end of his reasoning, he arrives at a contrast between time as measure within the mind of man and eternity as timelessness within God. This contrast Augustine, ever the dualist, ever the parallelist, reworks in variations. Metamorphosing his theory into vision, he reveals time tenacious in its hold over men yet transcended by those freed, with faith, to embrace eternity. Applying his theory to writing autobiography, he assesses his life doubly, judging temporally and judging transcendentally.

The decisive step that permits Augustine to put time in the mind of man is achieved with his example of poetic meter, and thus measure, in the line "Deus Creator Omnium." Asking how he knows which syllables are short and which long, Augustine finds he must compare their sounds to measure them and cannot once they are spoken, for then they no longer exist. Hence, because indeed he measures the syllables, Augustine determines: "I must be measuring something which remains fixed in my memory" (11.27). By analogy to this one example of temporal measurement, all others follow, and Augustine can pronounce on the nature of time:

> It is in my own mind, then, that I measure time. I must not allow my mind to insist that time is something objective. I must not let it thwart me because of all the different notions and impressions that are lodged in it. I say that I measure time in my mind. For everything which happens leaves an impression on it, and this impression remains after the thing itself has ceased to be. It is this impression that I measure, since it is still present, not the thing itself, which makes the impression as it passes and then moves into the past. When I measure time it is this impression that I measure. (11.27)

The future seems unaccounted for in this theory of time that depends on a concept of memory. But Augustine is able to make the future too an impression measured in the mind with the aid of an analogy between the future and the past, the expectation of the one and the remembrance of the other. The analogy is not explicit, but by means of repeatedly balancing—logically and grammatically—his comparisons of the future and the past, Augustine makes it evident: "In the mind there is both expectation of the future and remembrance of the past" (11.28); of "the two faculties of memory and expectation, the one [looks] back . . . the other [looks] forward" (11.28); and each determines the measure of time appropriate to it, for "it is not future time that is long, but a long future is a long expectation of the future; and past time is not long, . . . but a long past is a long remembrance of the past" (11.28).

Between the future and the past is a present in which the "mind's attention persists" (11.28), regulating the process by which the future becomes the past. Augustine's example is a man reciting a poem: by performing the simple act of recitation, "the man's attentive mind, which is present, is relegating the future to the past" (11.27). Moving, once again, from specific illustration to general declaration, Augustine succeeds in placing under the dominion of the mind's attentiveness all time, which—undoubtedly a process—he shows, decisively, to be a psychological process: "the mind, which regulates this process, performs three functions, those of expectation, attention, and memory. The future, which it expects, passes through the present, to which it attends, into the past, which it remembers" (11.28).

Pushing proof by analogy to its limits, Augustine, by explaining in detail the process by which a psalm is recited, achieves an explanation for "any longer action" in a man's life, "a man's whole life," and "the whole history of mankind" (11.28):

> Suppose that I am going to recite a psalm that I know. Before I begin my faculty of expectation is engaged by the whole of it. But once I have begun, as much of the psalm as I have removed from the province of expectation and relegated to the past now engages my memory, and the scope of the action which I am performing is divided between the two faculties of memory and expectation, the one looking back to the part which I have already recited, the other looking forward to the part which I have still to recite. But my faculty of attention is present all the while, and through it passes what was the future in the process of becoming the past. As the process continues, the province of memory is extended in proportion as that of expectation is reduced, until the whole of my expectation is absorbed. This happens when I have finished my recitation and it has all passed into the province of memory.
>
> What is true of the whole psalm is also true of all its parts and of each syllable. It is true of any longer action in which I may be engaged and of which the recitation of the psalm may only be a small part. It is true of a man's whole life, of which all his actions are parts. It is true of the whole history of mankind, of which each man's life is a part. (11.28)

It is wise, perhaps, to halt at the analogy to a "man's whole life," at least for the purposes of a study of autobiography.[15] As an analogy, it must not be taken too literally and too logically, for if it is, Augustine soon needs a sentence disclaiming his analogy like that serving for his odd simile of memory like a stomach: "Perhaps the simile is unjustified, because the two processes are not alike in all points" (10.14). Not to quibble, but a man living his whole life is not like a man reciting a psalm "in all points," for the man living his life does not know all that is to pass in his life as he knows all the words to the psalm he recites. To query Augustine, then, how—if not literally, not logically—does he mean his analogy to answer for man's existence?

Figuratively, for in book II, chapter 29, Augustine metamorphoses his analogy into a figure, actually two complementary figures, to make it speak of greater things—of Christian hope and mortal despair. In the two paragraphs of 11.29, Augustine presents his two figures, each representing a mode—with or without faith—of existing in time:

> But to win your favour is dearer than life itself. I see now that my life has been wasted in distractions, but your right hand has supported me in the person of Christ my Lord, the Son of man, who is the Mediator between you, who are one, and men, who are many. He has upheld me in many ways and through many trials, in order that through him I may win the mastery, as he has won the mastery over me; in order that I may be rid of my old temptations and devote myself only to God's single purpose, forgetting what I have left behind. I look forward, not to what lies ahead of me in this life and will surely pass away, but to my eternal goal. I am intent upon this one purpose, not distracted by other aims, and with this goal in view I press on, eager for the prize, God's heavenly summons. Then I shall listen to the sound of your praises and gaze at your beauty ever present, never future, never past.
>
> But now my years are but sighs. You, O Lord, are my only solace. You, my Father, are eternal. But I am divided between time gone by and time to come, and its course is a mystery to me. My thoughts, the intimate life of my soul, are torn this way and that in the havoc of change. And so it will be until I am purified and melted by the fire of your love and fused into one with you. (11.29)

The man living his life is apparent, but not the man reciting a poem, the linguistic side of Augustine's former analogy. Yet it is here—transformed—in the biblical verses cited. All of the biblical citations, except three (from Philippians), are from the Book of Psalms. Augustine does not recite the Psalms word by word in time as an analogy for his temporal existence; he cites them as the Word, which is eternal, which enlightens his existence. Not their sequence, but their significance is his focus.

The ardent first paragraph, containing all but the last of the citations from the Psalms, reveals Augustine's vision of the afterlife, but also, importantly, his vision of his life in time, below, imperfect beside it, when his spiritual gaze is on this "eternal goal." Augustine's past in time is forgotten, his future in time "will surely pass away," his present is gathered to "this goal in view": human time is transcended by Christian faith. Augustine, "intent upon this one purpose," knows what is to come to pass in his veritable life, his afterlife; he knows the Word that, enduring, illuminates all his life.

"But now my years are but sighs": this is the last citation from the Book of Psalms, the last citation from any book of the Bible, and it announces Augustine's turning away from his heavenly vision. Time reasserts itself as a power over Augustine, which tears his soul "this way and that in the havoc of change," and as a problem for him, the course of which "is a mystery." Augustine's vision in this second paragraph is of his mortal life; it is a vision that reveals Augustine "divided between time gone by and time to come." In the snare of time, Augustine knows nothing of the meaning of what happens in his life; such must be his ignorance, if he relies on other words than the Word to explain his life.

Augustine sustained or Augustine despondent, his life ruled by God's will or by indeterminate change—what differentiates between his moods, between his two modes of living is God's eternity that, in his belief, frames all human time.[16] In the analogy of the psalm, which he takes up again, it is God who is "endowed with such great power of knowing and fore-knowing that all the past and all the future [are] known to [Him] as clearly as [Augustine knows] a familiar psalm" (11.31). But the recitation of a psalm is in time, and knowledge of all time might well be in time; and time is change; and God is "eternally without change" (11.31). The logic of Augustine's renewed analogy fails, and he insists it does; as it did for men, so it must certainly for God. God does not "know all the past and all the future merely in this way. [His] knowledge is far more wonderful, far more mysterious than this" (11.31). Neither analogy nor figure suffices for Augustine's evocation of God's omniscience, and, invoking eternity, he returns to simplicity. To frame with eternity his meditation on time, which puts time in the mind of man, Augustine has recourse to an all-encompassing statement: God is "the truly eternal Creator of minds" (11.31).

To mortals, though, omnipotence is abstract and omniscience distant. The subject that makes salient all the contrasts Augustine accentuates between time and eternity is death, and yet death is little discussed in his theory of time in book 11. Only in Augustine's narrative does death have its due. There Augustine makes temporality felt as mortality, and he makes of eternity a continually giving "source of all life" (9.10). In his narrative Augustine experiences his abstractions, and he incarnates, rather than explicates, his two figures for existing in time.

When Augustine writes, in book 4, of his early sorrow at a young friend's death, he makes of his despair then an occasion for a discourse on friendship, of the sorrow it brings those who love their friends "outside God and outside the soul" (4.10) and of the joy it brings those "who love them in one who is never lost, in God" (4.9). The contrast between mortality and eternity cannot but follow, and it is in expressing it that Augustine compares transient lives to words that follow one another in speech. The context of the comparison is Augustine's evocation of the course in this life of "things of beauty" and his injunction not to turn to them, away from God, and cling to them, "outside of God" (4.10):

> Like the sun, they rise and set. At their rise they have their first begin-
> ning; they grow until they reach perfection; but, once they have reached
> it, they grow old and die. Not all reach old age, but all alike must die. . . .
> This is all that you have appointed for them, because they are parts of a
> whole. Not all the parts exist at once, but some must come as others go,
> and in this way together they make up the whole of which they are the
> parts. Our speech follows the same rule, using sounds to signify a
> meaning. For a sentence is not complete unless each word, once its
> syllables have been pronounced, gives way to make room for the next.
> Let my soul praise you for these things, O God, Creator of them all; but
> the love of them, which we feel, through the senses of the body, must not
> be like glue to bind my soul to them. For they continue on the course
> that is set for them and leads to their end, and if the soul loves them and
> wishes to be with them and finds rest in them, it is torn by desires that
> can destroy it. (4.10)

In his youth, Augustine "did not know this" (4.13). In his grief, he was "convulsed with tears and sighs that allowed [him] neither rest nor peace of mind" (4.7). His only salvation, and it was no true salvation, was to enter all the more deeply into the flow of time and cling all the more closely to things of beauty. But this solution, the only one for the faithless man he then was, was a cycle leading back to sorrow:

> Time came and it went, day after day, and as it passed it filled me with
> fresh hope and new thoughts to remember. Little by little it pieced me
> together again by means of the old pleasures which I had once enjoyed.
> My sorrow gave way to them. But it was replaced, if not by sorrow of
> another kind, by things which held the germ of sorrow still to come. . . .
> My greatest comfort and relief was in the solace of other friends who
> shared my love of the huge fable which I loved instead of you, my God.
> (4.8)

"Old pleasures," "other friends," all so many "transient things, which pass from their alotted beginning to their alotted end" (4.10), all so many words sounding in time. And their meaning "misled" Augustine further into the "huge" Manichean "fable," so that he did not "entrust to the Truth all that the Truth [had] given to [him]" (4.11). Therein, in the "day after day" of the "things which held the germ of sorrow still to come," in the words that gave way "to make room for the next" words, is the figure for the snare of time, and Augustine caught in it.

"'But do I pass away elsewhere?' says the Word of God" (4.11): the contrast between words and the Word is there in book 4. But it is not until book 9, chapter 10, where he writes of his mother's last days, that Augustine writes at length about his vision of the Word. To introduce his vision at Ostia, Augustine has recourse to the same scriptural citation, chapter and verse, he uses to speak of his yearning for life out of time in his theoretical book on time. He amends, though, Philippians 3:13 from a singular to a plural subject—"We had forgotten what we had left behind and were intent on what lay before us"—for he and his mother share the vision at Ostia. Reading on in Philippians, one comes to this verse: "For our conversation is in heaven, from whence also we look for the Savior, the Lord Jesus Christ" (3:20). A very appropriate allusion, for Augustine and his mother attain their vision in a conversation, "serene and joyful" (9.10) but bound by time, to which Augustine contrasts the "conversation . . . in heaven," which sounds beyond time: "And while we spoke of the eternal Wisdom, longing for it and straining for it with all the strength of our hearts, for one fleeting instant we reached out and touched it. Then with a sigh, leaving our spiritual harvest bound to it, we returned to the sound of our own speech, in which each word has a beginning and an ending—far, far different from your Word, our Lord" (9.10). Language snatches away the "spiritual harvest" of the vision, but Augustine continues to struggle with it to explain what could only be "reached out" to and "touched" beyond his and his mother's own souls:

> suppose that we heard [God] himself . . . just as in that brief moment my mother and I had reached out in thought and touched the eternal Wisdom which abides over all things; suppose that this state were to continue and all other visions of things inferior were to be removed, so that this single vision entranced and absorbed the one who beheld it and enveloped him in inward joys in such a way that for him life was eternally the same as that instant of understanding for which we had longed so much—would not this be what we are to understand by the words "Come and share the joy of your Lord?" (9.10)

Paradoxes abound: language that takes place in time takes Augustine and Monica beyond time; and talk that sounds aloud is the medium for their apprehension of silence in eternity (God's voice mutes into vision); and eternity that endures is glimpsed only in an "instant of understanding," "brief," "fleeting." But paradoxes are integral to the human condition, as 1 Corinthians 13:12, so often quoted by Augustine, explains: "For now we see through a glass darkly; but then face to face: now I know in part; but then shall I know even as also I am known."[17] By a series of substitutions and translations, "in part" and imperfect, Augustine makes his vision of "then" inform his writing "now." His mother's death instead of his own death, described in terms of the Word instead of his own words, permits Augustine the kaleidoscopic closure that illuminates his personal history: Monica, the mother who gave him earthly life, dying, gives Augustine the vision of life everlasting with which he, living on, judges his existence.

Grief-stricken after his young friend's death and solaced by the Word at the time of his mother's death—Augustine contrasts the two experiences to contrast much more by them. But mourning only accentuates the differences between Augustine the man lost in time and Augustine the man looking to eternity. These differences well-defined, every experience in the *Confessions* reveals Augustine to be living the one figure for time or the other.

In his early struggles for philosophical understanding, in his ambitions for achievement, in his beguiling but increasingly bitter enjoyment of his senses, in any and all of his early attempts at wisdom and pleasure, young Augustine knew only of time in transit and of truths stable nowhere in time's trajectory. "All the time [he] had been telling [himself] one tale after another" (6.11). And he grasped at, one after another, the latest truths told to himself by himself. And one word gave way to the next, one ephemeral wonder to the next—Faustus, the Academics, even the Platonists—and not with all his method, all his mind, could Augustine make one endure. Such is the snare of time. Examine any one of Augustine's early narrative experiences, and therein, in this temporal predicament so purposefully and repeatedly described by the mature Augustine, is the young Augustine.

But the misleading multiplicity of all the intellectual wonders yielded for Augustine to the simplicity of a vision of eternity, and all the tales were abandoned by him for the Truth. The words Augustine came to write were no longer only his own; they were his echoes of the Word. And in them Augustine came to see all his former truths, all the meanings he had given to his memories, in the light of this one Truth. When the metaphor is made methodical, inelegant but exact, it means that every sensual, intellectual, emotional, and spiritual impression in the "great storehouse" of Augustine's memory came to be explained to him newly, and finally, by his faith. And all the vicissitudes that his existence still held for him, Augustine did not need to fear for their significance, for they too would be illuminated by the same truth, the Truth that judges the ephemeral by eternal standards. Such security in a stable truth belongs to few men. Fully believed and fully practiced by a man with faith, it is Augustine's figure for the transcendence of time.

Of the two life figures Augustine himself incarnates, in his narrative doubly documented as before and after conversion, only this latter figure for transcendence determines his judgment of his life. For inflexibility and irony are the rule in Augustine's theory of time and eternity. Inflexibility in that Augustine allows the measure of a man's life to be in his mind, while he insists that the models by which a man judge his life exist outside of time. Irony in that a man's power over time is thus aggrandized, even as his potential for independent judgment in time is minimized. To Augustine's mind, a man interpreting his life without the Truth is a man telling tales, all individual and all invalid. Only a man relying on the Truth is a reliable narrator of his life. Reliable, Augustine would say, because the stable truth grants him a sure judgment of his life. Restricted, some might say, because a stable truth yields always the same judgment of a life. A judgment that is personal, as faith is personal, but a judgment that is persistent, not subject to reconsiderations of falsehood and "truth," of sin and serving God, of the Christian view of this world and faith in the next.

A pattern to the faithful . . . rousing them to imitation

In book 11, language as a concept serves Augustine handily in his figures for life with faith, thus with form, and life without faith, endlessly formless. But not until books 12 and 13 does Augustine go beyond the concept of language to issues concerning its concrete usage, the reading and writing of actual words on actual pages in the Book and his book. Genesis continues to be Augustine's text in books 12 and 13 as, moving from temporal to interpretive theory, he tests transmutations—life into language, language into life. And, tirelessly, he varies his life visions into images, parables, and parallel life stories. Thus Augustine confronts the principal dilemma a Christian faces when reading and writing in the faith: How is the transcendent Truth to be understood and written in the temporal medium of language?

Augustine's answer he receives from God, as inspiration, as God's voice speaking in his spirit: "'Man, O man,' [God's] voice [rings] out, 'What my Scripture says, I say. But the Scripture speaks in time, whereas time does not affect my Word, which stands for ever, equal with me in eternity. The things which you see by my Spirit, I see, just as I speak the words which you speak by my Spirit. But while you see those things in time, it is not in time that I see them. And while you speak those words in time, it is not in time that I speak them'" (13.29). A man seeing and speaking by the Spirit, his comprehension and annunciation resounding from eternity into time—these are mystical ideas. But Augustine grounds them with one phrase: "What my Scripture says, I say." In the words of the Word, time and eternity converge: the man who sees and speaks by the Spirit is the man who reads and writes by the Scriptures. Inspiration, to Augustine's understanding, is less mystical than it is hermeneutical.

Announcing the Scriptures as his inspiration—"I know no written words as pure as these, none that have induced me so firmly to make my confession to [God]" (12.15)—Augustine entreats the Lord that both the substance and the style of his *Confessions* be in accord with the Scriptures: "If . . . I am to speak the truth, let me utter not what is mine, but what is yours" (13.25). Consequently, Augustine embodies his ideas in contrasting scriptural images. Inevitably also, for he derives the dualism in his thought and his style from the Scriptures: "For it is in the Scriptures that [God speaks] to us, teaching us to distinguish between the things that only our minds can know and those that the flesh can perceive, between souls that are wedded to the spirit and those that cling to worldly things, just as we know the difference between day and night" (13.18). Augustine's variations in dual imagery—all contrasting faith and faithlessness—are many. Here he invokes the mind and body, spirituality and worldliness, day and night. Elsewhere—the Gospels his inspiration and Jesus his healer and his home—he contrasts health and sickness (2.7, 7.8), satiety and hunger (3.1, 6.10, 7.17), cleanliness and uncleanliness (4.6, 6.16), waking and sleeping (7.14, 8.5), sanity and madness (8.8), home and wandering (2.10, 4.1, 4.16), new life and death (8.6, 8.8, 9.2, 9.4).

Narrated and extended, these contrasting images become parables of sinning and serving God. Usually Augustine tells these in allusions and asides, more as sketches than as stories, but always he supplies their moral.[18] And always it is the same moral, which the parable of the Prodigal Son epitomizes. The wanderer in a "far country," wasting "his substance with riotous living," returning in shame to a father who shows "compassion" (Luke 15): these scenes Augustine evokes (1.18, 4.16). And his variations abound: the wanderer as sea voyager, buffeted by every wind, until brought by his divine helmsman to safe haven (4.14, 6.5); the wanderer as quester, roaming trackless wastes, before discovering the high road (2.10, 4.1, 7.21); and the wanderer as divided self, lost, until he comes home to himself in God (5.2, 6.1, 8.8). All of these parables illustrate the diversity of paths from God and the unity of the path to God. Other parables offer corporeal imagery: the man feeding his sensual appetites, yet starving until he finds the "food of the soul" (3.1); the sleeping man ready with his many excuses for not waking to God (8.5); the ailing patient, stricken with ulcers, sores, unnamed illnesses, awaiting the healing hand of his divine physician (7.8). Again, these illustrate the diverse ways to fall from God and the one way to be saved by Him. Augustine's own figures for a man living only in time and a man living in the hope of life after time, the tale after tale told by he who is without faith, the one Truth held by he who believes; again, the invariable conclusion. Stripped of figurative complexity down to simplicity: the diversity of error and the unity of truth, this is the moral to be drawn from every one of Augustine's parables of sin and saving grace.

When Augustine sketches the many paths away from God, the parables suffice, but when he charts the straight and narrow path, he draws on the lives of the Apostles. History thus enhances allegory. In the hierarchy of the faithful, which Augustine sets forth in book 13, the Apostles are symbols of unity in truth. In their earthly and exemplary lives, they "follow the example of Christ" and are followed by the faithful "[imitating]" them (13.21). In their sanctity, they are as "lights shining in the firmament," intermediaries between heaven and earth, "possessed of the word of life" to be told to the world of the living (13.19).

Paul, particularly, is singled out by Augustine in citations and allusions. Quoting Galatians 4:12, Augustine discloses the reason: "Be as I am, says Paul, for I am no different from yourselves" (13.21). Augustine in his conversion is like Paul.[19] And others, of all persuasions, may be too: "For I am the least of the apostles, that am not meet to be called an apostle, because I persecuted the church of God." Augustine does not quote 1 Corinthians 15:9, but in his very humility he preaches the example of Paul.

But the limits of imitation, and of what little presumption there is in Paul and in Augustine echoing Paul, are decidedly set. "We must live good lives"—lives patterned on the Apostles' lives—"so that the living soul may come to life in us" (13.22). Then "'there must be an inward change, a remaking of [our] minds'" (Romans 12:2) (13.22), and this not according to "the example of someone better than ourselves" (13.22):

"The reason for this is that when [a man] has remade his mind and can see and understand [God's] truth, he has no need of other men to teach him to imitate his kind. [God shows] him and he sees for himself 'what is [God's] will, the good thing, the desirable thing, the perfect thing'" (Romans 12:2) (13.22). Preliminary to—and perhaps productive of—the "inward change" is the Augustinian version of the apostolic teaching. The Book of Psalms provides Augustine with much of his dualistic imagery and many of his addresses to God, but the New Testament, particularly Paul's Epistles, provides Augustine with the matter of his work, men's lives, and with the models for his message to men.

By the pattern of the Apostles' lives, Augustine measures in his narrative the lives of those he meets, assessing the divergence of non-Christian lives and the parallels between Christian lives. Erring in individual ways before their right course is set, various Christian lives are hardly reduced by Augustine to identity, but all are subject to comparison with his own life and to trial by his version of scriptural truth. His judgments determine the design of his narrative. As again and again he tells of lives similar to his own, either in errors or in coming to conversion, the principle of his decisions and their design becomes apparent.[20] It is the principle of the diversity of error and the unity of truth, become more than the extremes of imagery, more than the moral of tales told, become—when all his work is subsumed under it—structural to Augustine's *Confessions*.

Early in his narrative, Augustine tells his first story of a life similar to his own. In book 3, chapter 12, he writes of a man telling of his own path to God and foretelling from it Augustine's similar path. The man is a bishop "who had lived his life in the Church and was well-versed in the Scriptures" (3.12); who, as a child, had been given to the Manichees for religious training by his "misguided mother" (3.12); who, later, by reading "almost all their books, . . . and even though no one argued the case with him or put him right, . . . had seen for himself that he ought to have nothing to do with the sect, and accordingly . . . had left it" (3.12). The parallels between the bishop's life and Augustine's are evident: the youthful infatuation with the Manichees, the later self-taught renunciation of their beliefs, the still-later entrance into the Church. To any remark about the detail that jars (the "misguided mother") and the detail de trop (the same rank of bishop for both Augustine and this unnamed bishop), the obvious rejoinder is that parallel Christian lives are not necessarily— rather far from—identical lives. What is essential in the bishop's story of his life, which is to be the story of Augustine's life, Augustine puts in the bishop's own words. Speaking of Augustine, the bishop foresees, "from his own reading he will discover his mistakes and the depth of his profanity" (3.12).

But several years are still to come during which Augustine reads himself into other delusions than his Manichean devotions, which begin to wane. For a while astrology captivates Augustine, then the Academics, then the Neo-Platonists; ambition holds him. Recounting these years in books 4–7, Augustine writes of others who shared his errors, condemning the similarities between their erring ways and his. There is the doctor who as a young man studied the textbooks of astrology; who later found that they were wrong, that only chance answered for correct foretellings of the future, and thus chose to give up astrology. The doctor, or rather God speaking through him, "imprinted on [Augustine's] mind doubts which [he] was to remember later, when [he] came to argue these matters out for [himself]" (4.3). There is Firminus, who provides Augustine with the decisive argument against astrology; who, oddly, against the evidence of his own argument, perseveres in seeking readings of the stars (7.6). There is the poor beggar, falsely happy in his drunken joy and as far from the "joy of hope" (6.6) as Augustine is in his anxious ambition; who, even so, Augustine claims, is happier and more honorable than he is. There are the friends who accompany Augustine in his pursuit of "shallow happiness" (6.6), who grasp as he does at worldly honours. "Often by observing them, [Augustine] was made aware of [his] own state, and [he] was not pleased with what [he] saw" (6.6). Alypius is among these friends, and Nebridius, and, with Augustine, they are all "perplexed to know what course of life [they] ought to follow" (6.10). Together they falter, and Augustine writes at length of their faltering; and together, later, they turn to God.

One conversion inspires another, among the friends and among other Christians also: such is the history Augustine records in his *Confessions;* such is the history of the Church. Augustine takes his position in this history in the sequence of conversion stories in book 8. It is a position of complexity, for Augustine was once the listener to these conversion stories, is now the teller of them, and is also the commentator on both his past and present responses to them. Listener, teller, commentator— Augustine emphasizes his roles, for he foresees others able to adopt them. Because "when converts are well-known, their example guides many others to salvation" (8.4).

These last words Augustine writes of Victorinus's conversion, the story of which was told to him by Simplicianus. Victorinus was a teacher of rhetoric, a man of great learning, both pagan and Christian. He translated the books of the Platonists that Augustine read in Latin, and he studied the Scriptures with care. And then he wavered, intellectually convinced of the Truth and emotionally unwilling to act on his conviction. "But later on, as a result of his attentive reading, he became resolute. . . . he gave in his name to be reborn through baptism" (8.2). Once he became a Christian and was constrained to choose between his profession and his faith, he gave up "his own school of words rather than desert [God's] Word" (8.5). Augustine's commentary on the story of Victorinus, on how he received it and why he retells it, is explicit: "When your servant Simplicianus told me the story of Victorinus, I began to glow with fervour to imitate him. This, of course, was why Simplicianus had told it to me" (8.5) Simplicianus could hardly have addressed more appropriately the pride and ambition of Augustine than by this story of one like him. The intellectual intent on reasoning his way to truth, with learned inquiry into the Platonists, then into the Scriptures; that was Victorinus, that was Augustine. The irresolute will, the time passing, then the emotional turn to conversion and the abandonment of all the words for the Word: first Victorinus took that course, then Augustine.

But not yet for Augustine the emotional turn to conversion, and this he explains in his analysis, which follows the story of Victorinus, of the "two wills within [him], one old, one new, one the servant of the flesh, the other of the spirit, [which] were in conflict and between them . . . tore [his] soul apart" (8.5). For his new will to win over his old, his spirit to gain ascendancy over his flesh, Augustine has need of more of the new, and it comes to him in a series of stories told by Ponticianus. The stories of Antony, of the monks living in the monasteries—"All of this was new" (8.6) to Augustine and Alypius listening, "amazed" (8.6), to Ponticianus the day that was to be the day of their conversions. But these stories Augustine does not retell—not directly, not in detail, and, the way he will use them, not yet. They become stories within another story, the story of Ponticianus's two friends converting to God.

The setting is Treves on a day of liberty for Ponticianus and his friends, who were all officials serving the state. While out walking together, two of the friends wander off and come to the home of "some servants of [God], men poor in spirit, to whom the kingdom of heaven belongs" (8.6). The echo is from the teachings of Jesus to his disciples, Matthew 5:3; thus the story of the monks enters, by allusion, into this story of the friends. In the house, the friends find a book containing the life of Antony; thus the story of Antony, though not retold, takes the central place in this story. One of the friends begins to read the book, and he finds in it inspiration and in himself the desire for emulation. He reads on, "labouring under the pain of the new life that was taking birth in him" and then "a cry broke from him as he saw"—the instant of understanding—"the better course and determined to take it" (8.6). He tells his resolution to his friend, who answers that he will stand by him. When Ponticianus and his other friend rejoin these two, they learn of their decision and respond with "all reverence" (8.6), but no similar resolution. Ponticianus and his friend leave for the palace and their worldliness, and the two friends remain at the house to enter God's service, "at the cost of giving up all they possessed and following [the Lord]" (8.6). Again the echo is from Jesus' teachings, Luke 14:33.

After retelling this story straight through, Augustine doubles back and tells of his responses as he listened to Ponticianus telling it. The story becomes a mirror of words in which Augustine sees what he is and detests, and what he would be and admires:

> While he was speaking, O Lord, you were turning me around to look at myself. For I had placed myself behind my own back, refusing to see myself. You were setting me before my own eyes so that I could see how sordid I was, how deformed and squalid, how tainted with ulcers and sores. I saw it all and stood aghast, but there was no place where I could escape from myself. If I tried to turn my eyes away they fell on Ponticianus, still telling his tale, and in this way you brought me face to face with myself once more, forcing me upon my own sight so that I should see my wickedness and loathe it. (8.7)

The mirror of words speaks of two friends, and Augustine turns to Alypius: "What is the matter with us? What is the meaning of this story? These men have not had our schooling, yet they stand up and storm the gates of heaven while we, for all our learning, lie here grovelling in this world of flesh and blood!" (8.8). All is contrast: of the rapidity of the friends' decision and the long delaying of Augustine and Alypius before the same decision; of the simplicity of the friends' resolution and the complexity of Augustine's and Alypius's still not taken; of the friends' less-lettered condition in life and Augustine's and Alypius's vain intellects and education.

Augustine stresses these dissimilarities between the two friends and himself and Alypius, before, in the chapters that complete the book, shading them into similarities. The transformation is the work of two conflicting wills in Augustine that take figurative form. The "mutterings" of his desires and of habit fighting for them seem "to reach [him] from behind, as though they were steathily plucking at [his] back, trying to make [him] turn [his] head when [he] wanted to go forward" (8.11). It is Satan incarnate in this will of Augustine's self: "Get thee behind me, Satan: thou art an offence to me; for thou savourest not the things that be of God, but those that be of men" (Matthew 16:23). And on the other side of Augustine's hesitation, within him as the will he would have win over habit, before him in a figure, is "Continence in all her serene unsullied joy" (8.11). She is surrounded by the "joys born of [her] Lord, her Spouse" (8.11), those who before Augustine had dedicated themselves to God, whose stories Augustine had read in the Scriptures and heard from such as Ponticianus.

Augustine's inner conflict ends in his crisis of tears. And then there is the singsong voice, "Take it and read, take it and read" ("Tolle, lege, tolle, lege") (8.12). But before Augustine obeys the divine command, he remembers—only now retold in its essentials, only here gaining Augustine's response to it—the story of Antony. How Antony had heard the Gospel "being read and had taken it as a counsel addressed to himself when he heard the words 'Go home and sell all that belongs to you . . . then come back and follow me'" (Matthew 19:21) (8.12). How by "this divine pronouncement he had at once been converted to [God]" (8.12). Then Augustine takes up Paul's Epistles, and reads, and—"in an instant . . . as though the light of confidence flooded into [his] heart" (8.12)—is converted.[21] Augustine tells his resolution to his friend, Alypius, who answers that he will stand by him. For Alypius takes up Paul's Epistles, reads, and is converted, his resolution being rapidly, simply, and emotionally taken, as was Augustine's, when finally realized. The two friends then tell others of their resolution—Monica, Verecundus, Nebridius. All respond with reverence, if not all with the same resolution.

The story within the story within the story, all are complete—except that they are, perhaps, to enter into other life stories of conversion. Antony hearing the words of Matthew was converted; the two friends reading of Antony's life were converted; Augustine and Alypius hearing their stories and reading the words of Paul were converted—the stories of all and the New Testament teaching that inspired them are in the *Confessions* to be read again, to move again others, perhaps, to resolution.

He who utters falsehood utters what is his alone

In the so many similar sequences of men turning sincerely and finally to God, Augustine writes of his conversion as one more among many that argues for the acceptance of God's Word. And Augustine's continuation in the faith, and his Christian theories of self-interpretation—neither, life story or philosophy, reveals Augustine vaunting his singularity. Undeniably individual, urgently personal, Augustine's *Confessions* are singular, but Augustine does not advance, nor would he appreciate, the claim. Because God's truth does not "belong to this man or that" (12.25); because it "belongs to us all" (12.25). The intimacy of Augustine's autobiography must not lead one to mistake or neglect its central tenet—the communality of the truth: "[God's truth] belongs to us all, because we all hear [God's] call to share it and [God gives] us dire warning not to think it ours alone, for fear that we may be deprived of it. If any man claims as his own what [God gives] to all to enjoy and tries to keep for himself what belongs to all, he is driven to take refuge in his own resources instead of in what is common to all" (12.25).

By relying on the Scriptures, not on his own resources, Augustine answers a great many questions central to autobiographical writing. A man's truths—the meanings he gives to his memories—changing over time, how does a man judge amongst his personal truths? How does he decide to award precedence and permanence to some and relegate others to lower orders or, with time, to a loss of all significance? Augustine's theory of memory answers, by revealing how reason rules a man's memory, ordering and judging his recollections by the one standard of scriptural truth. God's will being eternal and without change, how does a man, if he would, come to see the truths of his life in the light of the everlasting Truth; how does he, if he would, come to understand the place of his temporal existence in the eternity of God? Augustine's theory of time and eternity is explicit: living in ever-changing time, which is in his own mind, a man must look to eternity to discern the design and direction of his life. A man's life being given form by his faith, how, if his truth is transcendent but his language is temporal, does he write of it? Augustine's *Confessions,* complete, are his response; from his narrative, which he patterns on timeless, scriptural parallels between Christian life stories, to his theories of self-interpretation, where he explains his efforts.

Augustine is able to answer these central questions because he resolves, to his satisfaction, an always potential problem of autobiography: falsehood. The Scriptures are again Augustine's resource, and his readers' too, for they teach the virtues that bind Christian writers to Christian readers in a pact of truth. "The two commandments on which . . . all the law and the prophets depend" (12.18) are those that guarantee the pact: "Thou shalt love the Lord thy God with all thy heart, and with all thy soul, and with all thy mind. This is the first and great commandment. And the second is like unto it, Thou shalt love thy neighbour as thyself" (Matthew 22:37–39). Writing, Augustine is certain that "if [God inspires him] . . . what [he says] will be the truth" (13.25); being read, he is certain that he will be believed "by those whose ears are opened to [him] by charity" (10.3). Quite simply, in Augustine's philosophy, sincerity of belief preserves the Christian writer from falsehood, and charity in the Christian community assures readers of his truths.[22]

The irony of a man studying and teaching how to speak, but not knowing what to say, that was the position of young Augustine, the rhetor. But when Augustine converted, when he abandoned the "chair of lies" (9.2), he "began to talk to [God] freely" (9.1)—and truthfully. In the simplicity of Augustine's belief—"I trust and trusting I find words to utter" (1.5)—is the resolution to his frequent opposition of style and content (3.4, 5.13), "mere eloquence and truth" (5.3). Style and content concur in the Scriptures, and also, Augustine dares to say, in the *Confessions*.

Truths assured—and the scriptural phrases, figures, and forms found for them—Augustine achieves what few autobiographers attempt: the complete explanation of a life. In his *Confessions*, nothing is fortuitous, nothing gratuitous, and what is mysterious is only so to Augustine, God having reasons for the least to the greatest event in his life. And even these reasons are rendered lucid, for Augustine shows divine will—God's guidance (4.14, 6.5, 7.10), His providence (5.6, 9.10), His mercy (5.13, 6.12, 6.16)—to be directing the seemingly random events of his life.[23] Making what is known of God's omnipotence stand in place of what is unknown to man's limited cognizance, Augustine's explanation of his life is valid for every Christian life. The Scriptures grant the truths, at once theological and autobiographical, that are to suffice for the faithful. Not only do the *Confessions* bear witness to the explanatory power of faith; they are a remarkable testimony to the human will to order.

2

MONTAIGNE
Essays (a) (b) (c)

The world is but a school of inquiry

A MAN WHO HAS NOT directed his life as a whole toward a definite goal cannot possibly set his particular actions in order. A man who does not have a picture of the whole in his head cannot possibly arrange the pieces."[1] Such a man is Montaigne, who decides no destination and determines no design for his life, who writes of his life as he lives it—in the present, deliberated about in (*a*) "pieces" (243) [320], written about in (*a*) "bits" (297) [388]. Accepting the worldliness and the disorderliness of his sources, his subjects, and himself speaking on them, Montaigne creates his *Essays* in the flux of earthly time so mistrusted by Augustine. The problems Augustine saw inherent in such a position—the difficulties of self-definition and design, the relativity and ephemerality of truths, the lack of communality in communication—Montaigne not only encounters, but embraces. To Montaigne's mind, perpetual change is perpetually interesting, and inquiry is the most natural of human activities, always instructive, though always inconclusive: (*b*) "Agitation and the chase are properly our quarry; we are not excusable if we conduct it badly and irrelevantly; to fail in the catch is another thing. For we are born to quest after truth; to possess it belongs to a greater power" (708) [906]. Purposefully, Montaigne turns away from the dark mirror of Corinthians, which gives form to this life with the promise of the afterlife, to peer into a still stranger mirror: a mirror that reflects diversity, not similarity; that multiplies the aspects of subjects—selves, others, events, theories—seen in it; that, consequently, renders problematic the identities of those looking therein. (*a*) "This great world . . . is the mirror in which we must look at ourselves to recognize ourselves from the proper angle" (116) [157].

Having trained himself since his youth to (*b*) "see [his] own life mirrored in that of others" (824) [1053], Montaigne as readily pronounces on others' lives as on his own. His judgment: (*a*) "We are all patch-work"—without a pattern, Christian or otherwise, to our lives—"and so shapeless and diverse in composition that each bit, each moment, plays its own game. And there is as much difference between us and ourselves as between us and others" (244) [321]. So diverse is the human spirit that in another "piece" Montaigne finds a (*b*) "ruling pattern" ["forme mais-tresse"] (615) [789] in himself, and in another he praises the (*b*) "common (*c*) human (*b*) pattern" (857) [1096]. He may be coaxed out of this contradiction by a careful accounting of where he writes of diversity in our lives, where of unity, in what context and to what end. But he will only stay clear for the space of a few pages. Because Montaigne speaks his meaning (*b*) "in disjointed parts, as something that cannot be said all at once and in a lump" (824) [1054], and no disjointed part dominates another, and none determines the whole. What coherence there is to the disparate pieces seen from different angles derives from Montaigne's ongoing selection of them to reveal his writing self. But this is no excuse for resolving Montaigne into continuity; after all, even Montaigne's "ruling pattern" becomes in another "piece" his (*c*) "ruling quality, which is ignorance" ["maistresse forme, qui est l'ignorance"] (219) [290]. And, anyway, it is illogical to decide for anything other than diversity and discontinuity in a mind of so many colors.[2] To anyone who decides against this diversity, in Montaigne or in himself, Montaigne rejoins: (*b*) "anyone who observes carefully can hardly find himself twice in the same state. . . . and whoever studies himself really attentively finds in himself, yes, even in his judgment, this gyration and discord" (242) [319].

This "gyration and discord" being in Montaigne, his *Essays* can hardly repose into order. A study of evolution in Montaigne's written thought imparts no pattern to the patchwork he makes of human lives. Probing into 1580(*a*), 1588(*b*), and 1595(*c*) strata—and even more scholarly distinc-tions and divinations of strata—in Montaigne's *Essays* does not reveal all his awareness of diversity, discontinuity, and disorder in human lives to be early, all his claims for similarity, continuity, and order to be late.[3] Perseus, king of Macedonia, in a late appearance in the *Essays,* single-handedly disrupts that pattern: (*c*) "What is remarked for rare in Perseus, king of Macedonia, that his mind, sticking to no one condition, kept wandering through every type of life and portraying such a flighty and erratic character that neither he nor anyone else knew what kind of man he was, seems to me to fit nearly everybody" (825) [1054]. "Sticking to no one condition," Montaigne's will and his reasoning (*b*) "are moved now in one way" (now he speaks out for diversity, discontinuity, and disorder), "now in another" (713) [913] (now he finds for similarity, continuity, and order).[4] And he will be (*a*) "different tomorrow, if [he learns] something new which changes [him]" (109) [147], or simply if he is moved again by his reason's (*b*) "accidental impulsions that change from day to day" (713) [913]. Time, for Montaigne, is the medium for (*a*) "mutations" (574) [737], but not evolution.[5]

Even the books Montaigne cites to shore up his written self are subject, in his use of them, to change in time. Their meanings shift as Montaigne's allegiances do. And the only book amongst them of unquestioned authority is the one Montaigne least employs. Augustine's source of "all truths" (13.31) for all men, Augustine's resource for the parallels that unite men in Christian self-analysis, Montaigne perfunctorily, if piously, dismisses, declaring the Scriptures off-limits for the (*b*) "brattish rabble of men that we are" (856) [1095]: (*b*) "the holy book of the sacred mysteries of our belief"; (*c*) "it is not everyone's study; it is the study of the persons who are dedicated to it, whom God calls to it" (232) [306]. Believing the Bible (*c*) "is not a story to tell, it is a story to revere, to fear, and adore" (232) [306], believing (*b*) "human speech has lower forms, and should not make use of the dignity, majesty, and authority of divine speech" (234) [308], Montaigne writes God's Word out of his words.

Not in the Bible, but amidst the Babel of many authors, Montaigne finds his voice for his *Essays*. He sets on his pages a (*a*) "diversity of idioms and languages" and a "discordance of opinions and reasons" (415) [535], the very confusion with which God punished the builders of the ancient Tower of Babel: (*a*) "It was for the chastisement of our pride and the instruction of our wretchedness and incapacity that God produced the disorder and confusion of the ancient tower of Babel. . . . The diversity of idioms and languages with which he troubled that work, what else is it but that infinite and perpetual altercation and discordance of opinions and reasons, which accompanies and embroils the vain construction of human knowledge?" (414–15) [535]. Through this clamor of many tongues and many theories, Montaigne criticizes the vanity and the folly of the "construction of human knowledge," but all the same he takes his place amongst its builders. For their words, cited, become his—(*c*) "I do not speak the minds of others except to speak my own mind better" (108) [146]—and their subjects, sounded, become his study of (*a*) "man" (481) [617], of (*c*) "myself" (273) [358].

Other authors, other selves, his self, his *Essays*—Montaigne sees them all swing with the (*b*) "perennial movement" (610) [782] of the world. And yet he tries to transcribe their very instability onto the printed page. His avowed reasons for the attempt are—no surprise—diverse. At one moment, his *Essays* are a search for truth; at another, merely an amusement for his friends; most often, they are to serve Montaigne himself, often in contradictory ways. How do these reasons—public, domestic, and private—stick in Montaigne's unstable world? Or—to bring the question back to his text—how do these reasons account for Montaigne's transcriptions, themselves unstable (the *a, b, c* texts), and the instability they together signify?

On "the truth" Montaigne never wavers—but only because he is careful to keep it out of his *Essays*. Montaigne writes (*a*) "not to establish the truth, but to seek it" (229) [302]; he offers not his (*a*) "teaching," but his "study" (272) [357]. A certain moral truth—(*c*) "the first and fundamental part of virtue" (491) [631]—he does allow into his *Essays*, but as a human quality, individual not abstract, and wholly relative to he who embraces it. When classical thought is his inspiration, Montaigne concludes that (*a*) "truth must have one face, the same and universal" (436) [562]: this in the "Apology for Raymond Sebond," his virtuoso demonstration that no subject seen by human minds has "one face, the same and universal." When his Christian faith informs Montaigne's writing on truth, it is not to legislate between human truths, not to impart learning, rather to give a warning: (*a*) "our ideas and reasonings: they have a certain body, but it is a shapeless mass, without form or light, if faith and divine grace are not added to it" (327) [425]. But Montaigne's master, He who dictates "the truth," is distant from Montaigne's matter; He has His (*a*) "place above these vain and human wranglings" (251) [330]. Divine truths are above and human truths are unreconcilable in Montaigne's *Essays,* which are, therefore, a quest for "the truth" certain of never attaining their goal. Such a quest is a quest for questing's sake. Which is not as purposeless an activity as it sounds, given the intellectual nature of the chase that exercises the mind all the more, the end being always elusive.

Expert in questing, essaying without deciding, Montaigne does not hesitate to assert the aptness of his art for others. Thus in one of his proudest claims for the *Essays,* "my" vying with "our," Montaigne essaying his mind in writing becomes Montaigne essaying the human mind:

(*c*) It is a thorny undertaking, and more so than it seems, to follow a movement so wandering as that of our mind, to penetrate the opaque depths of its innermost folds, to pick out and immobilize the innumerable flutterings that agitate it. And it is a new and extraordinary amusement, which withdraws us from the ordinary occupations of the world, yes, even from those most recommended.

It is many years now that I have had only myself as object of my thoughts, that I have been examining and studying only myself; and if I study anything else, it is in order promptly to apply it to myself, or rather within myself. And it does not seem to me that I am making a mistake if—as is done in the other sciences, which are incomparably less useful—I impart what I have learned in this one, though I am hardly satisfied with the progress I have made in it. There is no description equal in difficulty, or certainly in usefulness, to the description of oneself. (273) [358]

Montaigne may be one more amongst the Babel of authors forming and watching fall the science he constructs, but he glories in the originality and the utility of his exercise. In a more modest moment, just before this outburst of confidence, he allows his *Essays* only (*c*) "by accident" (272) [357] to be useful to others. But either way, rating his *Essays* (*b*) "now low, now high, very inconsistently and uncertainly" (718) [918], Montaigne extrapolates from his psychological science a public good.

What, then, of Montaigne's 1580 Preface that claims so much less for his *Essays,* not this high-minded quest, rather (*a*) "no goal but a domestic and private one" (2) [9]? A preface that bids adieu to its readers asks not to be taken straight, so by what twist is Montaigne's public goal in publishing also a domestic and private goal? Private and public complement each other endlessly, if elusively, when Montaigne universalizes himself into man, but the (*a*) "relatives and friends" (2) [9] for whom Montaigne writes are still more elusive. Montaigne's living, close family are women, whose intellects he hardly solicits, believing the little good of women's abilities that he does. Montaigne's closest friend, Etienne de La Boétie, is dead, giving birth to the many psychological explanations of why Montaigne writes.[6] The penury of biographical material, perhaps, but few notable "relatives and friends" claim Montaigne's book. There are the five women Montaigne directly addresses in five essays, and his literary executrix known to him in his last years.[7] But beyond these few, only the readers whom Montaigne dismisses are here to spend their (*a*) "leisure on so frivolous and vain a subject" (2) [9].

Who these readers are is a historical question, but who Montaigne thinks they are is a textual question, which, answered, reveals more about Montaigne than about his readers. Imagining a reader for himself, Montaigne desires him a (*b*) "worthy man," "a friend" (750) [959], learning of Montaigne's humors and won over to him in the very act of reading the

Essays. Montaigne's desire is a metamorphosed memory. An earlier book, La Boétie's *La Servitude volontaire,* served as the medium for Montaigne's admiring and meeting his friend; La Boétie's book gave Montaigne the (*a*) "first knowledge of his name, thus starting on its way [their] friendship" that became "so entire and so perfect" (136) [182]. If La Boétie had written more, and at a more mature age, if (*a*) "he had adopted a plan such as [Montaigne's], of putting his ideas in writing, we should see many rare things" (135) [182]—indeed, we should see rare things very like Montaigne's *Essays*. In Montaigne's wished-for, replayed friendship, Montaigne takes on La Boétie's role as author while his reader is to take on Montaigne's own as eager and admiring friend. The relationship, in Montaigne's mind, is one of virtual identity, for in the friendship Montaigne prizes, souls (*a*) "mingle and blend with each other so completely that they efface the seam that joined them, and cannot find it again" (139) [186]. Montaigne asserts that such a friendship is too rare to be repeated. But then Montaigne would have even his more formal readers less learned than wise, subtle but sensible, with souls (*c*) "regulated and strong in themselves" (498) [640][8]—in short, so many more friends, so many more Montaignes. The chapter in which this thinly veiled wish appears? "Of Presumption."

Montaigne's "domestic and private" goal, hardly restrictive of his readership, reveals, rather, his desire to address personally a various public, to carry over the intimacy of his friendships into the informality of his *Essays*. When, in "Three Kinds of Association," Montaigne's subject is discussion, its participants and its pleasures, again he extols the qualities of wisdom, subtlety, and independence of spirit. And again he betrays how in his mind the identity of his friends, possessors of these qualities, merges into that of his readers, potentially as excellent:

> (*b*) The men whose society and intimacy I seek are those who are called talented gentlemen; the idea of them spoils my taste for the others. It is, if you take it rightly, the rarest type among us, and a type that is chiefly due to nature. The object of this association is simply intimacy, fellowship, and conversation: exercise of minds, without any other fruit. In our talks all subjects are alike to me. I do not care if there is neither weight nor depth in them; charm and pertinency are always there; everything is imbued with mature and constant good sense, and mingled with kindliness, frankness, gaiety, and friendliness. (625) [802]

Speaking, Montaigne supplely moves with the give and take, the "exercise," of discussion; writing, he creates a similar space for interchange with his cited authors and his wished-for readers. To Montaigne speaking "all subjects are alike," as to Montaigne writing (*b*) "any topic is equally fertile" (668) [854]. "Charm and pertinency are always there," in the discussion between friends animated with human qualities, in the *Essays* that Montaigne assures are his (*a*) "absurdities" and characterized by the "same bearing and the same air" as his "conversation" (595) [763]. Informal, laden with neither learned "depth" nor pedantic "weight," and frank, dedicated to "intimacy, fellowship, and conversation"—the characterization serves as well for Montaigne's written discussions, his *Essays*. For Montaigne speaking becomes Montaigne writing as Montaigne's interlocutors are replaced by the numerous authors whose opinions he considers and the kindred readers whose responses he solicits.[9]

But even lacking the others—the lively talkers, the learned authors, and the kind readers—Montaigne is sociable in his solitude. His soul (*a*) "can be turned upon itself; it can keep itself company" (177) [235]. In phrase after phrase of "I . . ." Montaigne identifies his soul's favorite activities: (*a*) "as for me, I turn my gaze inward, I fix it there and keep it busy. . . . as for me, I look inside of me; I have no business but with myself; I continually observe myself, I take stock of myself, I taste myself. . . . as for me, I roll about in myself" (499) [641]. Listening to his soul while he records it, Montaigne makes the celebrated (*c*) "book consubstantial with its author" (504) [648]. When it is time to speak his soul, Montaigne speaks (*b*) "to [his] paper as [he speaks] to the first man [he meets]" (599) [767], with (*a*) "a simple, natural speech, the same on paper as in the mouth" (127) [171]. And when it is time to respond—to renew an argument, reverse a thought, or record another reverie—Montaigne's writing method allows him always another say, another (*b*) or (*c*) addition, in his ongoing discussion with himself. And with others. For Montaigne asserts, (*a*) "we must sequester ourselves and repossess ourselves" (176) [234]; he asserts (*a*) "we must reserve a back shop all our own, entirely free, in which to establish our real liberty and our principal retreat and solitude" (177) [235]. But in this solitude suited to (*a*) "our ordinary conversation [which] must be between us and ourselves" (177) [235], Montaigne still succumbs to (*a*) "the gregarious instincts that are inside us" (176) [234]. Writing, he may have a "domestic and private" goal (perhaps defensively, perhaps defiantly so), but, publishing, Montaigne not only permits his readers to overhear his inner "conversation," he implicates them in the sounding of his not-so-private soul.

This many-faced soul that speaks to itself, that makes friends of readers and Montaignes of all men—this is what Montaigne's world mirror shows him of individuality in himself and variety and dissimilarity in the world. With a subtlety and standards all his own, Montaigne, who will not presume to pronounce on other people's truths, who will not dictate to them tracts and the terms of "the truth," will declare on the workings of their minds. We are all patchwork, we are all Perseus, and we are all subject to the same mental "gyration and discord" as Montaigne. Clamoring about diversity amongst men only to claim their similarity to him, thus Montaigne poses his central riddle. A riddle that yields to solution— but only when similarity is shown to be different from identity.

What is Montaigne's own and what he holds in common with others is not an identity; there can be no real identity in a world as unstable as Montaigne's. What there can be are similarities in human activities—in thinking, speaking, writing, and reading. Similarities that can end—with no paradox—in great dissimilarities between individuals' decisions, discourses, writings, and interpretations. The way he and we think, speak, write, and read is more Montaigne's subject than what he or we think, speak, write, and read, or why, or wherefore. This is why, reading, Montaigne's (*b*) "humor is to consider the form as much as the substance, the advocate as much as the cause" (708) [906]. This is why, writing, Montaigne emphasizes the manner, not the matter, of his knowledge— (*a*) "let attention be paid not to the matter, but to the shape I give it" (296) [387]—the manner that mirrors mental motion, the "exercise" and inner "conversation" of our minds.[10] And this is why—when he universalizes himself into man, when he makes friends of readers—Montaigne's call is, not to sectarian, but to subtle minds, decisive in themselves, as his is. Here a contrast with Augustine is pertinent: while Montaigne's method illustrates how men think, Augustine's doctrine shows them what to think; while Montaigne follows the very formlessness of thought, Augustine informs it with Christian content. Put sects aside—and stations, educations, ambitions, all that men take to themselves to identify themselves—and look to the inner movement of the (*a*) "marvelously vain, diverse, and undulating object" (5) [13]; then there is sense to Montaigne's celebrated saying: (*b*) "Each man bears the entire form of man's estate" (611) [782].

Each man alone has all—authors, people, self, the entire world—to take his measure of, to make his own. Working similarly from experience through to words, thus the Babel of authors, the patchwork of people, the Perseuses of all stripes come to invest the world with their diversity. If most often they attend only to their conclusions, Montaigne reminds them of their hesitations, as he too—exploring and experiencing, hesitating and reconsidering, deciding and recording—works through to his individuality. And to his paradoxical originality, which lies in demonstrating this universal activity of thinking in his idiosyncratic writing. Montaigne's world mirror, so often reflecting himself in others, has this last individual realm of investigation and reflection: over a thousand pages and a whole lifetime scintillating in its glass. As Montaigne's *Essays* speak of Montaigne particularly, as they speak not only of the way he experiences but of what, and of why, and of how he thus realizes his individuality, they are his (*b*) "memoirs" (751) [961], his (*a*) "confession" (495) [636], the record of his (*b*) "thoughts" (721) [922], (*b*) "the story of [his] life" (749) [958]—his autobiography. And for them Montaigne metamorphoses his mirror metaphor to make it more nearly traditional: (*c*) "The true mirror of our discourse is the course of our lives" (124) [168].

For lack of a natural memory I make one of paper

The "great storehouse of memory," which is the usual resource for autobiography, is empty in Montaigne. But no matter, for Montaigne traces (*c*) "the course of [his life]" (124) [168], not in what he remembers of past experience, but in what he reaps from it. The day-to-day actions of his life, he disdains writing: (*c*) "My actions would tell more about fortune than about me. They bear witness to their own part, not to mine, unless it be by conjecture and without certainty: they are samples which display only details" (274) [359]. The soldier, the chatelain, the mayor—these are roles Montaigne plays, made up more of masks, robes, and rituals than of Montaigne himself. If we believe Montaigne, he forgets them, for to remember them would reveal too much respect for fortune, too low a bow to outer appearances and insignificant details. His (*c*) "cogitations, a shapeless subject . . . not [lending] itself to expression in actions" (274) [359], this is the movement in Montaigne's mind that reveals his self, that declares (*a*) "the measure of [his] sight, not the measure of things" (298) [389]. And "the measure of [his] sight"—not the memories of his lifetime, but the intellectual hierarchy of his mind—for Montaigne is the essential in his autobiography.

Mockingly, Montaigne reserves for himself the honor of the most absent memory: (*a*) "in this . . . I think I am singular and very rare, and thereby worthy of gaining a name and reputation" (21) [34]. But from his particularity he soon, as so often, generalizes, arguing that (*b*) "excellent memories are prone to be joined to feeble judgments" and that "the magazine of memory is apt to be better furnished with matter than that of invention" (22) [35]. Montaigne can but win in the implied exchange, for presumably the greater the lack of memory, the greater the gain in judgment and invention. And thus his self-depreciation becomes—in an exchange frequent in the *Essays*—self-glorification. Montaigne reverts to his theory of compensation often, never again so blatantly, but over and over again subtly. For he disparages his memory often, but his judgment rarely. And when his invention is in question, Montaigne often ridicules its fantasies, but rarely its free activity.

His memory, (*a*) "monstrously deficient" (21) [34], does much for Montaigne's *Essays*. Not only does it incline Montaigne, his past being effaced, to mirror his present life in his *Essays,* its very weakness strengthens the mental faculties he most wants to display. Understanding, judgment, appreciation, invention—all are set the more to work the less that memory substitutes its acquisitions for their activities.[11] For to he who forgets what he knows, all is new and to be newly considered. When not recalled but reexperienced, (*b*) "places and books"—and all encounters in life—"always smile with a fresh newness" (23) [36] and always require a fresh evaluation. Learning is not acquired, but neither is it much desired, by a mind thus set in motion. For free from received knowledge, such a mind may all the more appreciate and essay its own resources. (*a*) "Like a runaway horse," Montaigne's mind may give birth to "chimeras and fantastic monsters," but they are of his own invention and the source of his *Essays:* "[my mind] gives itself a hundred times more trouble than it took for others, and gives birth to so many chimeras and fantastic monsters, one after another, without order or purpose, that in order to contemplate their ineptitude and strangeness at my pleasure, I have begun to put them in writing, hoping in time to make my mind ashamed of itself" (21) [34]. To his greatly deficient memory, Montaigne owes much of his intellectual liberty and creativity.

At times, however, Montaigne's hierarchy of memory low, judgment high, and invention, if not lofty, at least free does not hold. Heedless of outer appearances and holding only to an inner sense of self, Montaigne is much subject to his moods, and when his mood is low or light, he mocks all. His thinking and writing show nothing but "ineptitude and strangeness"; his judgment and invention are no better than his (*a*) "other faculties [which] are low and common" (21) [34]. Montaigne makes a confession about this sort of self-belittlement: (*c*) "If it did not seem crazy to talk to oneself, there is not a day when I would not be heard growling at myself: 'Confounded fool!' And yet I do not intend that to be my definition." As a moral here, Montaigne wryly offers: "No quality embraces us purely and universally" (173) [230]. As to what to make of his truism, Montaigne, so changeable, counsels, (*a*) "we must consider how our soul is often agitated by diverse passions" (173) [229–30].

Taking Montaigne's counsel involves tracing the effects of his emotions on (*a*) "the measure of [his] sight" (298) [389]. His "diverse passions" alter his meanings for judgment and invention, and the two terms, traditionally distinct, are only provisionally so in Montaigne's usage. Traditionally, judgment is concerned with all the subjects of the world, and invention, only with self-generated subjects. Hence judgment focuses the mind outside of itself, while invention occupies the mind within itself. In this sense, Montaigne writes: (*a*) "so it is with minds. Unless you keep them busy with some definite subject that will bridle and control them, they throw themselves in disorder hither and yon in the vague field of imagination. . . . And there is no mad or idle fancy that they do not bring forth in this agitation. . . . The soul that has no fixed goal loses itself; for as they say, to be everywhere is to be nowhere" (21) [33–34].

Giving it a goal, judgment controls the soul, keeping it from wandering, and for this excellence Montaigne's praise of judgment is frequent and generous. Focusing his soul, Montaigne's judgment focuses—to a degree at least—his identity amidst his changing diversity: (*b*) "Judgment holds in me a magisterial seat, at least it carefully tries to. It lets my feelings go their way, both hatred and friendship, even the friendship I bear myself, without being changed and corrupted by them. If it cannot reform the other parts according to itself, at least it does not let itself be deformed to match them; it plays its game apart" (823) [1052]. The stake in judgment's game is high, for when Montaigne's judgment wavers, so too does his identity defined against the world's diversity. The magistrate becomes a fool, as Montaigne, on the very page before his high praise of judgment, bluntly indicates: (*b*) "He who remembers having been mistaken so many, many times in his own judgment, is he not a fool if he does not distrust it forever after?" (822) [1051]. An emphatic "yes" would be Augustine's response. But often Montaigne is just the self-confident "fool" he describes, when forgetful of his mortal vacillations, when magisterial in evaluating subjects by his own standards.

But when, in another mood, he finds the world imposing on him, reflecting its diversity in him, then Montaigne hesitates: is he judging the world or inventing it? Knowing (*b*) "even . . . his judgment" to be subject to "gyration and discord" (242) [319], Montaigne knows himself to be all diversity, as, in the rhetoric of "Raymond Sebond," he argues: (*a*) "Finally, there is no existence that is constant, either of our being or of that of objects. And we, and our judgment, and all mortal things go on flowing and rolling unceasingly. Thus nothing certain can be established about one thing by another, both the judging and the judged being in continual change and motion" (455) [586]. By this reasoning, (*b*) "all our dreams" and "reveries" are found in "philosophy" (408) [528], and all the world is found, falsified, in our minds: (*a*) "Now, since our condition accommodates things to itself and transforms them according to itself, we no longer know what things are in truth; for nothing comes to us except falsified and altered by our senses" (453–54) [584]. Unsure of his authority, Montaigne takes to calling his *Essays* the (*a*) "reveries of a man who has tasted only the outer crust of sciences" (106) [144], the (*a*) "fancies" he records to reveal his "natural and ordinary pace, however off the track it is" (297) [388], the (*a*) "so many chimeras and fantastic monsters" (21) [34]. In this mood, his at-once diffident and derisive mood, Montaigne devalues judgment along with everything else. Judgment becomes just a presumptuous word for yet another falsifying faculty, and hardly distinct from invention.

Which, then, are Montaigne's *Essays*: the proof that his (*a*) "judgment is not unshod, of which these are the essays" (495) [637], or the (*b*) "most profound and maddest" (668) [854] of his reveries he captures in writing? The question is rhetorical, for its response is an ever-ready version of his adaptable reasoning: (*b*) "If I speak of myself in different ways, that is because I look at myself in different ways" (242) [319]. Montaigne's inconsistency he believes no different from others', and he himself counsels the best method to adopt for its analysis: (*b*) "Nothing is harder for me than to believe in men's consistency, nothing easier than to believe in their inconsistency. He who would judge them in detail (*c*) and distinctly, bit by bit, (*b*) would more often hit upon the truth" (239–40) [316]. Studying Montaigne's judgment and invention "in detail and distinctly, bit by bit," one finds the two faculties regain, if only transiently, their traditional functions. They are distinguished by the focus of their activities and by their contributions to Montaigne's sense of self.

As his substitute for the duration of memory, Montaigne keeps his judgment and his invention in continual motion, reading, reflecting, and recording judgments, entering his reveries and writing them. Experience, often book-learned, best tests Montaigne's judgment, and writing his thinking mind best tries Montaigne's invention. Language read and language written, these are the principal foci of Montaigne's judgment and invention, his self-claimed cardinal qualities. From the continuity of his intellectual activity, Montaigne argues—intermittently, never consistently—for a certain development in his sense of self. Reading, Montaigne forms one version of himself; writing, another; and they conflict.

Reading, Montaigne essays his judgment by gamely meeting other minds and resolutely refusing to be mastered by them. Reading, his interest is in the activity, not in the acquisition of ideas. Were he to acquire any ideas by reading, he would forget them: (*c*) "if I am a man of some reading, I am a man of no retentiveness" (296) [387]. Even his borrowings for the *Essays* he hardly retains: (*a*) "Some of this sticks to this paper; to myself, little or nothing" (107) [144]. All Montaigne's profit from the ideas of others he gains in his pursuit—not his possession—of learning. His own mind wakened to questioning, weighing, and judging, this is profit enough for Montaigne and amply compensatory for his lack of memory. For as he sharpens his judgment against the ideas of others, Montaigne sharpens his sense of self.

"Of the Education of Children" elucidates how judgment becomes Montaigne's master trait, and that of any well-educated man. There Montaigne recommends his nonretentive, always interrogative method of reading to an ideal tutor charged with forming the judgment of a noble child. What with Montaigne calling his *Essays,* not his (*a*) "teaching," but his "study" (272) [357], and his comparing himself to children setting forth (*c*) "their essays to be instructed, not to instruct" (234) [308], it is easy to see Montaigne in "Of the Education of Children" in the double role of counselor and child, advocating the education he is already undertaking. The principle of this education is to avoid passivity: to set the child, the man, to deciding, not receiving, judgments. In this its context, Montaigne's often-quoted simile of bees plundering flowers to make honey as the child ought to plunder books to make his judgment says much for how closely Montaigne allies the formation of judgment to the formation of self. For the child, for the man, memory merely enshrines other people's ideas; but judgment makes them—not (*a*) "on mere authority and trust" (111) [150], but by intellectual daring—his own: (*a*) "For if he embraces Xenophon's and Plato's opinions by his own reasoning, they will no longer be theirs, they will be his. . . . He must imbibe their ways of thinking, not learn their precepts. And let him boldly forget, if he wants, where he got them, but let him know how to make them his own" (111) [150]. The Montaigne-like child, his judgment formed and his education well along, (*c*) "will not so much say his lesson as do it. He will repeat it in his actions" (124) [167]. As Montaigne does: (*a*) "My art and my industry have been employed in making myself good for something; my studies, in teaching me to do, not to write. I have put all my efforts into forming my life. That is my trade and my work" (596) [764]. The child's study will become his self, as Montaigne's book is consubstantial with himself.

Yet, at times, Montaigne would have his readers believe that, wholly uninstructed, he is wise with centuries of thought. Without his studies, without his citations, he would speak just as he speaks, for the classics merely confirm the convictions held by him, unchanged, since his birth. Montaigne earnest in his studies has been quoted; here is Montaigne presumptuous: (*a*) "the firmest and most general ideas I have are those which, in a manner of speaking, were born with me. They are natural and all mine. I produced them crude and simple, with a conception bold and strong, but a little confused and imperfect. Since then I have established and fortified them by the authority of others and the sound arguments of the ancients, with whom I found my judgment in agreement. These men have given me a firmer grip on my ideas and a more complete enjoyment and possession of them" (499) [641–42], "Confused and imperfect" ["trouble et impartaicte"], these are the sorts of adjectives that characterize Montaigne's reveries, the (*a*) "chimeras" (21) [34] of his invention And "crude and simple" ["crues et simples"], these are among Montaigne's favored words for describing his ideas in writing. His (*c*) "cogitations" being a "shapeless subject" (274) [359], it is little wonder that he calls on the ancients to polish what in his mind is "confused and imperfect," that he allows his ideas to be "established and fortified" by theirs. But Montaigne's claims are hardier by far. Not only is he strident about his originality; his "firmest and most general ideas" he equates with the ideas of the ancients. He is a self-invented man who thinking for himself—as it happens—judges as the ancients judge.

Montaigne's mood can answer for which man he is: the diligent man, studying the ideas of others, sharpening his judgment, and forming himself; or the proudly confident man, creating his own ideas, exulting in his invention, and owing himself only to himself. And in another mood, mocking, he can undercut the self-satisfaction of both self-images. But more than Montaigne's moods must answer for why, repeatedly, he raises the issue of what is another's and what is his; why, willfully, he obscures the distinction between the two; and why, inevitably, his judgment and his invention merge in his mind.

What must answer is the common ground for Montaigne and his chosen authors—language—where both Montaigne's judgment and his invention have their work. To explain his "more complete enjoyment and possession" of his ideas in the language of others, there is the "authority," the "[argument]," the style—in short, there is the language that, formed to the thoughts of the ancients, forms Montaigne's thoughts too. And Montaigne's own language, all interwoven with the ancients' in quotation, has the same function of fixing the formless: (*c*) "In order to train my fancy even to dream with some order and purpose, and in order to keep it from losing its way and roving with the wind, there is nothing like embodying and registering all the little thoughts that come to it. I listen to my reveries because I have to record them" (504) [648]. Without language, Montaigne's (*b*) "most profound" and "maddest" reveries, and those that he likes best, are lost; into nothingness, they "suddenly vanish, having nothing to attach themselves to on the spot" (668) [854]. If reading calls Montaigne's judgment to resolution, writing forces his reveries to precision. And if, reading, Montaigne finds authors who suit him, then, writing, he lets them speak for him: (*c*) "I make others say what I cannot say so well, now through the weakness of my language, now through the weakness of my understanding" (296) [387]. Language, his own or others', is Montaigne's way into his mind. The autobiographical experience Montaigne shares with his readers is largely about words.

Writing his own words, citing the words of others, and continually confounding them all, Montaigne, even as his end is to express his selfhood, is hardly strict about authors' ownership.[12] Quite the contrary. Horace and Virgil, Lucretius and Juvenal, Montaigne's many citations and his many comments on them—these are Montaigne's study and, according to Montaigne, are revelatory of both his judgment and his invention, and hence his self. The argument is credible and the material is autobiographical when allusion in writing is valued as highly as expression. The borrowed, the indirect, and the half-said statement being among his favorite ways of speaking, Montaigne, partisan as he is, proclaims their excellence. Of his many borrowings, Montaigne repeatedly asserts their ability to reveal his thought. He picks his citations, places them, and exploits them to his own ends, and they in new service no longer speak the minds of old masters. Occasionally, Montaigne derides his mendicant ability, but most often he proudly avows the liberties he takes with other authors: (*c*) "I, among so many borrowings of mine, am very glad to be able to hide one now and then, disguising and altering it for a new service. At the risk of letting it be said that I do so through failure to understand its original use, I give it some particular application with my own hand, so that it may be less purely someone else's. . . . We naturalists judge that the honor of invention is greatly and incomparably preferable to the honor of quotation" (809) [1034]. Changing the context of a phrase, Montaigne may change its content; thus, even while he quotes, he may invent. Approving or disapproving a cited sentiment, Montaigne may clearly, if indirectly, make known his sentiments. But when clarity is not his aim—rather subtlety, ambiguity, or veiled audacity—then all the more Montaigne lets his borrowings speak for him:

> (c) And how many stories have I spread around which say nothing of themselves, but from which anyone who troubles to pluck them with a little ingenuity will produce numberless essays. Neither these stories nor my quotations serve always simply for example, authority, or ornament. I do not esteem them solely for the use I derive from them. They often bear, outside of my subject, the seeds of a richer and bolder material, and sound obliquely a subtler note, both for myself, who do not wish to express anything more, and for those who get my drift. (185) [245]

His cherished classical authors provide ample examples of Montaigne speaking his "subtler" self through others' words. Cicero on the loftiest of friendships is a central voice in Montaigne's "Of Friendship," and Lucretius does much to define man's limits in the "Apology for Raymond Sebond." But it is rare that Montaigne allows any one author to dominate an essay. Chosen as he likes, unidentified and intermingled one with another, Montaigne's classical authors champion as he decides the ideals and philosophical ideas he most admires. Quoted on fighting, they reveal his fascination with war, the nobleman's profession that he praises greatly but practices little. Quoted on dying, and so often, they articulate his obsession with his own death, which he wishes so studied and seemly. And perhaps the deaths of the ancients, destined by fortune or determined by chance, "sound obliquely" Montaigne's unacknowledged religious doubt.

Citing the classics, Montaigne follows, and flaunts, the intellectual fashion of his time, but his intimacy with the ancients betrays a deeper motivation for his love of quotation: his nostalgia for a lost world of heroics and high morals.[13] Their Latin set off from his vernacular, their verse from his prose, Montaigne's cited authors accentuate the contrast he laments between ancient times and his own times. Where his corrupt age will not change, Montaigne will—on paper and in person, his literary inspiration serving his life ambition. Learning from the ancients, from their books (a) "fuller and stronger" (297) [389] than those of the moderns, Montaigne studies, beyond heroics and heritage, the ethics of self:

(*a*) "if I study, I seek only the learning that treats of the knowledge of myself and instructs me in how to die well and live well" (297) [388].

Reading, Montaigne forms himself; reading, he merely seconds himself. Writing, Montaigne teaches his reveries (*c*) "some order and purpose" (504) [648]; writing, he merely records them (*a*) "without order and purpose" (21) [34]. His *Essays,* the showcase of his reading and writing, are proof of Montaigne's judgment—and the product of his invention. All of these inconsistencies are subject to Montaigne's reasoning: (*b*) "If I speak of myself in different ways, that is because I look at myself in different ways" (242) [319]. Resolutely, Montaigne refuses to allow that his judgment and his invention are, in the last analysis, distinguishable. But he insists that both faculties, their abilities recorded in lieu of memories, are decidedly autobiographical. For written by him in his present, the decisions of Montaigne's judgment and the daydreams of Montaigne's invention, with time passing, become his past, his paper memory, his autobiography.

My history needs to be adapted to the moment

Making a memory of paper, Montaigne makes a complicated pact with time. His past, he lets go; his future, too death-shadowed, he leaves distant; eternity, he respects but keeps unreal, above and uninformative; only his present Montaigne claims, finding it ample for his living and his writing. And this even though he is a man obsessed with death: (*a*) "never did a man so distrust his life, never did a man set less faith in his duration" (61) [86]. Indeed, the more he feels his life slipping away, the more Montaigne works to seize and savor its every moment: (*b*) "The shorter my possession of life, the deeper and fuller I must make it" (853) [1092]. But not in desperation, rather with satisfaction, Montaigne meditates on the moment and manages his life: (*b*) "It takes management to enjoy life. I enjoy it twice as much as others, for the measure of enjoyment depends on the greater or lesser attention that we lend it" (853) [1092]. Of time, he writes, (*b*) "I do not want to pass it; I savor it, I cling to it" (853) [1091]. Montaigne privileges the present, not because it is fleeting, but because it is full.

Philosophers praise the present, and Montaigne cites several (Seneca, Cicero, and Epicurus (8–9) [18]),[14] but few men listen. Most fall prey to the call of the future rather than the past, perhaps because Montaigne thinks his generalized multitude as forgetful as he is, more likely because

Montaigne, criticizing, writes too early to know Romantic and modern memory. What men lose rushing into the future, he maintains, is what is and what they are. Divination is a (*a*) "notable example of the frenzied curiosity of our nature, which wastes its time anticipating future things, as if it did not have enough to do digesting the present" (27) [42]. And dissatisfaction keeps men gaping after future fancies (225) [296–97], as ambition sets them striving for more than they are (857) [1096]. Insistently, Montaigne asserts the incompatability of a future-oriented outlook with an inward-looking gaze: (*b*) "We are never at home, we are always beyond. Fear, desire, hope, project us toward the future and steal from us the feeling and consideration of what is, to busy us with what will be, even when we shall no longer be" (8) [18]. Explaining the cause of this (*b*) "commonest of human errors" (8) [18], this wasteful anticipation, Montaigne indicates his desired destination in life: (*c*) "Every man rushes elsewhere and into the future, because no man has arrived at himself" (799) [1022]. To arrive at oneself, this for Montaigne is wisdom, this the achievement of its greatest precept: "Know thyself." Resisting the future to remain in the present, reducing his expectations to sharpen his concentration, Montaigne stays "at home" to see clearly and continually into his copious self.

Montaigne's self-absorption in the present is hardly a Christian preoccupation, encouraged as it is by pagan philosophers rather than by the injunctions of the Scriptures. Devoted to the present as the place for self-inquiry and all worthwhile activity, and disdainful of the future as fit for little more than ambition, vain emotion, and thwarted satisfaction, Montaigne reveals only worldliness in his relation to time. When, exceptionally, he looks to eternity, to (*a*) "the grandeur of [the] sublime and divine promises" of the Scriptures, he declares them "unimaginable, ineffable, and incomprehensible" (385) [499]. Stopping speculation short with superlatives, Montaigne praises eternity greatly to dismiss it completely. As a defense for this dismissal, he argues: (*a*) "Man can only be what he is, and imagine only within his reach" (387) [501]. Hence Montaigne stays in his beguiling present; hence he allows the future to block at death, with no apparent door opening onto eternity. The closing words of Augustine's *Confessions,* "We must knock at [God's] door. . . . only then will the door be opened to us" (13.38), are foreign to the very feel of Montaigne's earthbound *Essays.* Montaigne declares himself a devout Catholic, believing, no doubt, that his God-given self will achieve stability in eternity, that then he will see "face to face" and will know even as he is known (1 Cor. 13:12). But Montaigne's belief urges him to no seeking, no centering, of himself in eternal types, nor does it forestall his striving to see, in all darkness, himself in all his volatility here below.

With reason, a Church censor could complain of Montaigne's (*c*) *"unsanctioned terms,* (*b*) 'fortune,' 'destiny,' 'accident,' 'good luck' and 'bad luck,' 'the gods' and other phrases" (234) [308], for they bespeak Montaigne's ready adaptability to this world ungoverned by the next. Here chance and change—hardly Christian "phrases," hardly Christian "gods"—rule. And on them Montaigne depends to spur his mind to the incessant activity that suits him best. Montaigne has need of constant stimuli—events, sights, and others, not only authors; his sort of nature, (*a*) "it wants to be stimulated; . . . not shocked; but roused and warmed up by external, present, and accidental stimuli. If it goes along all by itself, it does nothing but drag and languish. Agitation is its very life and grace" (26) [41]. To set his (*c*) "spirited mind" (818) [1045] to the chase, Montaigne counts on chance: (*b*) "I have little control over myself and my moods. Chance has more power here than I. The occasion, the company, the very sound of my voice, draw more from my mind than I find in it when I sound it and use it by myself" (26) [41]. Even withdrawn into his tower, Montaigne hardly subscribes to scholarly rigor in "Il Penseroso" seclusion: (*b*) "There I leaf through now one book, now another, without order and without plan, by disconnected fragments. One moment I muse, another moment I set down or dictate, walking back and forth, these fancies of mine that you see here" (629) [806]. "Without order and without plan," the phrase is the leitmotiv repeating as Montaigne gives himself over, again and again, whether in solitude or in society, to chance and to change.

Responding to the world, Montaigne is adaptable; training his judgment, enjoying his invention, he is stable. Montaigne mutable in the moment or Montaigne imperturbable in time: the contradiction is central to the *Essays.* To demonstrate its extent, and the degree of Montaigne's vacillation, two (*b*) strata serve well. Montaigne's existence is subject to the "wind of accident," and endlessly divisible:

> (*b*) Not only does the wind of accident move me at will, but, besides, I am moved and disturbed as a result merely of my own unstable posture. . . . I give my soul now one face, now another, according to which direction I turn it. . . . All contradictions may be found in me by some twist and in some fashion. Bashful, insolent; (*c*) chaste, lascivious; (*b*) talkative, taciturn; tough, delicate; clever, stupid; surly, affable; lying, truthful; (*c*) learned, ignorant; liberal, miserly, and prodigal: (*b*) all this I

see in myself to some extent according to how I turn. . . . I have nothing to say about myself absolutely, simply, and solidly, without confusion and without mixture, or in one word. *Distinguo* is the most universal member of my logic. (242) [318–19]

Montaigne's existence is firmly in his control, and all of one piece:

(*b*) I customarily do wholeheartedly whatever I do, and go my way all in one piece. I scarcely make a motion that is hidden and out of sight of my reason, and that is not guided by the consent of nearly all parts of me, without division, without internal sedition. My judgment takes all the blame or all the praise for it; and the blame it once takes, it always keeps, for virtually since its birth it has been one; the same inclination, the same road, the same strength. And in the matter of general opinions, in childhood I established myself in the position where I was to remain. (616) [790]

How is chance to be reconciled with essence, and Montaigne's passing, mutable in the moment, reconciled with his being, which persists? A metaphor important to the *Essays* offers a solution.

(*a*) "It is myself that I portray" (2) [9], Montaigne announces in his Preface, introducing his readers at the start of his *Essays* to the portrait-painting metaphor he writes into all their strata. And already, as he equates his portrait with the pages of his *Essays,* Montaigne plays the potential for variability and ambiguity in his metaphor:

(*a*) I want to be seen here in my simple, natural, ordinary fashion, without straining or artifice. . . . My defects will here be read to the life, and also my natural form, as far as respect for the public has allowed. Had I been placed among those nations which are said to live still in the sweet freedom of nature's first laws, I assure you I should very gladly have portrayed myself here entire and wholly naked. Thus, reader, I am myself the matter of my book. (2) [9]

Nature and art are in conflict here, and ironically so. Montaigne portrays his "simple, natural, ordinary fashion"—but constrainedly out of respect for the public, but composed in an art form, but completely other than as he would desire ("entire and wholly naked"). "Thus, reader," how much of Montaigne's "natural form" is "the matter of [his] book"? Doubts arise, and the dilemma of which to trust, nature or art. Nature being so persistently praised, art—constraining, composing, falsifying—must be the ousted value. But what, then, of the portrait Montaigne presents? It is devalued before it is even seen. And later showings of Montaigne's portrait receive little more respect: (*a*) "this dead and mute portrait, besides what it takes away from my natural being, does not represent me in my best state, but fallen far from my early vigor and cheerfulness, and beginning to grow withered and rancid" (596) [764–65]; (*c*) "my portrait is a cadaver on which the veins, the muscles, and the tendons appear at a glance, each part in its place" (274) [359]. "This dead and mute portrait," "a cadaver"—Montaigne's portrait is far from capturing the lifelikeness of his "natural form." And Montaigne, in a well-known disclaimer, acknowledges as much:

> (*a*) As I was considering the way a painter I employ went about his work, I had a mind to imitate him. He chooses the best spot, the middle of each wall, to put a picture labored over with all his skill, and the empty space all around it he fills with grotesques, which are fantastic paintings whose only charm lies in their variety and strangeness. And what are these things of mine, in truth, but grotesques and monstrous bodies, pieced together of divers members, without definite shape, having no order, sequence, or proportion other than accidental? . . . I do indeed go along with my painter in this second point, but I fall short in the first and better part; for my ability does not go far enough for me to dare to undertake a rich, polished picture, formed according to art. (135) [181–82]

Nature and art being age-old antagonists, and, in Montaigne's time, nature being the habitual victor, Montaigne does nothing notable in finding for truth in his simple and natural, not his polished and portrayed, self.[15] But in the more subtle play of his portrait-painting metaphor, Montaigne subverts the traditional opposition of nature and art. He places emphasis, not on his portrait, but on his painting of it, and with this distinction, seemingly slim but repeatedly stressed, Montaigne wins for art a higher valuation. Received artistic forms, which require "straining and artifice," are rejected, but self-determined artistic modes are praised and to be practiced. As an activity not an artifact, a process not a product, art is seen to be expressive of the individual; hence art becomes admirable because—in its practice—"natural." There is a hint of this appreciation in the Preface, in the verbs of choice Montaigne emphasizes. And in the grotesques, vibrant with "variety and strangeness" and more vividly depicted than the "rich, polished picture, formed according to art," invention freely works. Even in Montaigne's "cadaver," where (*c*) "one part of what [he is] was produced by a cough, another by a pallor or a palpitation of the heart," there the natural man, if "dubiously" (274) [359], determines his art.

But Montaigne's reappraisal of art as an activity is better seen in a later essay that testifies not only to the emphasis in his portrait-painting metaphor but to the moral philosophy it implies. "Of Repentance" is where Montaigne, extending his metaphor, encompasses—and entangles—the roles of chance and essence in his life, as he experiences the present and as he endures over time:

> (*b*) Others form man; I tell of him, and portray a particular one, very ill-formed, whom I should really make very different from what he is if I had to fashion him over again. But now it is done.
>
> Now the lines of my painting do not go astray, though they change and vary. . . .
>
> I cannot keep my subject still. It goes along befuddled and staggering, with a natural drunkenness. I take it in this condition, just as it is at the moment I give my attention to it. I do not portray being; I portray passing. Not the passing from one age to another, or, as the people say, from seven years to seven years, but from day to day, from minute to minute. My history needs to be adapted to the moment. I may presently change, not only by chance, but also by intention. This is a record of various and changeable occurrences, and of irresolute and, when it so befalls, contradictory ideas; whether I am different myself, or whether I take hold of subjects in different circumstances and aspects. So, all in all, I may indeed contradict myself now and then; but truth, as Demades said, I do not contradict. (611) [782]

"I do not portray being; I portray passing": these are the conciliatory (and celebrated) sentences in Montaigne's long elaboration of contradictions.

"I do not portray being." Montaigne does not, because he must pose for a portrait of being, and he, living and changing in the present, cannot keep still. The Montaigne who is already portrayed, and particularly poorly, is ensconced, metaphorically, in paint; historically, in print. He belongs to the past: "it is done." Montaigne cannot repent of or reform this past self who, though once his "to fashion," is now finished, and forgotten; who is no more. He cannot repent or reform because neither hindsight nor foresight, what he was or what he would be, communicate Montaigne's being to Montaigne. Montaigne has no continuity of identity in time. And, besides, repenting and reforming are suspect activities. In the terms of his metaphor, they are artful and deceptive, like polishing and perfecting his portrait, not natural and representative, like his varying painting in rhythm with (*b*) "the world [that] is but a perennial movement" (611) [782].[16] "I do not portray being," Montaigne insists, because, in the words of his "Apology," (*a*) "we have no communication with being" (455) [586].

"I portray passing." In the always-passing present is time enough for

Montaigne's encounters with the world and with his work. The changing circumstances of the chance-ruled world, Montaigne meets in the moment, with his own changes brought about "not only by chance, but also by intention." And he paints the interchange in the lines of his portrait that "change and vary." All is in flux—as phenomena. Yet the flux is so attentively assessed ("from day to day, from minute to minute") that its movement achieves a certain duration—in Montaigne's mind: a duration wholly inner; not determinative of Montaigne's identity, but dependant on Montaigne's consciousness, on Montaigne, persistently, judging and inventing. (*c*) "My trade and my art is living" (274) [359]: this is Montaigne's metaphor in its quintessence. His ever-varying self ever vigilant to his variations: this is Montaigne's essence.[17] Mutable in time, Montaigne meets and moves with the vagaries of chance in his world, his work, his self; persisting in time, Montaigne, as he judges, as he creates, simply continues meeting and moving with these "various and changeable occurrences." In the moment, chance and essence—the forces that animate Montaigne's life—have their reconciliation.[18]

Making his home in the moment, Montaigne lives to participate in the world's perpetual movement and writes to keep abreast of it. As time slips him forward to new moments, Montaigne, writing without a plan or a promise, shifts his focus too, recording the later moments in later essays and later additions to the *Essays*. Time animates Montaigne's active, additive art. Time is the medium for his metamorphoses as, practicing his art, Montaigne models—as well as his *Essays*—his self: (*c*) "In modeling this figure upon myself, I have had to fashion and compose myself so often to bring myself out, that the model itself has to some extent grown firm and taken shape. Painting myself for others, I have painted my inward self with colors clearer than my original ones" (504) [647–48]. Not as a portrait, but as a process, is Montaigne's (*c*) "book consubstantial with its author, concerned with [his] own self, an integral part of [his] life" (504) [648]. Montaigne's *Essays* are always in progress because he always is: (*b*) "we go hand in hand and at the same pace, my book and I" (611–12) [783]. It is thus that his writings in the present—accumulated, augmented, and kept always current with his life—faithfully paint Montaigne's self-portrait, the rendering of his being in its unremitting passing.

A thousand contrary ways of life

Generalizing, Montaigne sets all men rambling, each on his own erratic route: (*b*) "Life is an uneven, irregular, and multiform movement"

(621) [796]. Of the instant, nothing more, is he sure—(*a*) "I guarantee no certainty, unless it be to make known to what point, at this moment, extends the knowledge that I have of myself" (296) [387]—which is all any autobiographer, anchored in the present for all his pronouncements on the past, can guarantee. But many an autobiographer takes the present as a vantage point from which to draw elaborate maps of meaning for his life. From this view Montaigne turns away, never claiming conversion to what he would be in order to contemplate what he was, never questing into the future for final knowledge of himself or into the past for the pristine experience of himself. Montaigne is a traveler in life, but not as the frequent autobiographical metaphor implies, not with a purpose or a plan for his voyage, only as he haphazardly and erratically travels:

> (*b*) My plan is everywhere divisible; it is not based on great hopes; each day's journey forms an end. And the journey of my life is conducted in the same way. . . .
> . . . I, who travel most often for my pleasure, do not direct myself so badly. If it looks ugly on the right, I take the left; if I find myself unfit to ride my horse, I stop. . . . Have I left something unseen behind me? I go back; it is still on my road. I trace no fixed line, either straight or crooked. (747, 753) [955, 963]

The (*b*) "road along which" Montaigne will go "as long as there is ink and paper in the world" (721) [922] cannot be a narrative route, so unforeseen and unsustained is his progress on it. Montaigne's mode of traveling, of living, exacts his desultory mode of writing. The "plan . . . everywhere divisible," demanding "no fixed line, either straight or crooked," directing none of Montaigne's numerous turns and many returns, is the non-narrative "plan" of Montaigne's *Essays*.

(*c*) "My style and my mind alike go roaming" (761) [973]: thus Montaigne vaunts his literary form.[19] His writing method—contradictory, changing, constantly turning back on itself—is as well-suited to following the mind's "roaming" movement as it is ill-suited to declaiming sure truths, which could hardly stand in his unstable (*a*) (*b*) (*c*) text. Montaigne can allow himself over the years to change his text as he changes his mind because his created "essay" form has no set contours. Without a solo subject to center him, an authoritative reference to check him, or a narrative to carry him along, Montaigne, writing, can go as he pleases, letting "fortune" arrange his "bits": (*a*) "As my fancies present themselves, I pile them up; now they come pressing in a crowd, now dragging single file" (297) [388].[20] To readily serve his wandering focus, Montaigne likes language (*a*) "succulent and sinewy, brief and compressed, (*c*) not so much dainty and well-combed as vehement and brusque . . . not pedantic, not monkish, not lawyer-like, but rather soldierly" (127) [171]. Such is the language Montaigne writes, only, supposedly, (*b*) "for few men and for few years" (751) [960], for he disdains hallowing language as inscription written to enshrine thought. His language, Montaigne stresses, is not the monument of his past thought, but the supple medium of his present thinking.

He would have preferred writing his *Essays* as letters (246) [185]; he berates himself for not keeping a daily journal (166) [221]: Montaigne admires literary forms permitting discontinuity, daily change, the always fresh start. His chosen form is better; for more than allowing, as letters and journals do, repeated access to the discontinuous present, Montaigne's *Essays* allow limitless access to any number of presents. His *Essays* are, as it were, revisitable; their subjects are, as it were, renewable. The distinction between revising and revisiting *Essays* Montaigne stresses—in theory, if not always in practice:

> (*a*) This bundle of so many disparate pieces is being composed in this manner: I set my hand to it only when pressed by too unnerving an idleness, and nowhere but at home. Thus it has built itself up with diverse interruptions and intervals, as occasions sometimes detain me elsewhere for several months. Moreover, I do not correct my first imaginings by my second—(*c*) well, yes, perhaps a word or so, but only to vary, not to delete. (*a*) I want to represent the course of my humors, and I want people to see each part at its birth. It would give me pleasure to have begun earlier, and to be able to trace the course of my mutations. (574) [736–37]

Sometimes, the truth is, Montaigne compromises his commitment to the present. He succumbs to the human proclivity to preserve and polish in words what passes in life, and his written register of the present, not simply and strictly added to, but altered, becomes a revision of the past. But, in principle, Montaigne resists this sort of revision; he resists a steady movement to improvement, continuity moving to conclusion.[21] Revisiting his *Essays* and renewing their subjects, he quickens to "birth" new ideas; he sets into motion new "mutations"—erratically. For to continually and consistently chart "the course of [his] mutations" is not Montaigne's, even wishful, intention.[22] Montaigne, according to Montaigne, does not develop; he digresses. And, to Montaigne's mind, this— "with diverse interruptions and intervals"—is the movement and all the interest of "the course of [his] humours."

Metaphorically, Montaigne takes to drink to capture in the metaphor his movement over the years: (*b*) "I add, but I do not correct. . . ."

> . . . I fear to lose by the change: my understanding does not always go forward, it goes backward too. I distrust my thoughts hardly any less for being second or third than for being first, or for being present than for being past. We often correct ourselves as stupidly as we correct others. (*c*) My first edition was in the year 1580. Since then I have grown older by a long stretch of time; but certainly I have not grown an inch wiser. Myself now and myself a while ago are indeed two; but when better, I simply cannot say. It would be fine to be old if we traveled only toward improvement. It is a drunkard's motion, staggering, dizzy, wobbling. (736) [941–42]

A drunkard judges poorly of which is best, his first, second, or third impressions, deciding usually for whichever is well within his inebriated vision. Montaigne's metaphor, unflatteringly, prompts disconcerting questions that deflate the pretensions of authors—particularly autobiographers and scholars. If a man splits into "indeed two," or several, or any number of selves, what are the criteria for judging him "now and , , , a while ago"? If later does not determine "better," what are the merits of autobiographical and scholarly hindsight and the hardiness of judgment it inspires? The confident stance of later judging earlier shaken, how does one chart the development of "a motion," not "toward improvement," but simply "staggering, dizzy, wobbling"? Indeed, why does one chart "a drunkard's motion," his every turning on a route that, crossing and recrossing, leads nowhere? Is there not work enough, and less manipulative, in recording his course "with diverse interruptions and intervals"?

A man's actions (*a*) "commonly contradict each other so strangely that it seems impossible that they have come from the same shop" (239) [315]: such is the difficulty most authors deny by imposing a design on diversity. Montaigne finds it (*a*) "strange to see intelligent men sometimes going to great pains to match these pieces" (239) [315]. And he criticizes (*b*) "even good authors [who] are wrong to insist on fashioning a consistent and solid fabric out of us" (239) [315]. And, more strongly, he criticizes (*b*) "even good authors" who "choose one general characteristic, and go and arrange and interpret all a man's actions to fit their picture; and if they cannot twist them enough, they go and set them down to dissimulation" (239) [315]. Artists, perhaps, might ably pattern a (*b*) "relatedness and conformity" (824) [1054] between a man's actions and his many aspects, but of their ability Montaigne is wary: (*b*) "I leave it to artists, and I do not know if they will achieve it in a matter so complex, minute, and accidental, to arrange into bands this infinite diversity of aspects, to check our inconsistency and set it down in order. Not only do I find it hard to link our actions with one another, but each one separately I find hard to designate properly by some principal characteristic, so two-sided and motley do they seem in different lights" (824) [1054]. If authors are unjustly authoritative, art—other than Montaigne's, that is—is, surely, manipulative.

Disdaining the (*a*) "common patterns" (169) [225], Montaigne distrusts the written form—the narrative form—in which they are commonly presented. He believes narrative, not serviceably descriptive, but subtly determinative of a man's life story. The links of causality, even of sequence, in a narrative, he believes, are, at best, inexact, at worst, falsely explanatory. Montaigne has an (*b*) "impulsive mind" (297) [389]; he loves (*b*) "the poetic gait, by leaps and gambols" (761) [973]; his mind is too impetuous for narrative: (*c*) "being a sworn enemy of obligation, assiduity, perseverance . . . there is nothing so contrary to my style as an extended narration. I cut myself off so often for lack of breath; I have neither composition nor development that is worth anything" (76) [105]. But where Montaigne cannot give "composition . . . worth anything," most likely most others cannot either. Writing (*c*) "without a plan and without a promise" (219) [289], Montaigne responds to the many aspects of his subjects; other writers, too often, cling to their own stubborn insistence on what is and what is not. Montaigne's example is historians of (*a*) "the commonest sort":

> (*a*) Those . . . spoil everything for us. They want to chew our morsels for us; they give themselves the right to judge, and consequently to slant history to their fancy; for once the judgment leans to one side, one cannot help turning and twisting the narrative to that bias. They undertake to choose the things worth knowing, and often conceal from us a given word, a given private action, that would instruct us better; they omit as incredible the things they do not understand, and perhaps also some things because they do not know how to say them in good Latin or French. (304) [397]

Autobiographers are hardly exempt from Montaigne's criticism. For he does not accord privileged subjective insight to those judging their own lives who would better arrange the pieces. Every person being (*a*) "so shapeless and diverse in composition," and "each bit, each moment" (244) [321] playing its own game, autobiographers who too diligently argue their raison d'être, artfully turning and twisting their life designs, they too falsify. Because Montaigne's conviction is that, unceasingly, (*a*) "there is as much difference between us and ourselves as between us and others" (244) [321]; because Montaigne's suspicion is that narrative, exacting sequence, encourages systemization, thus falsification: hence to Montaigne's mind, autobiographer, biographer, any writer is an undependable narrator of human lives.[23]

Montaigne's generalizations are weighted with autobiographical implications, which he argues in images of suffocation and freedom:

> (*b*) Men do not know the natural infirmity of their mind: it does nothing but ferret and quest, and keeps incessantly whirling around, building up and becoming entangled in its own work, like our silkworms, and is suffocated in it. *A mouse in a pitch barrel* [Erasmus]. It thinks it notices from a distance some sort of glimmer of imaginary light and truth; but while running toward it, it is crossed by so many difficulties and obstacles, and diverted by so many new quests, that it strays from the road, bewildered. (817) [1044–45]

The autobiographer who trusts to his (*h*) "second or third" "thoughts" just because they are not first, who corrects himself "as stupidly" as he corrects "others" (736) [941]—he keeps "incessantly whirling around, building up and becoming entangled in [his] own work." Forming a too (*b*) "consistent and solid fabric" (239) [315] of his written life—he "in [his] own work, like our silkworms, . . . is suffocated." A "glimmer of imaginary light and truth" may be that of an autobiographer's self-interpretation, which he—too diligently designing his life—too persistently pursues. Thus in his autobiography he turns away from discovery: (*a*) "for once the judgment leans to one side, one cannot help twisting the narrative to that bias" (304) [397]. Refusing, "while running toward" his sighting of truth, to accommodate the "difficulties" and "obstacles" he encounters, such an autobiographer refuses change to hold to his construct; he denies his present life as he lives it to hold to his past life as he would write it.

While writing a life, liberty must be kept if "new quests" are to be met. Montaigne, ever his own example, demonstrates. Freedom of subject, he secures: (*b*) "Any topic is equally fertile for me" (668) [854]. And the forethought of system and structure, he abjures: (*b*) "the heart and the core of the matter I am accustomed to leave to heaven" (713) [912]. Thus Montaigne refuses self-imposed restrictions; and those imposed by others, notably discretion, he skirts: (b) "in these memoirs, if you look around, you will find that I have said everything or suggested everything. What I cannot express I point to with my finger" (751) [961]. Montaigne may have (*c*) "some personal obligation to speak only by halves, to speak confusedly, to speak discordantly" (762) [974], but whatever his obligation, it is hardly a limitation, for he finds indirection an excellent means of self-expression: (*b*) "I go out of my way, but rather by license than carelessness. My ideas follow one another, but sometimes it is from a distance, and look at each other, but with a sidelong glance. . . . It is the inattentive reader who loses my subject, not I. Some word about it will always be found off in a corner, which will not fail to be sufficient, though it takes little room" (761) [973].

The minutiae of his thinking, which would be neglected in a narrative of events, and (*a*) "the course of [his] mutations" (574) [737], which would be smoothed in a narrative given to explanation—his *Essays*, Montaigne maintains, respond to these nuances. Thus Montaigne reveals his (*a*) "natural and ordinary pace, however off the track it is" (297) [388], into which written movement he easily slips his subsequent mutations. They are but later stages in his endless quest, which is never advanced on any road to "the truth," which is always "off the track" and so always able to turn aside for a new thought. And others (*b*) "in this hunt for knowledge" (818) [1045] fare as Montaigne does. If they think themselves well advanced, (*c*) "it is a sign of contraction of the mind . . . or of weariness" (817–18) [1045]. If they think themselves unconcerned, (*b*) "it is only personal weakness. . . . There is always room for a successor, (*c*) yes, and for ourselves" (817) [1045].

Incessantly, men must think; their "natural infirmity," their instinct to ferret and quest, allows them no stillness. But if their intellectual activity be a bane or a blessing, this is of their choosing. Either "incessantly whirling . . . building up and becoming entangled," men must stifle in their ideas; or meeting "difficulties," "obstacles," and setting off on "new quests," they must stray from their ideas. Such are the options Montaigne offers in his two images. *"A mouse in a pitch barrel"* or Montaigne on always new routes, such are the analogies Montaigne suggests. Intellectual imprisonment or intellectual freedom: the choice, thus presented, is no choice. Men will always hanker after a "glimmer of imaginary light and truth" and hasten after what they cannot have, but rather than stubbornly insisting on this illusory certainty, they do better by far to wander far, wherever leads their minds' (*b*) "irregular perpetual movement, without model and without aim" (818) [1045]. As many as are the (*a*) "contrary ways of life" (169) [225], so many are the "new quests" to be undertaken: (*c*) "A spirited mind never stops within itself; it is always aspiring and going beyond its strength; it has impulses beyond its powers of achievement. If it does not advance and press forward and stand at bay and clash, it is only half alive. (*b*) Its pursuits are boundless and without form; its food is (*c*) wonder, the chase, (*b*) ambiguity" (818) [1045]. Montaigne's declaration is an invitation. (*b*) "In this hunt for knowledge" (817) [1045], whether the prey be self or other subjects—(*b*) "for all subjects are linked with one another" (668) [854]—there is always a (*b*) "road in another direction" (817) [1045] for those willing to continually seek, rather than too hastily secure, knowledge.

So many interpretations disperse the truth

Questing, judging, inventing, interpreting—in short, thinking—men share, never a common truth, only a common endeavor, fated, as the Tower of Babel, to failure. No matter. Montaigne's *Essays* are his evidence that truth is not for men, that men are capable only of secular, historical, individual, ephemeral interpretations, found and as soon lost on the (*a*) "thousand different roads" (387) [501] of their worldliness (*a*) "How diversely we judge things! How many times we change our notions!" (423) [546]. The exclamations are rhetorical: all the challenge is to write such versatility, to read such diversity, to speak at all one to another.

The only means of communication between men, the only mainstay of their community, is sincerity, which Montaigne allows in theory to lament its scarcity in practice: (*a*) "Since mutual understanding is brought about solely by way of words, he who breaks his word betrays human society. It is the only instrument by means of which our wills and thoughts communicate, it is the interpreter of our soul. If it fails us, we have no more hold on each other, no more knowledge of each other. If it deceives us, it breaks up all our relations and dissolves all the bonds of our society" (505) [650]. Language is central, but—having no sure reference in the Scriptures or other authority, serving only individuals' relative, ephemeral, and perhaps dishonorable intentions—words may interpret, or they may dissimulate, souls. Montaigne's desire for intimacy is matched by his doubts of its feasibility. And his suspicions hardly help the communication, for while he asserts his honesty, he distrusts that of others: (*a*) "But whom shall we believe when he talks about himself, in so corrupt an age, seeing that there are few or none whom we can believe when they speak of others, where there is less incentive for lying?" (505) [649]. Cautious, Montaigne does not assume his communication with others, and he does not trust their interpretations of him. He finds men more given to twisting interpretations to suit their own interests than to trying to decipher another's intended meanings: (*a*) "there is no sense or aspect, either straight or bitter, or sweet, or crooked, that the human mind does not find in the writings it undertakes to search. . . . For there are so many means of interpretation that, obliquely or directly, an ingenious mind can hardly fail to come across in any subject some sense that will serve his point" (442) [569–70]. But misinterpretation is not always malicious, and Montaigne, with humor, admits as much. Knowingly, he identifies the advantages of (*c*) "a cloudy and doubtful style," wherein an author may "express himself, through stupidity or shrewdness, a bit obscurely and contradictorily: he need not worry. Numerous minds, sifting him and shaking him, will squeeze out of him a quantity of meanings, either like his own, or beside it, or contrary to it, which will all do him honor" (442) [570].

Knowing he will be misread, or perhaps unread, Montaigne posits himself as his own reader. But even Montaigne is unsure of understanding Montaigne. As a writer, he prides himself on his plain speaking, but, as a reader, he retrieves his own meanings with difficulty. Distanced from the immediacy of writing, Montaigne appreciates the difficulties of interpretation. He acknowledges that he too, like any reader, can lose himself in the labyrinth of interpretation: (*c*) "This also happens to me: that I do not find myself in the place where I look; and I find myself more by chance encounter than by searching my judgment. I will have tossed off some subtle remark as I write. . . . Later I have lost the point so thoroughly that I do not know what I mean; and sometimes a stranger has discovered it before I do. If I erased every passage where this happens to me, there would be nothing left of myself" (26–27) [41–42]. Montaigne had best not erase his *Essays,* for thus he erases his paper memory. He had best not correct his *Essays,* for thus he risks change for the worse (425–26) [549].

Few are the privileges Montaigne reserves for himself as author; at most, the paternity of his book, but not—time passing, distance gained—authority over it: (*c*) "To this child [this book], such as it is, what I give I give purely and irrevocably, as one gives to the children of one's body. The little good I have done for it is no longer at my disposal. It may know a good many things that I no longer know and hold from me what I have not retained and what, just like a stranger, I should have to borrow from it if I came to need it" (293) [383]. Writing done and interpretation begun, Montaigne accepts the role of stranger to his own meanings, similar to any reader of his written thoughts, because he believes that before the finished work, author and reader—if (*a*) "able" (93) [126]—are equal. Fortune, Montaigne's catchall phrase for the way the world must be, makes the author take his place beside the reader: (*a*) "Fortune shows still more evidently the part she has in all these works by the graces and beauties that are found in them, not only without the workman's intention, but even without his knowledge. An able reader often discovers in other men's writings perfections beyond those that the author put in or perceived, and lends them richer meanings and aspects" (93) [126]. With a modern insistence, though not a modern vocabulary, Montaigne believes texts multivalent, and he argues—ungraciously when his sincerity is in question, zealously when his profundity is the issue—that neither author nor reader is the possessor of their many meanings. Not even the autobiographer as author and reader of his own words has access to all meanings. In Montaigne's hermeneutical theory, language is democratically problematic.

The *Essays*—(*c*) "these little notes, disconnected like the Sibyl's leaves" (838) [1071]—are obscure to Montaigne too. But no matter, for what Montaigne does not understand, he essays again. Time stealing his earlier meanings, time gives him changes for new meanings. Borrowing from more authors, recording more reveries, writing newly into his *Essays*, Montaigne easily ends in inconsistency. But inconsistency, as he likes to repeat, is central to his character, and Montaigne makes of it an intellectual virtue: (*c*) "To treat matters diversely is as good as to treat them uniformly, and better: to wit, more copiously and usefully" (377) [490]. Montaigne never lacks matter, for he may study all—all knowledge being relative—in himself: (*b*) "I study myself more than any other subject. That is my metaphysics, that is my physics" (821) [1050]. His psychological/metaphysical/physical science proves nothing but uncertainty, yet he hardly minds. He knows the excellence of uncertainty, the incentive to the quest. He enjoys the hermeneutical abyss, the (*c*) "wonder, the chase, (*b*) [the] ambiguity" (818) [1045] keeping him questing. (*b*) "What do I know?" (393) [508] is Montaigne's motto. And in a (*c*) "book consubstantial with its author" (504) [648], to ask "What do I know?" ["Que sçay-je?"] is to ask "Who am I?" ["Qui suis-je?"]." Continually questing, this is the question—the quintessential autobiographical question—to which Montaigne essays, again and again, new solutions.

3

ROUSSEAU
Confessions, Dialogues, Reveries

A Rousseau in society, and another in seclusion

ROUSSEAU ANNOUNCES individuality as the touchstone of autobiography, but he hardly finds its expression easy. "The truth" he believes is personal, not Christian and communal, not even secular and philosophical. "I feel my heart"[1] [5]—emotionally, sensually, intellectually: this is Rousseau's autobiographical truth. Defining himself to himself, Rousseau need not submit to the Scriptures nor spar with the secularists, but depicting himself for others, he must. The emphatic individual must portray himself in the language common to all; and therein, for Rousseau, is the paradox and the problem of autobiography. Early, in the first preamble to the *Confessions,* Rousseau recognizes the problem: "For what I have to say I would need to invent a language as new as my project; because which tone, which style should I take to sort out the immense chaos of emotions, so diverse, so contradictory, often so vile and sometimes so sublime, which has ceaselessly agitated me?" [1153]. "Which tone, which style" does Rousseau take? First that of an ardent narrative replete with Christian figures, which are reassigned Rousseauian values. Then defensive dialogues with a wished-for reader, both questions and answers provided by the author. Then solitary meditations written as essays, in which thinking and writing are to keep rhythm together. Yet in the later pages of these late essays, Rousseau admits his "emotions" and "sensations" poorly served by literary signs. Writing autobiographically throughout his last fifteen years—*The Confessions,* the *Dialogues, The Reveries*—Rousseau increasingly finds his self-translations into language unsatisfactory.

Rousseau undertakes his *Confessions* confident of the truth of his life ("I will be truthful"), his ability to express it ("I will tell all"), and the success of his autobiographical project ("I will rigorously fulfill my title") [1153]. He will write "the life of a man," "his true life," which has never before been written: "Histories, lives, portraits, character studies! What are all those? Ingenious novels built on a few actions, a few speeches relating to them, and subtle conjectures in which the author seeks rather to shine himself than to find the truth. Seizing upon the main traits of a character, he links them with invented traits, and as long as the whole makes a portrait, what does it matter if it is like?" [1149]. Concerning earlier *Confessions*, Rousseau is silent.[2] Of an earlier self-portraitist, he is summary: "Montaigne paints himself like, but in profile" [1150].[3] Biographers and autobiographers, those "falsely sincere writers" [1150]: the former are too ignorant and the latter too reticent to write of truth other than as it is habitually, partially, and imperfectly seen in "Histories, lives, . . . all those." Rousseau will expose in his *Confessions*—out of the confessional, unveiled before all—truth never before shown. And he will order and explain his individual truth in a more than autobiographical work, in a secular work "unique and useful" [1150], "a book precious to the philosophers" [1154].[4] Searching his own heart, he will virtually inaugurate "the study of the human heart" [1154], exposing, ordering, and explaining "the good, the bad, indeed, all" [1153]. Since selectivity is a form of autobiographical falsity, surely narrative completeness must communicate "the truth."

But "indeed, all" is more easily promised than achieved, and bravado does not produce books. Even before he finishes the *Confessions,* Rousseau's emotional weather clouds over. And he must write autobiographically again, trying again—changing tone, changing style—to reveal "the truth." The clarity Rousseau confidently claims for the *Confessions* darkens as his insecurity deepens, giving way, gradually, to obscurity—to the hesitations at the end of the *Confessions,* to, eventually, the repetitions without reason of the too-long *Dialogues.* The narrative completeness so essential to the *Confessions*—"so thoroughly all holds together, and is one in [his] character" [1153]—is fragmented in the *Dialogues,* as is Rousseau. *Rousseau, juge de Jean-Jacques* reveals Rousseau, the anxious author, writing to correct Jean-Jacques's "lying reputation" [1153]. But so theatrical is Rousseau's authorial voice, and so eerily absent is Jean-Jacques, "he . . . [whom] the public misrepresents and slanders at will" [665], that Rousseau, as autobiographer, is hardly in the *Dialogues.* Certainly, Rousseau's suspicions are revelatory of his self, but amidst the "shadows" and "mysteries" of his haunted imagination, Rousseau judging Jean-Jacques is strangely otherworldly, a posthumous presence writing the autobiography of his reputation. Only when he sacrifices his manuscript of multiple selves—on the altar of Notre Dame, at the hands of false friends, to chance and to the years to come—only then does Rousseau, as auto-biographer, take on flesh and blood again. Laying to rest his too many roles, Rousseau ceases to dialogue, interminably, with his enemies. No longer writing their history, he can take up his own.

Again, differently. At the end of his life, "detached" from his "fellow-men" and "the whole world" (*R*27) [995], Rousseau has yet to attempt an autobiographical work for himself, a work that does not originate as a countermove to society. His *Confessions* have been made to his readers; they have also been shaped to meet and modify the expectations of those readers. Rousseau's continual concern for the "order" and "sequence" of his *Confessions* reveals, in part, his respect for the norm of chronological narrative, a norm that works both for and against his self-knowledge. Carefully ordering his life for presentation in the *Confessions,* Rousseau sacrifices, to a degree, introspection for exposition. Desperately defying public opinion in the *Dialogues,* he sacrifices his first person *I* for the third person split of Rousseau and Jean-Jacques. Expository writing serves Rousseau's social interests well, both the defenses he makes of himself in his *Confessions* and *Dialogues* and the attacks he makes on society in his philosophical works. But writing defensively or assertively, Rousseau cannot write interrogatively. Writing his self for others, Rousseau can-not—quite—write his self. Only by banishing the audience of others from his mind, by dispensing with the linear narrative and defensive dialogues designed to win them—only then does Rousseau hope, in his last autobiographical work, to mirror the movement of his mind and memory. Then, perhaps, he may evoke on paper his own presence; then, he may discover, there at last, his elusive self.

For yet to be revealed is the real Rousseau. As early as the first pre-amble to the *Confessions,* Rousseau announces a split: "There was a Rous-seau in society, and another in seclusion who did not resemble him in the least" [1151]. In the *Dialogues,* Rousseau tries, vainly, to unify the public and private versions of his self. By the start of the *Reveries,* Rousseau is, paradoxically, several and solitary—persecuted under many guises in the world and isolated in his self-righteousness. Who, then, is Rousseau? The *Confessions* are finished, the narrative that is to reveal "a portrait in every way true to nature" (*C*17) [5]. *Rousseau, juge de Jean-Jacques* is finished, the dialogues that are to judge "the for and against" of this "truth" [663]. Yet the Rousseau of "the study of the human heart" [1154] or the Rous-seau completely "other" [5], he of the first preamble to the *Confessions* or he of the last, and his successors in *Rousseau, juge de Jean-Jacques*—none, it seems, is the real Rousseau. For at the start of the *Reveries*, Rousseau has still to ask, "But I, . . . what am I?" and he has to answer, "This must now be the object of my inquiry" (*R*27) [995].

Another literary form—a cross between journal entries and essays, a record of daydreams and thoughts—is to do Rousseau's work of self-discovery. In these *Reveries*, the "thread" (*C*379) [407] of confessional narrative is to be dropped; the "for and against" [663] of judicial dialogues renounced. Without "order," without "method," Rousseau will record the "variations of [his] soul" (*R*33) [1000]. His findings will prompt no philosophy, for no longer Augustinian in his moral certainty, Rousseau will no longer contribute to the study of man. Adversity, though hardly humility, restricts him to the study of only Rousseau: "I have nothing left in the world to fear or hope for, and this leaves me in peace at the bottom of the abyss, a poor unfortunate mortal, but as unmoved as God himself. . . . Such an exceptional situation is certainly worth examining and describing, and it is to this task that I am devoting my last days of leisure" (*R*31, 33) [999, 1000]. Denounced by men, Rousseau disdains them; ostracized by society, he is self-sufficient. Thus, all the better, he will succeed in his self-study. Keeping "a formless record of [his] reveries" (*R*32) [1000], he will record those that best reveal himself to himself, the reveries of his solitary hours, wherein, he assures, "I am completely myself and my own master, with nothing to distract or hinder me, the only ones [wherein] I can truly say that I am what nature meant me to be" (*R*35) [1002].

No longer ambitious, Rousseau does not even claim—much—originality. More or less accurately, he places himself in the autobiographical tradition. He acknowledges, though evasively ("if sometimes"), that he too, though unknowingly ("involuntarily"), painted himself in the *Confessions* "in profile" (*R*77) [1036]. And he acknowledges Montaigne his predecessor in his latest autobiographical endeavor: "My enterprise is like Montaigne's, but my motive is entirely different, for he wrote his essays only for others to read, whereas I am writing down my reveries for myself alone" (*R*33–34) [1001]. Never mind that Montaigne declares for his *Essays*, as stridently as Rousseau does for his *Reveries*, "no goal but a domestic and private one,"[5] Rousseau insists on the originality of his readership. After all, Montaigne published his essays while alive; Rousseau will not. Rousseau's is the braver isolation—so he argues, repeatedly, too vigorously, while, like Montaigne, scrupulously preserving his last papers for later eyes. The "solitary person" (*R*32) [1000], "with one accord . . . cast out by all the rest" (*R*27) [995], cannot resist leaving behind further evidence of his innocence, final papers contributing—like all the others—to his defense. The reader looking over his shoulder: Montaigne wrote for him, and Rousseau—however "formless" his "record" (*R*32) [1000]—does so too.

Social and philosophical in the *Confessions,* set upon and anxious in the *Dialogues,* solitary and ardent in the *Reveries*—whatever his emotional constellation, Rousseau would have his reader sight him through the lens of his prose: "The facts are public knowledge and anyone can know them, but what is important is to find their secret causes. Naturally, no one could have seen these better than me; to show them is to write the history of my life" [1151]. Not to write is to leave to posterity an impostor, "a character who is foreign to me" [1153]. A public Rousseau, a private Rousseau; one a stranger, one secret: the truth of Rousseau's life is polarized. Hence he works all the harder to present—to impose—his version of "the truth."

Witness Rousseau's attitude—emblematic or symptomatic, as you will—to spoken and written language. Spoken and written language are to Rousseau two very different means of self-expression: the former is uncontrollable, often deceptive, always inadequate; the latter, by craft, can be made to express truth.[6] Introductions made in person, impromptu speeches before a group, the give-and-take of conversation—all of Rousseau's speech in society reveals him, he insists, "not only at a disadvantage but in a character entirely foreign to me" (*C*116) [116]. Thus Rousseau chooses to control the impression he gives by making himself known in writing to Madame de Warens in "a fine letter in a rhetorical style" (*C*55) [48]; to Madame de Broglie by "an epistle in verse" (*C*273) [290]; to Madame Dupin in an ill-advised love letter (*C*274) [292]; to Monsieur de Malesherbes in four autobiographical letters; to the public in the *Confessions* and the *Dialogues;* to, curiously, himself, his only supposed reader, in the *Reveries of the Solitary Walker.* "Let the last trump sound when it will," Rousseau will come before God Himself, "this work [*The Confessions*] in [his] hand" (*C*17) [5].

Yet making fine verbal appearances, perhaps Rousseau falsifies his substance. Manipulating words well, perhaps he misleads—his very control of prose serving him ill. Rousseau himself becomes suspicious when, well into the *Reveries,* still seeking his ever-elusive self and the style to speak him, he comes to question his language that has gone before. Writing ever newly his autobiographical *I,* Rousseau has repeatedly found his written selves inadequate, as what is private in him has gone public to be wrongly interpreted; as what he has written, the style obedient to his will, has let complexities slip from his grip. He has persevered, only to find that his elegant verbal selves become strangers as they are read by others, only to find, time and again, that his words belong to the world and he is all alone, still untold. Rousseau acknowledges that "the 'Know Thyself' of the temple at Delphi was not such an easy precept to observe as [he] had thought in [his] *Confessions*" (C63) [1024], that "the real and basic motives of most of [his] actions are not as clear to [him] as [he] had long supposed" (R94) [1051], that "the self-knowledge which [he has] devoted [his] last hours of leisure to acquiring" (R107) [1061] is an endless study. But, more and more, to do his ongoing work of self-discovery, Rousseau turns away from the literary signs of his autobiographical expertise to the sensations of his past experience. Autobiographer several times, Rousseau ends his career still seeking another—this one solitary, surely "the true" one—of the selves of his creation. And occasionally, but fleetingly, he communes with this Rousseau, alive in his memory and ineffable, with whom he speaks a symbolic, wholly nonverbal language.

Public and private versions of the self: are they the same, similar, estranged? knowable or not? communicable? Rousseau articulates questions that all autobiographers, overtly or not, answer. Augustine and Montaigne expressly interpret themselves in the Christian and classical traditions; they translate themselves into the phrases, figures, and forms of the Scriptures or the ancient authors. Addressing God, Augustine knows no inner division; reading and writing by the Scriptures, he describes and unites public and private versions of himself. Playing off secular authors, Montaigne, writing and quoting, willfully confounds the worldly and the intimate, in himself, in his *Essays*.

Rousseau is the first to cleave, completely, a schism between his public and private selves. And the longer he writes autobiographically, the sharper he cuts the divide. All arrogance at the start, Rousseau borrows from the autobiographical tradition to explore the expectations and limitations of what went before. And he rejects the learning and accepted self-translations of other ages and other authors to insist on the essence of his inner reality, his autobiographical individuality. Then he too learns the difficulty of translating memory into metaphor, essence into expression; he too learns the limits of self-writing. At the start, Rousseau rewrites autobiographical conventions—public *Confessions* in a tell-all narrative, private essays in a loudly public voice—but, ultimately, he rejects any and all conventions to lapse into symbolic silence. Language—

scriptural, secular, whichever style, whatever substance—Rousseau finds less and less serviceable as he finds his soul ever clearer and more austere; until, finally, he insists that language fails—never his own depths.

Continually changing autobiographical forms, Rousseau learns over the years the inescapable—and modern—autobiographical lesson: language may help or language may hinder self-knowledge. At the start of each autobiographical work, Rousseau swears his language will say all. At the end of each, he finds his language as inexpressive as the silence of his auditors or readers. Rousseau explores, he describes, he analyzes his changing styles. And autobiographer several times over, he ends by writing not only his autobiography but a literary theory. A theory in which language splits down the same fault line as self: there is public language and private language, and communication is no more assured to one than self-revelation is to the other. A theory in which what society writes and reads is not what the self writes and reads, and the difference is to be recognized, sometimes lamented and sometimes exploited. A theory in which control—by the writer of the reader—is often at issue in the relations between self and other. And in the relations between self and self, for Rousseau the autobiographer is also Rousseau his own reader and under the sway of his own words. The moving tale of his innocence and the world's abuse, be it fact or be it fiction, is an artful autobiographical story. And Rousseau is perhaps the first and the last to read with ardent conviction what in it may well be only fiction.

The decision I made to write and to hide

At his autobiographical start, how pronounced is the schism between Rousseau and the world; how profound are its consequences? The two Rousseaus of the *Confessions* (before their further division in the *Dialogues,* before their renunciation in the *Reveries*)—he who is solitary, elegantly written, well under control, and he who is social, impromptu, fallible; Rousseau as he likes and writes himself, and Rousseau as the world sees and styles him:[7] does their doubleness engender Rousseau's duplicity? A duplicity perhaps reprehensible given his philosophy in the *Confessions,* perhaps desirable given his defensive position in the world. A duplicity perhaps even inevitable given Rousseau's zealous rhetorical efforts to woo and win his readers. Early, Rousseau's readers learn to negotiate between extremes, and, early, they learn to question Rousseau's many—and contradictory—argumentative and narrative means.

Rousseau confesses all, Rousseau merely alludes to all: in a clear and honest narrative, he reveals his soul; in a narrative necessarily obscure, he cunningly conceals his truth. The revealed and the concealed--much of Rousseau's autobiographical theory is in this imagery.[8] His usual version of the revealed and the concealed is simplicity itself: his enemies hide; Rousseau is all in the open. Rousseau's unfailing honesty in the face of a malevolent society—the simple extremity of the view renders it suspect. Very occasionally, and evasively, with numerous qualifications, Rousseau confesses to concealment. And the rarity and incongruity of these avowals renders them significant. And ironic too, for Rousseau subtly admits to concealment, in passage after passage, where he declaims loudest his autobiographical frankness.[9]

One quotation may speak for Rousseau's narrative innocence, another for his wariness and literary experience. With good intentions, Rousseau promises simplicity and openness in his *Confessions:* "I should like in some way to make my soul transparent to the reader's eye, and for that purpose I am trying to present it from all points of view, to show it in all lights" (C169) [175]. But intentions meet counterintentions, the light of sincerity encounters the darkness of conspiracy, and Rousseau acknowledges the troubled secrecy surrounding his writing:

> I would give everything in the world if I could enshroud what I have to say in the darkness of time. Being forced to speak in spite of myself, I am also obliged to conceal myself, to be cunning, to try to deceive, and to abase myself to conduct that is not in my nature. The ceiling under which I live has eyes, the walls that enclose me have ears. Uneasy and distracted, surrounded by spies and by vigilant and malevolent watchers, I hurriedly put on paper a few disjointed sentences that I have hardly time to re-read, let alone to correct. (C263) [279]

Ironically, Rousseau will light the very dark of "the darkness of time" with "the truth": "I know that despite the huge barriers which are ceaselessly erected all round me, they are always afraid that the truth will escape through some crack. How am I to set about piercing those barriers?" (C263) [279]. Transparency and obscurity, revelation and mystification—the extremes, ungracefully, refuse balanced reconciliation.

Rousseau's "objectivity" continually at odds with his subjectivity is another clash in his textual discord. Rousseau attempts an objective account of his fall from public grace, which is revelatory and admonitory:

> In relating . . . the events that concern me, the treatments I have suffered and all that has happened to me, I am in no position to trace them to their prime mover or to assume reasons when I state facts. . . . If there

are any among my readers generous enough to try and probe these mysteries till they discover the truth, let them carefully re-read the last three books [9, 10, 11]. Then let them apply the information in their possession to each fact that is set down in the book which follows, and go back from intrigue to intrigue and from agent to agent till they come to the prime movers of it all. I am absolutely certain what the result of their researches will be, but I lose myself in the obscure and tortuous windings of the tunnels which lead to it. (C544) [589–90]

Rousseau knows the end his readers will reach because he creates the obscure route leading to it. Having lost the personal papers that were to aid in writing part 2 of his *Confessions,* he has only one guide through the past—his feelings. From what he felt, and still feels, he recreates what must have been: "I have only one faithful guide on which I can count; the succession of feelings which have marked the development of my being, and thereby recall the events that have acted upon it as cause or effect. . . . I may omit or transpose facts, or make mistakes in dates; but I cannot go wrong about what I have felt, or about what my feelings have led me to do; and these are the chief subjects of my story" (C262) [278]. Rousseau's inner version of the past decides which events he describes, why and in what way, and which letters he cites, with what commentary. His later years offering him nothing but "misfortunes, treasons, perfidies, and sad, heart-rending recollections" (C263) [279], Rousseau smoothly, suspiciously, attributes all the evil to the conspiracy, citing dates and details and, most disarmingly, whole letters from his "self-styled friends," to document the "memorable epoch in [his] life, which gave birth to all [his] other misfortunes" (C262) [278]. Rousseau's "objectivity"—completely emotional—is illusory in practice.

And it is misleading in theory. Seemingly, Rousseau would leave his readers free to discover "the truth." Thus his endeavor to render his "soul transparent" (C169) [175]; thus his endeavor to leave his reader further at liberty, even to create "the truth": "by relating to him in simplest detail all that has happened to me, all that I have done, all that I have felt, I cannot lead him into error, unless wilfully; and even if I wish to, I shall not easily succeed by this method. His task is to assemble these elements and to assess the being who is made up of them. The summing-up must be his, and if he comes to wrong conclusions, the fault will be of his own making" (C169) [175]. Rousseau's openness is hardly ingenuous, for he grants his reader the minimum in interpretative freedom: the freedom to fail or to agree with Rousseau, who keeps the cipher for translating

Rousseau. For writing his "feelings," his "inner thoughts," "the history of [his] soul" (*C262*) [278], Rousseau painstakingly creates "the being who is made up of them" (*C169*) [175]. And, despite his protests, he repeatedly asserts, "'Such is my character'" (*C169*) [175].

Rousseau is the master of autobiographical theory that he never follows. Precisely because it is contradictory. And because it is impracticable ("all that has happened, . . . all that I have done, all that I have felt"), improbable ("simple detail" in telling "all"), unattainable (rendering a "soul transparent" in words), and unimaginable (readers genuinely charged with "the summing-up" of his work). Rousseau will have it all ways, and not one as he says. The simplicity and completeness of "all" is to leave readers free to discover truths other than those according to Rousseau. And they do, but neither because Rousseau is simple nor because Rousseau tells all. Rousseau's simplicity is stylized; his "all" is a tautly told tale; and the argument behind his ideal of autobiographical openness equaling autobiographical objectivity is decidedly sophisticated—and sophistical. As for the interior of his soul, Rousseau is all the more artful in his skillful control of what to show, what not to show. Either way—revealing or concealing—Rousseau is manipulating, never letting go the idea of a right and wrong "summing-up," conclusion, reading of himself.

Asserting his clarity, avowing his secrecy, affirming his objectivity, then his subjectivity—Rousseau betrays in his very swing between extremes the impetus to falsity in both his psychology and his literary theory. On the side of candor, Rousseau insists his emotions speak truly and outspokenly, hence how can he, even should he wish, dissemble? On the side of cunning, Rousseau claims, merely cleverly, to hide "the truth" in obscure meanings. His motive is not, of course, deceit; rather the defense of his "truth." His means, he insists, are far from desirable, to him wholly unnatural: "forced . . . in spite of [himself], obliged to conceal [himself], to be cunning, to try to deceive ["reduit . . . à [se] cacher, à ruser, à tâcher de donner le change"], he lowers himself to "conduct that is not in [his] nature" (*C263*) [279]. His candid nature belied, necessity becomes Rousseau's tutor as his strange, and estranged, place in the world obliges him to stoop to subterfuge. Secrecy clouds over his transparency of soul, and an essential, lamentable, subtlety comes to characterize his *Confessions*.

Thus writes the autobiographer of his *Confessions,* justifying his literary tactics to his readers. Writing of his past experience, Rousseau confesses to quite another behavior, to dissembling that has nothing to do with the defense of the daring philosopher, nothing to do with the world of power and diplomacy that persecutes him. He confesses to the dissembling of a mere little boy, a lying little boy—become now a man. The youthful Rousseau, the child born for liberty, the later philosopher of nature, does not improve under the tutelage—read the restraint—of society. Both fine and flawed in his youth, he does not exchange his virtues and vices for those more seemly to his age or his occupation as philosopher, novelist, autobiographer. Thus Rousseau insists, in his *Confessions,* his *Dialogues,* his *Reveries,* his personal letters, his autobiographical fragments: he—inside, his success aside—is the same Rousseau as ever. This unalterable Rousseau is he to whom belongs a decided tendency to evasion, fiction, and deception when in difficult situations.

The behavioral pattern is set early in Rousseau's life; the telltale linguistic pattern, early in his written life. In the third book of the *Confessions,* Rousseau writes, "the decision I have made to write ["écrire"] and to hide ["me cacher"] is precisely the one that suits me" [116].[10] To write and to hide, the verbs are curiously balanced. In the next sentence, Rousseau implies the subordination of one verb to the other: "If I had been present, people would not have known my value" (C116) [116]. By implication, Rousseau absent, or hidden, would make known his real worth. But before this second sentence is read, before this context determines the ambiguous content of the first sentence, the reader of the *Confessions* has learned to associate the verb "to hide" ["se cacher"] with such verbs as "to lie" ["mentir"], "to dissemble" ["dissimuler"], and "to be silent" ["se taire"]. For such, inevitably, are Rousseau's evasive maneuvers in situations where he encounters injustice or indifference, and where he feels a need for secrecy.

Young, Rousseau learns artifice. When first expelled by adult injustice from his childhood paradise—after the mystery of the broken comb and his unmerited punishment—Rousseau and his equally ill-treated cousin take to hiding behind appearances:

> We lived as we are told the first man lived in the earthly paradise, but we no longer enjoyed it; in appearance our situation was unchanged, but in reality it was an entirely different kind of existence. No longer were we young people bound by ties of respect, intimacy, and confidence to our guardians; we no longer looked on them as gods who read our hearts; we were less ashamed of wrongdoing, and more afraid of being caught; we began to be secretive, to rebel, and to lie [nous commencions à nous cacher, à nous mutiner, à mentir]. (*C*30–31) [20–21]

When apprenticed to the engraver, Rousseau learns under the "tyranny" of his master "vices" that in a fairer situation, he claims, "I should . . . have despised" (C40) [31]: "I learnt to covet in silence, to conceal, to dissimulate, to lie, and finally to steal" ["j'appris à convoiter en silence, à me cacher, à dissimuler, à mentir, et à dérober"] (C40–41) [32].

Not only injustice sends Rousseau into hiding behind lies; the perception of hidden motives in others causes him to redouble his defensive maneuvers:

> Dry and cold questionings, without any sign of approval or blame at my answers, gave me no confidence. When there was nothing to show whether my chatter pleased or displeased I was always in a state of fear, and tried less to reveal my thoughts [je cherchois moins à montrer ce que je pensois] than to avoid saying anything that might injure me. . . . A man who is interrogated begins for that reason alone to be on his guard; and should he suppose that one has no real interest in him but merely wants to make him talk, he lies or keeps quiet or redoubles his caution [il ment, ou se tait, ou redouble d'attention sur lui-même], since he would rather be taken for an idiot than be the dupe of another's curiosity. (C84) [81–82]

The reserve of Madame de Vercellis, in whose house Rousseau served as a valet, occasions these remarks on the opening and the hiding of his heart. Quite another demeanor is Rousseau's before those who treat him with kindness or, at the least, honest interest. Before the Comte de Gouvon and "his very kind reception," Rousseau is truthful: "He questioned me with interest and I replied with sincerity" (C94) [93]. Before those whom he loves, Rousseau thinks and speaks honestly, effortlessly, his heart all openness. Madame de Warens is Rousseau's continual example: "For I should have found it impossible to keep anything secret from her: my heart was open before her as before God" (C185) [191].

The secret Rousseau keeps, the secret of the innocent maid Marion accused instead of him of stealing the ribbon? Shame rules Rousseau in that incident from start to finish, from his initial lying to his later rewriting of the scene in which to confess. Reproach, even justified reproach, elicits Rousseau's evasive responses. Accused of theft, Rousseau turns accuser; guilty, he lies his way to public, but provisionary, innocence. And he lies all the more energetically as he from whom he would most hide his culpability—"as a thief, a liar, and a slanderer" ["voleur, menteur, calomniateur"]—is himself: "I should have rejoiced if the earth had swallowed me up and stifled me in the abyss. But my invincible sense of shame prevailed over everything. It was my shame that made me impudent, and the more wickedly I behaved the bolder my fear of confession made me. I saw nothing but the horror of being publicly proclaimed, to my face, as a thief, a liar, and a slanderer" (*C*88) [86]. The incident could have had two outcomes: what happened (Rousseau unjust and hiding in his lies) and what should have happened (Rousseau finding the heart in which to confess himself). Rousseau defensive, and before everyone, was stubborn; Rousseau before a sensitive person, and taken aside, would have told all: "If I had been allowed time to come to my senses, I should most certainly have admitted everything. If M. de la Roque had taken me aside and said: 'Do not ruin that poor girl. If you are guilty tell me so,' I should immediately have thrown myself at his feet, I am perfectly sure" (*C*88–89) [86–87]. Rousseau before Madame de Vercellis or Rousseau before the Comte de Gouzon; before a heart closed and cold or before a heart questioning and kind: Rousseau's audience determines all, his hiding or his honesty, his telling convincing tales or his telling the truth.

And which sort of heart have Rousseau's imagined readers? They who—by their very silence—evince no "real interest" (*C*84) [82], who let slip no "sign of approval or blame" (*C*84) [82], who, perhaps, work surreptitiously against him, who, worse, might unjustly and publicly accuse him. The readers whom Rousseau wishes heavenly and just, whom he fears to be all too earthly, whom—his imagination running on—he foresees, generation after generation, incomprehensibly cruel to the most amiable of men: what face does Rousseau put on them? None. His suspicions cloud his imaginative vision, and Rousseau sees others only as strangers; their actions are suspect, their feelings secret, their thoughts inscrutable—enshrouded as they are in his imagery of secrecy, which is, as always, revelatory.

Not by chance do the concealed interests of Madame de Vercellis and her household, and the concealed guilt of Rousseau in that household, recall to Rousseau's mind the shadowy intrigues he believes still haunt him. A few months youthful service, and Rousseau marks an epoch in his life: "I believe that it was then that I was first the victim of that malicious play of intrigue ["ce jeu malin des intérets cachés"] that has thwarted me all my life" (*C*85) [82]. The coincidence of events is hardly accidental, the lesson gleaned from them hardly surprising. Ending his apprenticeship in deceit and entering his mastery of lying, Rousseau discovers the world, not surprisingly, deceitful and full of lies. Having learned subtlety, he finds others sly; having learned to hide the truth, he finds much obscure. The "malicious game of hidden interests" [82], Rousseau criticizes its rules, but, early, he enters the play. Whatever metaphoric form this intrigue takes, whether he imagines it as "the work of darkness" (*C*544) [589], "the abyss of evil" (*C*544) [589], or "the horrible mystery" (*C*574) [622], Rousseau senses it always as half hidden, as something he cannot clearly see. At the time he writes his *Confessions,* he is the victim of these hidden interests, of a worldwide conspiracy—so he believes. And so his readers—as, reading on, they learn "more of [his] life . . . [and] get to know [his] disposition" (*C*45) [37]—know Rousseau's characteristic response to such a situation. "The decision [Rousseau] made to write ["écrire"] and to hide ["se cacher"] is precisely the one that suits [him]" [116]. To write and to hide: the verbs are balanced because they represent parallel acts. Rousseau does not only write in hiding, he hides in writing.

One can only judge me after reading me

At the start of both parts 1 and 2, Rousseau presents himself, in almost identical phrases, as the incarnation of his words:

Whether Nature did well or ill in breaking the mould in which she formed me, is a question which can only be resolved after the reading of my book [c'est ce dont on ne peut juger qu'après m'avoir lu]. (*C*17) [5]

After two years of patient silence, in spite of my resolutions I take up the pen once more. Suspend your judgment, reader, as to the reasons that force me to it. You cannot judge them till you have read me to the end [Vous n'en pouvez juger qu'après m'avoir lu]. (*C*261) [277]

Read, then judge: such is the order Rousseau would have his readers observe; such is the order he fully expects them to reverse. Rousseau's request seems reasonable, yet, considered strictly, hardly feasible. As if reading, and for that matter writing, can be clearly separated from judging. As if his "truth" exists in a vacuum, and is not, as it is read, written, and assessed, unavoidably verbal—his figures forming, his style embodying, his language defining the "true" Rousseau. The unvoiced issue, then, is whose words to believe, others' learned elsewhere or—read, then judge—Rousseau's. Language being partisan, Rousseau's request is far from innocent. If his rhetoric have effect, Rousseau is really—that "which can only be resolved after the reading of [his] book" (*C*17) [5]— the words of his autobiography, indisputably, and emphatically not the "wicked" Rousseau of the world.

To efface the worldly Rousseau, misunderstood and maligned, to replace him with the inner Rousseau who is simple and sincere, Rousseau offers all his memory—and artistry:

I never promised to present the public with a great personage. I promised to depict myself as I am; and to know me in my latter years it is necessary to have known me well in my youth. As objects generally make less impression on me than does the memory of them, and as all my ideas take pictorial form, the first features to engrave themselves on my mind have remained there, and such as have subsequently imprinted themselves have combined with these rather than obliterated them. There is a certain sequence of impressions and ideas which modify those that follow them, and it is necessary to know the original set before passing any judgments. I endeavour in all cases to explain the prime causes, in order to convey the interrelation of results. (C169) [174–75]

Working so that the "certain sequence of impressions and ideas"—as in his mind, so in his readers'—"modify those that follow them," Rousseau orders his narrative that "the interrelation of results" be, from first to last, in his service. By assigning to certain events the value of "causes" and to others the value of "results," Rousseau accents selected experiences in his life and thus patterns his self-presentation. And—if his effort to influence ("I endeavour in all cases . . . to convey") is successful—thus Rousseau patterns his readers' reception. His confidence in "sequence," "causes," and "the interrelation of results" (C169) [174–75] is far from rare, his narrative method far from random. Rousseau's method is no less, and considerably more, than the method of every well-ordered argument, every narrative with a purpose. His readers may reach their own "conclusions" (C169) [175], but only if they distance themselves from Rousseau's narrative voice, only if they determine for themselves what in Rousseau's life were causes and what were effects, what in his written life is to be believed and what not, and identify and judge, by their own system of values, Rousseau's virtues and defects.

Rousseau, for one, passionately believes himself true to his words. From his earliest youth, he shows himself unusually sensitive, emotionally subject, to the influence of language. Learning to read, Rousseau learns who he is: "I know nothing of myself till I was five or six. I do not know how I learnt to read. I only remember my first books and their effect upon me; it is from my earliest reading that I date the unbroken consciousness of my own existence" (C19) [8]. Still a child, Rousseau's character is admirably formed by his reading the *Lives* of Plutarch: "It was this enthralling reading, and the discussions it gave rise to between my father and myself, that created in me that proud and intractable spirit, that impatience with the yoke of servitude, which has afflicted me throughout my life, in those situations least fitted to afford it scope"

(*C*20) [9]. Novel reading gives Rousseau his first—and lasting—lesson in who others are. From novels, he acquires passion without experience and knowledge without understanding:

> In a short time I acquired by this dangerous method, not only an extreme facility in reading and expressing myself, but a singular insight for my age into the passions. I had no idea of the facts, but I was already familiar with every feeling. I had grasped nothing; I had sensed everything. These confused emotions which I experienced one after another, did not warp my reasoning powers in any way, for as yet I had none. But they shaped them after a special pattern, giving me the strangest and most romantic notions about human life, which neither experience nor reflection has ever succeeded in curing me of. (*C*20) [8]

Feeling is Rousseau's test for truth, for the emotional accuracy of his memories, even their factual exactitude, and his sense of the just and the unjust in his experience. But "the truth" Rousseau writes is often heroic, dramatic, romantic, poetic, picaresque—in short, whether banal or bizarre, decidedly literary.[11] For reading, always eclectic, forms—and writing enshrines—Rousseau's sensibility. And—inversely, inseparably—Rousseau's sensibility, from youth to old age, dictates his very literary autobiographical "truth."[12]

No stranger to the power of a text, Rousseau perfects his own art of persuasion. Acknowledging his susceptibility to his preferred master, implicitly, he acknowledges his ambition: "Continuously preoccupied with Rome and Athens, living as one might say with their great men, myself born the citizen of a republic and the son of a father whose patriotism was his strongest passion, I took fire by his example and pictured myself as a Greek or a Roman. I became indeed that character whose life I was reading" (*C*20–21) [9]. Such a transformation of his readers into "the character" of his text is something Rousseau works hard for in his *Confessions*. Rousseau's higher goal is "a work . . . useful . . . for the study of men" [3]; his more self-serving end is to justify his ways, not to God, but to men.[13] What better way to justify than by inciting his readers to identify—though he has vices as well as virtues (thus he serves his purposes)—with his "proud and intractable spirit" (*C*20) [9], his, "as one might say," "Greek or . . . Roman," admirably high-minded self? Both like and unlike other men, Rousseau appeals to his readers both as everyman and as the unique individual he believes himself to be. Since his readers' role is to judge, knowing themselves similar to Rousseau, to everyman, they, seemingly, must judge Rousseau's all too human faults leniently. How much more leniently they must judge if they, as it were, become Rousseau.

Opening his *Confessions* with the judgment day, Rousseau announces by assertion alone what he hopes to effect by his narrative. In a reversal of textual time, beginning with the ending he has in mind, he creates the scenario in which his readers become Rousseau and, naturally, approve Rousseau. "My purpose is to display to my kind . . ." (*C*17) [5]: from the start, Rousseau, though he is "different" (*C*17) [5], addresses himself to his fellows. His character is unique, but let his readers "hear [his] confessions," "groan at [his] depravities," "blush at [his] misdeeds" (*C*17) [5], and they will share Rousseau's unworthiness and know they are no better than him. The book Rousseau holds in his hand as he stands before God is the book his readers hold before their eyes. If they continue to read, Rousseau's *Confessions* will become their own. They will lose the innocence of their difference from Rousseau. Rousseau's actions and emotions will become part of his readers' experience; they will recognize in Rousseau's faults their own faults, and as Rousseau confesses himself in writing, his readers will confess themselves in reading. The plural of Rousseau's title will take on new significance, for each of his readers must reveal "his heart . . . with equal sincerity" (*C*17) [5]. Rousseau's confession will be but one among the many that his readers, "the numberless legion of [his] fellow men" (*C*17) [5], will make. Such is the scenario Rousseau would have enacted in his readers' minds, the closing line of which is the unvoiced, because untrue, statement, "'I was a better man than he'" (*C*17) [5].

To coerce his readers into identifying with him, Rousseau takes them back to his childhood, the time of his natural innocence. He leads them forward then through a description of his youth that charms by the very details he fears, or pretends to fear, will weary his readers. In his adventures and his aspirations, his follies and his forays into adulthood, Rousseau's readers may trace the lineaments of their own youthful experiences. And as his narrative advances, they may share Rousseau's pursuit of happiness as they may then share his enjoyment of it, then his loss of it.[14] What Rousseau says to Thérèse when driven from France, he may well be understood to say to his reader: "you must arm youself with courage. You have shared the good days of my prosperity. It now remains for you, since you wish it, to share my miseries" (*C*538) [583]. To arm his readers with courage, Rousseau makes of his "good days" so "touching and simple [a] tale" (*C*215) [225] that his readers—far from being wearied, as Rousseau worries—would wish, as Rousseau does, to prolong it. Indeed, Rousseau does prolong it, not so much by his accumulation of remembered and well-loved details, nor so much by his leisurely description of a delightful day like any other day at Les Charmettes, as by his frequent allusions to this "short period of [his] life's happiness" (C215) [225]. Les Charmettes, recurring, becomes a leitmotiv evoking lost happiness. Before arriving there in his narrative, Rousseau foreshadows the beauty and brevity of his pastoral existence by telling his prophetic daydream of such happiness (C106–7) [107–8]. Then his reverie becomes real, and Rousseau, lingering, remembers and writes the happiness that was fleeting. After, narrating the labyrinthine details of the conspiracy that thwarts his later life, Rousseau pauses time and again to recall the gentle world he has lost: before moving to the Hermitage, "I had not ceased to regret my dear Charmettes and the pleasant life I had led there" (C374) [401]; at the Hermitage, "[I exclaimed] to myself sometimes with a sigh: 'Ah, this is not what life was like at Les Charmettes'" (C396) [425]; on the island of Saint-Pierre, "to these amusements I added another [bringing in the harvest], which recalled to me the delightful life at Les Charmettes" (C594) [644]. Rousseau's nostalgia for what is past is so "touching and simple" (C215) [225], and he writes so well of what he claims cannot be described, the "happiness . . . [that] lay in no definable object" (C215) [226], that his readers, perhaps joining in Rousseau's nostalgia, perhaps remembering personal happiness they have lost, may arm themselves not only to share Rousseau's "miseries" but to share his view of those who inflict them.

Rousseau may or may not lose Les Charmettes innocently in his life, but he loses it designedly in his written life. For Les Charmettes is won and lost at the chronological and emotional, literal and symbolic, veritable rhetorical center of Rousseau's *Confessions*. Broadly, figuratively, Rousseau writes of extremes, of before and beyond paradise. Before is Rousseau's innocence; after, his experience. Before are the six bright books of Rousseau's youth; after, the six dark books of the conspiracy. Before Rousseau is simple and unassuming; after, he creates his philosophy, his personal reforms, his romances, his autobiographical writings—all that commands his place in history. And Rousseau's response to simplicity and success is insistent distress at all that his creative genius achieves: "After favouring my wishes for thirty years, for the next thirty fate opposed them; and from this continual opposition between my situation and my desires will be seen to arise great mistakes, incredible misfortunes, and every virtue that can do credit to adversity except strength of character" (C261) [277]. Exile from paradise, alone, might wreak such havoc, but, amassing metaphors, Rousseau claims more.

Whatever tradition serves, Rousseau uses. And more as a pagan than as a Christian, he is driven from his pastoral paradise. True, Rousseau acknowledges wrongdoing; he nods in the direction of sin and guilt, confessing to sexual and worldly knowledge that deprived him of Les Charmettes. But, then, his faults, he argues, were foibles, and inadvertent at that. Thus begins Rousseau's habitual sequence for effacing sin: Could he truly have sinned if he sincerely did not wish to sin? And if he could have sinned, perhaps did, he regrets it. And if he is sorry, sad, and suffering, then he has atoned. And if he has atoned, surely, forgiveness must follow. The sequence is nowhere clearer than when Rousseau absolves himself of stealing, lying, and slandering, all for the stolen ribbon (C89) [87].[15] How much surer the sequence and more assured the absolution if, not sinning but sinned against, Rousseau does no more than reluctantly leave his pastoral home.[16] He is confident: "strong in [his] innocence alone," he in the world dares "openly to speak the truth to men" (C214) [223]. Notwithstanding his moralizing, Rousseau is less righteous than literary, less the repentant sinner than the unhappy lover. Notwithstanding his paradisiacal imagery, Rousseau is less Adam than Coridon.[17] And such is the strength of his sincerity and his loving disposition that Rousseau, according to Rousseau, is virtually assured his natural and inalienable innocence. And this though his use of Christian symbolism is far from innocent: if not deceptive, at least self-serving.

Telling traditional tales, Rousseau tells them all aslant. Rousseau is also the prodigal son, who long wandering—sampling the life of a watchmaker, engraver, convert, servant, music master, many-faced bourgeois—returns home to Maman. But he is not welcome. In that moment, he is lost: "In one moment I saw the happy future I had depicted for myself vanish for ever. . . . It was a frightful moment; and those which followed it were just as dark" (C249) [263]. From then on, misery is his: "that fatal moment . . . was to bring the long procession of my misfortunes in its train" (C247) [260]. For, again and always, he is condemned to wander the routes of worldliness. Rousseau is the inspired convert, struck by his vision on the hot and dusty road to Vincennes as he happens to read—"tolle, lege, tolle, lege"—the question "Has the progress of the sciences and arts done more to corrupt morals or improve them?" (C327) [351]. "The moment [he] read this," Rousseau—his a secular sortilege—sees "another universe" and becomes "another man" (C327) [351]. And he is lost. Deciding to share his vision, to write for the good of others, from then on, Rousseau suffers: "from that moment I was lost. All the rest of my life and of my misfortunes followed inevitably as a result of that moment's madness" (*C*328) [351]. For he is the prophet whose message is not heeded, who sacrifices himself to teaching those who will not listen. The *Discourses, The Social Contract, The New Héloïse,* Rousseau describes their creation only to dismiss their importance, to announce, once again, the ever-shifting moment of his first "misfortunes" (*C*247) [260]: "But it is time to come to the great revolution in my destiny, to the catastrophe which divided my life into two such different parts, and which from a trivial cause produced such terrible effects" (*C*441) [474]. What was the "revolution," "catastrophe," "cause" with "such terrible effects"? Not Rousseau's published philosophy, but his falling out with Madame d'Epinay and his philosopher friends. As usual, Rousseau looks beyond the philosophical to the personal, and anchors, however askew, the abstract in the concrete. Of the later *Emile* and the *Confessions,* Rousseau identifies the latter as "the real cause of the storm which was raised" (*C*574) [622] to hound him from Switzerland, then from one country after another. Thus the convert, not to God and the Christian community, but to nature and simplicity, is persecuted; thus the prophet is driven into the wilderness.

Rousseau's many personae, implicitly, meet—as figures complementing and clashing one with another, as images shifting in and out of focus in kaleidoscope fashion—when part 1 closes and part 2 opens on Rousseau having set out from Les Charmettes. Adam exiled, Coridon unloved, the prodigal son rebuffed, the worldly one to be chosen, the visionary about to see: all are Rousseau, who then escapes the symmetry—and consistency—of his own autobiographical design, of innocence and experience, of conversion for the worst. For, in part 2, repeatedly, Rousseau sees and is silenced, falls and suffers. And, repeatedly, he regains paradise—at the Hermitage (*C*376) [403–4], at Montmorency (*C*483) [521]. Until, all but closing his *Confessions,* Rousseau comes full circle, to the pastoral, to tranquil days he can call his own, to his innocent life on the island of Saint-Pierre, in paradise regained, and enjoyed—to be lost again.

The more Rousseau becomes entangled in inconsistencies of figure and story, cause and effect, the more he struggles to control his narrative. His metaphors betray his struggles. Early in the *Confessions,* Rousseau's metaphors for his narrative are images of order; of a methodical voyage through the past, recreating all, gay and sad (*C*62, 65) [57, 59]; of narrative riches to be taken up and left at will (*C*31) [21–22]; of "sequence" and "interrelation" in his life as he lives and writes it (*C*169) [174–75]. Later, as the conspiracy comes to dominate his autobiographical story, Rousseau's same images are distorted: figuratively entangled, the voyager is lost in "the obscure and tortuous windings of . . . tunnels" (*C*544) [590], his "faithful guide" (*C*262) [278] become a tenuous "thread" (*C*542) [587], twisting and unsure, through the maze of the past (*C*503, 553, 574, 585) [544, 599, 622, 634].

Rewriting traditional symbols, Rousseau thwarts traditional expectations and sidesteps traditional values. And he does so so subtly that readers may accept his manipulation of emotional symbols uncritically, even unconsciously; succumbing to the persuasion of scriptural figures and forms set—personally, philosophically, smoothly—to secular uses. Many remark the religious, often Augustinian, figures in Rousseauian guises.[18] But Rousseau's subtlety is less in his figures than in their odd usage. Their very oddities bespeak his personal politics as Rousseau inconsistently assigns, and invariably reassigns, meanings to his recurring figures—never quite fixing the sequence of his life's events, even the epochs of his "happiness" and his "misfortunes," never quite fixing the significance of his individual symbols, even those as central as his innocent and experienced selves.[19] Thus changeably, serviceably, none too strictly, the religious becomes Rousseauian to serve earthly rhetorical ends. The sinner trumpeting his innocence, the prodigal son willfully wandering, the prophet crying for himself in the wilderness of his own words: these, too, are Rousseau—seen without sympathy. But Rousseau coaxes his readers to share his sensibility, to feel compassion for the sinner (though he deny his sinning), admiration for the prodigal son (though he refuse his "Maman" service), and moral outrage for the persecuted prophet (though he isolate himself in his pride and paranoia).

Readers may willingly suspend their benevolence, even their belief, but Rousseau's narrative—and increasingly as it lengthens—will work against the effort. On an argumentative level, the "sweet memories" (*C*261) [277] of the first part behind and the "darkness" (*C*544) [589] of the second enveloping them, his readers must all the more depend on Rousseau. The simple truths of Rousseau's youth, truths his readers, from their own experience, may have recognized and seconded, are past. In the second part of the *Confessions*, the truth is in two; there is Rousseau's version and his enemies'. And the truth is particular; readers can bring nothing from their own lives to illuminate the ins and outs of the Holbachian conspiracy. On a psychological level, the sincerity of Rousseau's tone, the way he confesses faults and fine points with simple candor, entices his readers early to admire him. The essentially attractive portrait Rousseau paints of his younger self entices them then to find his older self, his suffering self, also admirable, not because he necessarily is so, but because he becomes too well known to be coolly assessed. On a stylistic level, the beauty of Rousseau's narrative, beauty in its detail and its design, draws readers from their distance as they read on. The disclosures, the cadenced development, the very length of the *Confessions* pulls readers, book by book, further from a dispassionate perspective. Many narrators seek these effects: "the interrelation of results" (C169) [175] Rousseau seeks is further reaching. Most narrators seek their readers' sympathy; Rousseau tries to govern it.

Consider how Rousseau's theory of "*The Morals of Sensibility*" (C381) [409] grew out of his observations on the development of character, his own and others':

> It has been observed that the majority of men are often in the course of their lives quite unlike themselves; they seem to be changed into quite different people. . . .
> Looking within myself and seeking in others for the cause upon which these different states of being depended, I discovered that they had a great deal to do with our previous impressions from external objects, and that, being continually a little changed through the agency of our senses and our organs, we were unconsciously affected in our thoughts, our feelings, and even our actions by the impact of these slight changes upon us. Numerous striking examples that I had collected put the matter beyond all dispute; and thanks to their physical basis they seemed to me capable of providing an external code which, varied according to circumstances, could put or keep the mind in the state most conducive to virtue. (C381) [408–9]

Never mind how difficult such "an external code" would be to maintain in reality. Rousseau attempts it, in images and scenes, in his *Confessions:* "Climates, seasons, sounds, colours, darkness, light, the elements, food, noise, silence, movement, repose: they all act on our machines, and consequently upon our souls, and they all offer us innumerable and almost certain opportunities for controlling those feelings which we allow to dominate us at their very outset" (C381) [409]. All offer Rousseau, writing of them, modulating the rhythm and the imagery in his language, a thousand opportunities to influence his readers' emotions. Subtly, Rousseau, writing, etches his idiosyncratic impressions—his revisions of tradition—in his readers' minds. Not so subtly, he highlights the beauty of what he loves and the blackness of what he hates. If Rousseau's theory of behavior functions as a theory of literature—and certainly he believes in the influence of art on morals and beliefs—Rousseau's objective is assured. By making known to his readers all that he experienced—the places he lived, the people he knew, the changes he underwent—Rousseau will make his memory his readers' own, and his readers, perhaps unconsciously, will experience a modification in their thoughts and feelings. The distance between narrator and readers will be all but obliterated, and readers, ending their reading, will judge Rousseau as Rousseau judges Rousseau.

For all his efforts, such is not the result that Rousseau knows and writes into his *Confessions*. Even he, finishing his *Confessions,* learns the failure of his theory in practice. Unable to end the story of his life with his death, Rousseau ends it with the literary equivalent, the falling into silence of his narrative voice. Recreating the scene of a worldly, and actual, reading of his *Confessions,* Rousseau stands before—if not the crowd of his "fellow men" (C17) [5]—a select and symbolic group of auditors. To them—ending his reading, ending his writing—Rousseau addresses with passionate defiance his, all the same, predictable refrain:

> I have told the truth. If anyone knows anything contrary to what I have here recorded, though he prove it a thousand times, his knowledge is a lie and an imposture; and if he refuses to investigate and inquire into it during my lifetime he is no lover of justice or of truth. For my part, I publicly and fearlessly declare that anyone, even if he has not read my writings, who will examine my nature, my character, my morals, my likings, my pleasures, and my habits with his own eyes and can still believe me a dishonourable man, is a man who deserves to be stifled.
>
> Thus I concluded my reading, and everyone was silent. Mme. d'Egmont was the only person who seemed moved. She trembled visibly but quickly controlled herself, and remained quiet, as did the rest of the company. (C605–6) [656]

The voice that is stifled is Rousseau's.[20] It is also that of his listeners, the voice that refuses its assent, perhaps even the voice that would dissent, that might well say things "contrary" to what Rousseau declares, but refuses "to investigate and inquire into" them. While writing, Rousseau can imagine his *Confessions* an impassioned monologue likely to move his listeners to compassion and admiration, or an elaborate dialogue with listeners who, though opposed to him, can be coerced and convinced before their turn comes to speak. But as Rousseau's writing and his several public readings of the *Confessions* end, with them ends his hope for an ideal audience. Rousseau's real, and he fears representative, audience reveals the experience of individuals that he, narrating, seeks to control and he, silent, learns he cannot control. Their symbolic silence is loud with judgment by values other than his. Thus Rousseau, though perhaps only Rousseau, hears silence speaking.

Clearly, Rousseau strikes the contrast between his opening and closing reading scenes: one prefiguring a judgment heavenly and as he would wish—wherein all humans second his soul; the other figuring a judgment earthly and far from satisfactory—silence. The contrast is the contrast of all the *Confessions:* of how Rousseau would have his readers read and of how he fears they read, of his version of the truth versus theirs, of—starkly—him against them. The truth that Rousseau hides in his writing that it might escape the vigilance of his enemies is, to his way of thinking, singular—"the truth." Yet in his readers' minds "the truth" may be interlocked with truths Rousseau hides from himself, truths that escape his control of the written word. These may be his enemies' versions of veracity, the result, surely, of their many intrigues; these may be diverse interpretations, the result, simply, of others seeing Rousseau differently than Rousseau sees Rousseau. There are, indeed, in the *Confessions* two orders of—to use Rousseau's vocabulary—"the truth": that which Rousseau would have his readers know and that which his readers will know in spite of Rousseau. Given his generous, though hardly guileless, autobiographical method in the *Confessions,* his readers have the means to find more than "the truth" according to Rousseau: witness the many psychological studies that come to conclusions different from Rousseau's concerning his character and his philosophy. But Rousseau? What Rousseau may not have realized until he wrote the *Reveries,* or may never have realized, was that the narrative tools he used were double-edged, that in attempting to control his readers' view of himself, he may have limited his own view, that in hiding the truth from his enemies—perhaps, for all his protestations, from his readers too—he may have hidden it from himself.

As I tried to recall so many sweet reveries . . .

Only when the "most sociable and loving of men" (*R*27) [995] is excluded from human society does he discover, if not the falsity, then the inadequacy of his self-presentations to others. Rousseau of the *Confessions,* Rousseau and Jean-Jacques of the *Dialogues,* the public selves set confessing and dialoguing with society, posterity, anybody listening—

none reveals the private Rousseau, the *Solitary Walker,* "detached . . . from them and from the whole world" (*R*27) [995]. "Wrenched somehow out of the natural order, . . . plunged into an incomprehensible chaos" (*R*27) [995], Rousseau nearing the end of his life is bereft of explanations—and obligations. Renouncing others, Rousseau metamorphoses as autobiographer: "I am devoting my last days to studying myself and preparing the account which I shall shortly have to render. Let me give myself over entirely to the pleasure of conversing with my soul, since this is the only pleasure that men cannot take away from me. If by meditating on my inner life I am able to order it better and remedy the faults that may remain there, my meditations will not be entirely in vain" (*R*32) [999]. The sequel to "the rigorous and sincere self-examination" (*R*32) [999] formerly called the *Confessions* will be of another sort. Rousseau will compose his inner life in spiritual order rather than his outer life in chronological order. Addressing his soul rather than public opinion of his soul, he will study his "successive variations" (*R*33) [1000] rather than his place in history and its implications. His *Reveries* will be didactic, scientific, artistic, but unschematic; they will be written without an overarching theory governing their occasional practice. Vacillating between the autobiographically grandiose and the personally humble, between revelation and rambling, Rousseau never quite sets the program of his last papers, though he never ceases envisioning their lesson. Innocent, but ignorant of who he is, here, "alone in the world" (*R*27) [995], is Rousseau. And only in his *Reveries,* without the desire for communication, without the help or the hindrance of convention, will Rousseau come to know Rousseau solo.

"Unfortunately, before setting out on this quest, [he] must glance rapidly at [his] present situation" (*R*27) [995], Rousseau's—never mind his denial—ongoing obsession. The end of his *Confessions* and *Dialogues* coinciding with the supposed end of his earthly affections, Rousseau summarizes his autobiographical progress for his new reader—Rousseau. Speaking having sufficed as penance and suffering having earned him pardon, he claims his *Confessions* have emotionally and morally cleansed him: "My heart has been purified in the crucible of adversity and the most careful self-examination can hardly find any remaining traces of reprehensible inclinations. What could I have still to confess when all earthly affections have been uprooted? I have no more reason now to praise than to condemn myself: henceforward I am of no importance among men, and this is unavoidable since I no longer have any real relationship or true companionship with them" (*R*33) [1000]. Society is lost, and posterity too, the *Confessions* to the former and the *Dialogues* with the latter equally vain. Henceforth, rigor, rhetoric, readers, all methods and motives will be suspect in Rousseau's projected study of his self:

> To accomplish it successfully I ought to proceed with order and method, but such an undertaking is beyond me, and indeed it would divert me from my true aim. . . . I shall perform upon myself the sort of operation that physicists conduct upon the air in order to discover its daily fluctuations. I shall take the barometer readings of my soul, and by doing this accurately and repeatedly I could perhaps obtain results as reliable as theirs. However, my aim is not so ambitious. I shall content myself with keeping a record of my readings without trying to reduce them to a system. (*R*33) [1000–1001]

Rousseau needs no system; he already knows the system that governs his soul. He has already in the *Confessions*, anticipating the judgment of others, passed judgment on himself; he has already determined what were his vices and what were his virtues, what their causes and what their effects. The "certain sequence of impressions and ideas" (*C*169) [174] he tries in the *Confessions* to impress on his readers, and does impress on his text, ends in the assertion of his essential innocence and goodness. He can no more forget what he wrote confessing, and speaking as *juge de Jean-Jacques,* than he can forget what his enemies wrote of him: he has opposed his texts to theirs. But in the state of a standoff, hoping to live out his days in peace, Rousseau is anything but peaceful. For justification does not ensure satisfaction, nor sincerity guarantee salvation. And be traying his lack of conviction, of calm, is Rousseau still writing. He asserts too often, too insistently, his indifference toward his persecutors, and he undertakes his *Reveries,* his attempt to counter in writing their still-pervasive influence, not on his generation and future generations, but on himself.

"Let [him] therefore detach [his] mind from these afflicting sights," sounds, thoughts, obsessions; Rousseau's "only remaining duty is to [himself] and this is all [he desires]" (*R*32) [999]. In the *Confessions,* carried along by "the thread of [his] narrative" (*C*379) [407], Rousseau describes the happy and the dark periods of his existence. In the *Dialogues,* divided by his for-and-against argumentation, he delineates the good and the bad sides of his character. Renouncing narrative and dialogue forms, Rousseau renounces with them the need to record any part of his past or himself that does not manifest itself in his creative

reveries or pleasant memories. What rules will govern his literary form—
be it ordered or not, "a faithful record" (*R*35) [1002] or "a formless
record" (*R*32) [1000]—will be of Rousseau's making. Loose, they will
give "free rein" (*R*35) [1002] to his spirit to stifle his pain as he pursues his
pleasure: "The free hours of my daily walks have often been filled with
delightful contemplations which I am sorry to have forgotten. Such
reflections as I have in future I shall preserve in writing; every time I read
them they will recall my original pleasure. Thinking of the prize my heart
deserved, I shall forget my misfortunes, my persecutors and my disgrace"
(*R*32) [999–1000]. Rousseau's enjoyment will be grounded in his imagination, in his ability to summon his meditations and memories vividly
into the moment. His guarantee will be language. His goal: "In telling
myself, I felt pleasure, I [will] feel pleasure again" [1174].

The pithy statement is from another of Rousseau's projected works,
perhaps begun as a substitute for the unwritten *Morals of Sensibility,*
perhaps abandoned in the very desire to perfect the art of pleasure.
Twelve fragments short, *The Art of Pleasure* goes unwritten while the
Reveries—autobiographical rather than abstract, practical rather than
pedantic—are introduced in the First Walk at greater length than all *The
Art of Pleasure.* But the optimism of the Walk of promises rapidly gives
way to the mysticism and the pragmatism of the Second Walk, as Rousseau's project is beset with difficulties even as it is begun.

Not the least of which difficulties is Rousseau's feeling that he undertakes his task too late in life: "My imagination has lost its old power, it no
longer takes fire at the contemplation of the objects that inspire it, nor
does the delirium of reverie transport me as once it did. Today there is
more recollection than creation in the products of my imagination, a
tepid languor saps all my faculties, the vital spirit is gradually dying down
within me, my soul no longer flies up without effort from its decaying
prison of flesh" (*R*35) [1002]. The "delirium of reverie," which transports
him above the ills that beset him, Rousseau still seeks in his walks, but
when he cannot create it in the present or call it from the past, he has to
satisfy his soul with the written approximation of its power. And if, to
foster his satisfaction, he elaborates pleasing variations (whether comforting delusions, rose-tinted recollections, or fantastic expectations), if
he supplements and adorns—in short, rewrites—reality and reverie and
memory, so, Rousseau reasons, be it.

For as sole reader of his *Reveries,* Rousseau enjoys new—or at least
newly acknowledged—autobiographical options. Such as fiction. Finding in reverie respite from harsh reality, Rousseau lets loose his imagina-

tion, to cross at will the line between reality and illusion, to create the harmless stories he formerly invented to amuse society and now creates for self-sustenance. Or, his imagination faltering, his cultivated fictions infertile, he turns to studying selected sensations and reviewing well-chosen recollections. Then the "gaps" in his memory he embellishes with "adornments" (R76) [1035], and with fine sentiments he invests the solitary waste of his heart. Whatever fills his spirit—be it originally fact or fiction—when written, accurately renders Rousseau. For when his creative escapes from his current situation are recorded, the chronicle, Rousseau asserts, is autobiographical.

In the Fourth Walk—a most rigorous argument of a "reverie"—Rousseau justifies his autobiographical largesse. There he develops, to deploy, a moral theory of "the truth": a theory by which he enjoys greater leeway with "the truth" than ever Rousseau of the *Confessions* allowed—or at least acknowledged. In the Fourth Walk, Rousseau is, as ever, exceedingly verbal about loving "the truth," but he envisions "the truth," not as a metaphysical entity, the white or black of fact, rather as a spectrum of subtle grays dictated by moral imperative. Opposing content and context, trivia and essence, the crucial distinction between factual and moral truth Rousseau relegates to justice: "the truth which we owe one another is that which concerns justice, and it is a profanation of the holy name of truth to apply it to trivial things of which the existence is a matter of general indifference and the knowledge totally useless" (R66) [1027]. Utility deciding morality, Rousseau decides the difference between lying and fiction, between memory and ornament, between "all the truth" of the *Confessions* and "all the truth"—necessary—in the *Reveries:* "everything which by being opposed to the truth offends justice in any way is a lie. . . . but everything which although opposed to truth does not affect justice in any way is no more than a fiction" (R70–71) [1030]. Between the "lie" that offends justice, decency, society, all humanity and the "fiction" that merely offends reality, the distinction is clear. But its implications? Particularly for the autobiographer of "all . . . all . . . all . . ." (C169) [175]? Exceptional, though conditional, liberty. Inasmuch as "to lie without advantage or disadvantage to oneself or others is not to lie; it is not falsehood but fiction" (R69) [1029]. Thus, appropriately innocent, the autobiographer may write what he will. No matter if he write what he has never said, seen, heard, done, lived, as long as he be free from reprehensible inclinations, as long as prejudice does not decide his presentation, nor self-interest undo the equilibrium of his fair-minded and clear-sighted—one is tempted to say—objectivity. But in the opposite sense tend the conclusions of Rousseau's theory: in determining "the truth," the autobiographer determines morality; in the process, his reason bows to his conscience; and the product of his efforts, his autobiography, is, indeed, all subjectivity.

Elaborating and illustrating his theory, Rousseau confesses to a little undesirable lying and much morally whitewashed fiction. His most frequent falls and flights from strict reality he experiences in conversation and in narration. In conversation, hurrying to fill awkward silences, he "invents stories rather than keep quiet" (*R*73) [1033]. In narration, he lingers over loved memories, re-creating as needed their forgotten details, replenishing the sadly bare regions of his memory. Of his *Confessions,* Rousseau acknowledges:

> I was writing from memory; my memory often failed me or only provided me with an incomplete picture, and I filled the gaps with details which I dreamed up to complete my memories, but which never contradicted them. I took pleasure in dwelling on my moments of happiness and sometimes I embellished them with adornments suggested to me by my fond regrets. I described things I had forgotten as I thought they must have been, as they perhaps really had been, but never in contradiction to my actual memories. Sometimes I decorated truth with new beauties, but I never used lies to extenuate my vices or lay false claims to virtue. (*R*76–77) [1035–36]

Easily, Rousseau admits, "I have often made up stories, but very rarely told lies" (*R*79) [1038]. And suavely he defends his stance, "I confess that anyone who holds a mere fiction against himself as a lie has a more tender conscience than I have" (*R*71) [1030].

Thus the *Confessions* themes of shame in public speaking and hiding in persuasive writing play again in Rousseau's theory of moral "truth." But as the writer of the *Reveries,* Rousseau exposes what before he merely let slip: the constraints of discursive language. Language forces and falsifies, charms and compromises, carries Rousseau along often too quickly, too glibly for reflection. Unthinkingly, he speaks to please others; pleasingly, he writes for his self as other. With either audience, either incentive, he risks error:

> If one must act justly towards others, one must act truthfully towards oneself. Truth is an homage that the good man pays to his own dignity. When my lack of small talk forced me to fill the silence with harmless fictions, I acted wrongly, because one should not debase oneself in order to amuse others, and when the pleasure of writing led me to embellish

reality with ornaments of my own invention, I acted even more wrongly, because to decorate truth with fables is in fact to disfigure it. (*R*80) [1038]

For his verbal facility, his brilliant and beautiful style, the price Rousseau pays is high: the sullying of his dignity and the compromise of his cherished "truth."

When the truth is disfigured will even its autobiographer recognize it? If to "the truth" the autobiographer lends "new beauties" (*R*77) [1036], are his efforts ever neutral? Yes, Rousseau argues, if he writes entirely "without advantage or disadvantage to [himself]" (*R*69) [1029]; if he writes free of justification, concern for his reputation, the temptation to aggrandization. If not, then he lies. Supposing he be free of all motives, fair or foul, well then, the autobiographer undoubtedly tells tales. Rousseau, at least, tells tales. Perhaps undermined by his "lies . . . dictated . . . always by weakness" (*R*80) [1039], perhaps enhanced by his own fables, is the autobiographer, once written, still "I"? And if he be inevitably "other," how innocently does he embrace his alter, his verbal, identity? So many questions, so many doubts, has Rousseau. Nevertheless, he persists in recording his reveries, knowing in his solitary soul that he has need of his creations, his written approximations of the past and his agreeable versions of the present.

He persists even as his reveries resist being written. All too soon, Rousseau comes, once again, to his earlier conclusion: "true joy defies description" (*C*330) [354]. Perhaps. But what he cannot render, Rousseau lengthily recounts—his fall into immortality in the Second Walk, his water reveries in the Fifth, his narrowing nature reveries in the Seventh, his cherished, but cut-short, reverie of "Palm Sunday . . . exactly fifty years [ago]" (*R*153) [1098]. All these, in their richness, Rousseau cannot transcribe into language: "how can I tell what was neither said, nor done, nor even thought, but only relished and felt, when I cannot adduce any other cause for my happiness but just this feeling?" (*C*215) [225]. In his zeal to record his reveries, this is the lesson Rousseau forgets, the lesson of the *Confessions* that he must learn again: "true happiness is quite indescribable; it can only be felt, and the stronger the feeling the less it can be described" (*C*224) [236]. "Happiness," "joy," "reverie"—all share this emotional, sensational essence, which is immeasurable, which is ineffable.

Rousseau reasons why. His reveries are more or less active or passive, more or less in focus or "vague" (*R*85) [1004]. Their different kinds are more or less sensual, intellectual, creative, or nostalgic—so many simplistic tags of limited service. For reverie confounds sense and the senses. For the inner geography of reverie has neither determined borders nor set spiritual destinations.[21] Whatever their slant—sensual, intellectual, creative, even recollective—reveries center Rousseau's soul in a duration like eternity wherein, self-sufficient as the Divinity, he enjoys his existence in its profundity. The extremity of the attribution is Rousseau's—Rousseau's of the Fifth Walk while soaring with confidence (*R*88–89) [1046–47]. But Rousseau of the failing imagination, of the self-doubts in the Second and Seventh Walks, of the self-criticism in the Fourth, acknowledges the fragility of his self-proclaimed deity. He acknowledges that language eclipses reverie, for writing intervenes, which relegates all experience of the present to the past, and time rules, which refuses all intimations of immortality.

Rousseau's confidence in reveries written—"every time I read them they will recall my original pleasure" (*R*32) [999]—fades to his sense of choice and compromise. Reveries are to be lived, or they are to be lost— at the least diluted—in language. Yet surely there is a difference between the reader who will never know the "true joy" of a writer's experience and the writer as reader of his own writing who will have access to the original experience. Yes, but the essential difference language in no way describes or defines. Imagination decides. Animating the moment, reverie offers pleasures in profusion, which agitate as they fascinate. Animating memory, reverie confounds remembering and dreaming, imaginatively remaking what was into what is, thus quickening the confusion and ruffling the spirit, thus "recollected in tranquility" with difficulty.[22] Mixing "memory and desire," reverie merges the past and the present, emotionally, sensually, creatively, but—in its immediacy—wordlessly. Whence the difficulty of charting in language its psychic territory.[23]

As early as the Second Walk, Rousseau pays homage to the sensuality and the inexplicability of reverie. The unlikely source of his "joy" is his accident, near fatal in the falling and remarkably literary in the writing. Downed by a Great Dane (not, like Montaigne, by a heavy horse), Rousseau, coming to, finds his thoughts, emotions, and sensations concentrated into an endless moment. Who he is, where, when, and why— all his questions are resolved into the simple awareness of his existence:

> In this instant I was being born again, and it seemed as if all I perceived was filled with my frail existence. Entirely taken up by the present, I could remember nothing; I had no distinct notion of myself as a person, nor had I the least idea of what had just happened to me. I did not know who I was, nor where I was; I felt neither pain, fear, nor anxiety. . . . I

felt throughout my whole being such a wonderful calm, that whenever I recall this feeling I can find nothing to compare with it in all the pleasures that stir our lives. (*R*39) [1005]

Absorption in the moment, such is the rare reward of profound reverie. But the mystery within, Rousseau cannot write, not without the aid of precedent. Montaigne's "Of Practice" serves, as Rousseau coerces authority and reverie, the prototypical and the inexplicable, into the same written moment; as Rousseau essays the unique and tells the ineffable: the irony is Montaignesque and manifest.

Even the reveries Rousseau calls "contemplations" (*R*32) [999], "meditations" (*R*34) [1001], or "thoughts" (*R*38) [1004] are compromised in the mesh of his words. The "delightful contemplations" he would "preserve in writing" (*R*32) [999], their very description—noun and adjective connotatively clashing—reveals Rousseau's refusal of a schism between mind and emotion. Indeed, the more Rousseau's meditations are strictly intellectual, the less they are enjoyable: "reverie amuses and distracts me, thought wearies and depresses me; thinking has always been for me a disagreeable and thankless occupation. Sometimes my reveries end in meditation, but more often my meditations end in reverie" (*R*107) [1062]. Rousseau's "ideas follow their natural course, unrestricted and unconfined" (*R*35) [1002]: they come as they come, "with as little connection as the thoughts of this morning have with those of last night" (*R*32) [1000]. Writing, Rousseau will order his meditations despite his intentions to the contrary, and his "joy" will end by yielding to his judgment. By putting the inner dispositions of his soul in "better" "order" (*R*32) [999], he will subject them to his intellect, and the meditations that were will be transformed into the meditations that ought to have been. Even if Rousseau were to put judgment aside, an unlikely feat on his part, his "joy" would never find expression in written language. The rules of style would encourage decorum, and the rules of grammar and syntax would circumscribe his freedom.

The more imaginative, the more creative his reveries, the more language limits and belies Rousseau's "joy." A passage in the *Confessions* prefigures the ecstasy and the difficulty in creative reverie. There Rousseau lets both go to continue his narrative; in the *Reveries,* he embraces and wrestles with the dilemma:

In thinking over the details of my life which are lost to my memory, what I most regret is that I did not keep diaries of my travels. . . . The sight of the countryside, the succession of pleasant views, the open air, a sound appetite, and the good health I gain by walking, the easy atmosphere of an inn, the absence of everything that makes me feel my dependence, of everything that recalls me to my situation—all these serve to free my spirit, to lend a greater boldness to my thinking, to throw me, so to speak, into the vastness of things, so that I can combine them, select them, and make them mine as I will, without fear or restraint. . . . If, in order to hold them, I amuse myself by describing them to myself, what vigorous brush-strokes, what freshness of colour, what energy of expression I bring to them. . . . Why do I not write them, you will ask. But why should I? I reply. Why rob myself of the present charm of their enjoyment, to tell others that I enjoyed them once? What did readers matter to me, or a public, or the whole world, while I was soaring in the skies? Besides, did I carry paper with me, or pens? If I had thought of all that, nothing would have come to me. I did not foresee that I should have ideas. They arrive when they please, not when it suits me. Either they do not come at all, or they come in a swarm, overwhelming me with their strength and their numbers.[24] Ten volumes a day would not have been enough. How could I have found time to write them? (*C*157–58) [162–63]

"Ten volumes a day" would not have sufficed for the younger Rousseau; ten, twenty, however many "Walks" will not suffice for the older Rousseau. When Rousseau, young or old, wholly immerses himself in his reveries, in the richness of their presence, he never writes them—not for his readers, not for himself. The older Rousseau explains: "Surrounded by such riches, how was I to keep a faithful record of them all? As I tried to recall so many sweet reveries, I relived them instead of describing them" (*R*36) [1003].

If words will never render their richness and time enough will never be found to restore their fullness, why then write reveries? The language that succeeds in sketching their outline destroys their presence. Why does Rousseau deprive himself of the present charm of "their enjoyment" to say to the older Rousseau, "I enjoyed them" (*C*158) [162]? To remind himself in future years. Certainly, but the exchange seems poor, and besides it must be mediated by what is unwritten in his memory, the sensations that actually revive the recollection: "The memory of this state [joyful reverie] . . . [brings] it back to life; if we completely ceased to experience it, we should soon lose all knowledge of it" (*R*36) [1003].

There are other reasons for, other pleasures to be had in, the exchange, and Rousseau, solitary writer, knows them: "I shall recall in reading them the pleasure I have in writing them and by thus reviving times past I shall as it were double the space of my existence. In spite of men I shall still enjoy the charms of company, and in my decrepitude I shall live with my earlier self as I might with a younger friend" (*R*34) [1001]. The pleasures are of two orders. In accordance with Rousseau's formula—"In telling myself, I felt pleasure, I feel pleasure again" [1174]—Rousseau, having transmuted the pleasure of the past into the pleasure of writing, recalls in reading his written language the enjoyment he felt writing it. Writing as a process gains new value in Rousseau's mind when, isolated from the world, writing his *Reveries,* he ceases to concern himself with controlling the judgment of others. Writing as a physical record, a collection of papers for posterity, theoretically, no longer interests him, but Rousseau still values the product of his efforts, exceedingly. He merely changes his audience, consciously—or at least rhetorically—from others to himself, and becomes the supposed sole consumer of his work. As such, when reading his own writing Rousseau experiences a second pleasure, one perhaps greater than the recollected pleasure of writing. He experiences "the charms of company" (his own) while living with a "younger friend" (himself). Written language—which cannot return Rousseau to his past (only sensations in his memory have that power), which cannot make him the "younger" Rousseau—can differentiate the older from the younger Rousseau and in so doing double his pleasure in his existence. The division that time and written language effect in Rousseau he welcomes, since atoning for his separation from society, it allows him to enjoy his past self, one mediated by his language, that he can read of, believe in, keep company with.

Cultivating the company of his "younger friend," Rousseau is increasingly tolerant and less strident. The influence of his senses on his heart is his "one torment" (*R*132) [1082] in life; if he can but avoid painful impressions, he believes he can master himself. Living retired from society, Rousseau hopes to avoid all unpleasant meetings with his enemies, but his paranoia populates even his solitude with their presence. It is not enough to forget "as quickly as [he] can and run away" from a "sinister look . . . [a] barbed remark . . . [a] malicious person" (*R*133) [1082], for though the turmoil in Rousseau's heart vanishes with the object that causes it, he has still to contend with "the fear of meeting some new cause of suffering" (*R*133) [1082]. Reveries and writing can vanquish the fear: the art of reverie centers Rousseau's mind on the present and banishes from his consciousness his recollections and anticipations of evil; the art of his writing in the *Reveries* takes him into the pleasant past, the place he purges of evil by his power over language.

Writing to ward off the malevolence of others, real and imagined,

Rousseau does not so much express his self in the *Reveries* as soothe it. By centering his attention on the happiest, the loveliest, the most innocent moments of his life, by making them appear again to him in language, Rousseau occupies his mind with the pleasure of writing and the pleasure of the past—as he selects and styles it. The writer who in the *Confessions* attempts to control the impressions he makes on all posterity is at no loss for means when he would reinforce his own sense of innocence. As he asserts his innocence for others in the *Confessions,* he reiterates it for his own benefit in the *Reveries.* As he charms his readers in the *Confessions,* he in the *Reveries* charms himself with the rhythm of his prose, the beauty of his descriptions, the vividness of his early memories. The literary practice of "*The Morals of Sensibility*" (C381) [409], of influencing ideas and emotions by the arrangement of images and scenes in the imagination, though never entirely successful when the reader is not the writer, proves more successful for the older Rousseau when, writing, he seeks to order his own mind. If carried along by "the pleasure of writing" his *Reveries,* Rousseau "[embellishes] reality with ornaments of [his] own invention" (R80) [1038], little matter, for he influences only himself. His responsibility is no longer to truth in the abstract and his readers in general, as in the *Confessions,* where he admits he did "decorate truth with fables" (R80) [1038]. If in his *Reveries* he hides aspects of himself and his situation behind the embellishments of his writing, he only alters his own distance from what he sees as sad truths. And, indeed, in light of his view of his situation—surrounded as he believes he is by enemies who watch him and wish him harm—hiding himself in writing from the vicissitudes, all unpleasant, of "the strangest situation which any mortal will ever know" (R35) [1002] can only do Rousseau good.

A diary of my expeditions

Reveries and the written record of his reveries can afford Rousseau a resting place in a world where "everything is in constant flux" (R88) [1046]. But reveries cannot endure, the world of others breaks in, and, more and more, Rousseau no longer feels "vigorous enough to swim in the chaos" of his "ecstasies" (R112) [1066]. And writing, the substitution for their presence, though the source of another pleasure, can never be more than the succession of signs that marks the absence of a "joy" Rousseau still seeks. Nearing the end of his life, forever trying to perfect the art of pleasure, Rousseau neglects both the pleasure of reverie and the pleasure of writing for another pastime, the last great passion of his life:

I have only just begun to write down all my long reveries and already I can feel that I shall soon have finished. Another pastime has taken over and now absorbs me so completely that I have not even time for dreaming. I abandon myself to it with an enthusiasm bordering on extravagance, and which makes me laugh when I think about it, yet I continue undeterred, because in my present situation I have no other rule of conduct than always to follow freely my natural leanings. . . . So I am left with my grasses to keep me going and botany to occupy my mind. (*R*105) [1060]

"Because in my present situation . . .": always Rousseau's concern is to counter the effect of his situation on his spirit. When first forced to face his sad fate, Rousseau had worried that it might even taint his imagination: "It was even to be feared that my imagination, alarmed by my misfortunes, might end by filling my reveries with them, and the continual consciousness of my sufferings might gradually come to oppress my heart and crush me finally under their weight" (*R*107) [1062]. Manifestly, Rousseau remains preoccupied with his "misfortunes," which, if they do not creep into his imagined reveries, do crop up in his written reveries. To escape from his obsession Rousseau has to escape even from his imagination: "In these circumstances an instinct that is natural to me averted my eyes from every depressing thought, silenced my imagination and, fixing my attention on the objects surrounding me, made me look closely for the first time at the details of the great pageant of nature, which until then I had hardly ever contemplated otherwise than as a total and undivided spectacle" (*R*107–8) [1062].

Creation of an inner world and observation of the natural world, both acts can quiet Rousseau's turmoil, but late in life, Rousseau considers the act of observation far the surer of the two. Reversing the tendency of a lifetime, Rousseau's love of botany takes him outside himself.[25] Lying on the ground, examining the structure of grass or moss, flowers of the field or the forest, Rousseau satisfies his sense and his spirit with what in all his imaginings and writings he can never grasp—nature herself alive in the moment. Not in her unity, but in her specificity, nature exhibits to Rousseau—on the simplest level—things. At the end of a long literary career, Rousseau, tiring of his manipulation of signs, of his own creations, finds, finally, his greatest solace in nature's creations.

In the middle of his life, Rousseau distrusts self-expression in spoken language; it is too uncontrollable, too untrue. At the end of his life, Rousseau, expressing and controlling his mind in written language, finds it also too untrue, too removed from his actual experience. As he is writing his last work, Rousseau is also "writing" another work:

> All my botanical walks, the varied impressions made by the places where I have seen memorable things, the ideas they have aroused in me, all this has left me with impressions which are revived by the sight of the plants I have collected in those places. I shall never again see those beautiful landscapes, those forests, those lakes, those groves, those rocks or those mountains, the sight of which has always moved me, but now that I can no longer roam in those happy places, I have only to open my flower collection to be transported there. The fragments of plant life which I picked there are enough to bring back the whole magnificent spectacle. This collection is like a diary of my expeditions, which makes me set out again with renewed joy, or like an optical device which places them once again before my eyes. (*R*120) [1073]

In a language of things, a language of immediacy, Rousseau composes his "diary." He has but to open it to be transported to the past he loves and has lost; he has but to hope to add to it to be off to the woods and the fields and his peace in the present.

4

WORDSWORTH
The Prelude—1799, 1805, 1850

Praise to the end, / Thanks likewise for the means

WORDSWORTH writes autobiography in which the events of his life are peripheral and the imaginative movement of his mind is essential as— one manuscript after or over another—he forms, but never finally, *The Prelude: 1799, 1805, 1850*.[1] He does not begin his life story, as Augustine, Montaigne, or Rousseau does, in response to conversion, skepticism, or some deep and novel resolution ending in self-justification; his is no inner need to preach, parade, or persuade while he rivals in philosophical scope Christian, Renaissance, or Enlightenment amplitude. Rather, simply, his is the need to write poetry. Or, more precisely, to discover why and how and for whom he can write poetry—while writing poetry. Yet as two parts become thirteen then fourteen books, Wordsworth becomes ever more moral in his message and biblical in his imagery, ever more august a personnage, as, "poet," he becomes "a pilgrim gone / In quest of highest truth" (1805, 11.391–92) and, finally, a "[Prophet] of Nature" (1805, 13.442). And even as his vital and vague metaphors of moving and wandering are honed to rhetorical sharpness, even as the idiosyncratic is made emblematic, Wordsworth's joy in his inspiration shades into judgment of his composition, and his conviction no longer cuts. As the *Prelude* to his philosophical work becomes his philosophical work, the poet, pilgrim, and prophet figures become ever more orderly and overt, and Wordsworth ends in 1850 with his autobiographical pattern well in place, but studied, unresponsive, even unfaithful, to his original poetic spirit.

The essential question—good for guesses and learned stories—is, why? The one for now—and more historical—is, according to whom? So diverse and self-determining are Wordsworth's readers that they freely pick and choose *Preludes:* as Victorian earnestness demands and early modern taste damns the prophet of 1850; as late modern oddity and love of ambiguity delights in the hesitations of the uncertain and youthful poet. Perhaps the pull of one *Prelude* or another for one generation or another derives from the different draw of memory, mimesis, and Christian metaphor, each in successive stages dominating a version of the evolving poem. Memory, sensual yet cerebral, unschematic yet deconstructable, owns most of 1799; and mimesis brings scene and story (the singularity of Cambridge, the Continent, and London) to meet muted communal metaphor in 1805; and metaphor, increasingly strict and structural, by 1850 tints the whole poem traditional Christian. All end more or less eerily reconciled in the three *Preludes,* but the judgment of whether admirably or strainedly is as the reader chooses to see. Memory being a modern obsession, mimesis but the classical heritage, and allegorical metaphor far from the current cult of ambivalence, by today's standards, the early Wordsworth decidedly outdoes the late.[2]

The common contemporary assessment of Wordsworth's genius—all bright in his early poetry and bedimmed, even eclipsed, in his late—easily encompasses *The Prelude*'s history. In the two-part *Prelude* of 1799 and the intermediate five-book version of 1804, the interest is recent and scholarly; their lines, preferred for their vigor and simplicity, being read as Wordsworth's core study in memory and imagination. In the full-length *Prelude* of 1805, memory, mimesis, and communal metaphor admirably meld into the classic of autobiographical poetry, as the realistic, be it landscape or cityscape, is understood to resonate between the mnemonic and the symbolic. If only the poem of the author's last wishes is valid, the delight of the Victorians introduces the dilemma of the moderns; for modern readers, from Wordsworth's twentieth-century editor on, regularly reject 1850, finding the earlier enigmatic vitality deadened by the later metaphoric message, the Christian symbolism finally too pervasive, too pat, and indistinguishable from dogma. By this assessment—here much exaggerated but mostly accepted—Wordsworth, his many *Prelude* manuscripts the cited evidence, fusses for over fifty years, inevitably exchanging youthful brilliance for artful balance for aged banality, 1799 for 1805 for 1850.

"Was it for this / That one, the fairest of all rivers, loved / To blend his murmurs with [his] nurse's song" (1799, 1.1–3), evoking and composing his poetic spirit? Yes, for inscribing and erasing, rewriting and rearranging his poetic statements, Wordsworth works in the rhythm of the river still flowing and his spirit still forming. He records his many meta-

morphoses and leaves his many manuscripts; with these he reveals, certainly, the stance of his philosophy, but more, by his very changeableness—for better and for worse—the suppleness of his creativity.

The method not the message: the emphasis is familiar. It is that of the
freely mnemonic, not very mimetic, idiosyncratically metaphoric autobiographical tradition; that of self-seekers given to working at cross-
purposes—meeting difficulties, meditating new quests—their minds
never at rest, their writings as discontinuous as true to (*b*) "our inconsistency" (824) [1054]: their ranks represented by Montaigne and the late
Rousseau of reverie and now, unwittingly, by Wordsworth. Unwittingly,
for Wordsworth's is a perplexing case in which his creative message being
best expressed by his ceaseless method, he—at least late in life—is not the
one to know. His (*b*) "food is (*c*) wonder, the chase, (*b*) ambiguity" (818)
[1045], but Wordsworth spends a lifetime slowing, caging, and explaining his prey, in 1799, 1805, 1850.

Wordsworth's preferred metaphors—travelers, wanderers, and pilgrims in scenes of landscape grandeur—accurately imply this progress
and effectively chart his life. But they do so ironically. Because, early, all
Wordsworth's care is for mnemonic vitality and shifting ambiguity in
personal poetry; yet Wordsworth's poetic progress, finally charted—
however zigzag the path—tells principally of chosen and communal
wisdom. Thus poetic cartography is a poor—because partial, paradoxical, even patently contradictory—metaphor for Wordsworth's changeable autobiography.

Early, Wordsworth's famous formulation of his poetic power rings
with his certainty that becoming is all:

> his mind,
> Even as an agent of the one great mind,
> Creates, creator and receiver both,
> Working but in alliance with the works
> Which it beholds.

> (1799, 2.301–5)

The subject of this eulogy is "the first / Poetic spirit of our human life"
(1799, 2.305–6). Its owner, the "Blessed . . . infant" (1799, 2.267), leads
Wordsworth via his "best conjectures" (1799, 2.268) back to the past, vivid
in his memory and his theory, the only viable source of his poetry. The
"first-born affinities that fit / Our new existence to existing things" (1799,
1.387–88), the "first" "sense of dim similitude which links / Our moral
feelings with external forms" (1799, 2.163–65), the "first creative sen-

sibility, / . . . by the regular action of the world / . . . unsubdued" (1799, 2.409–11)—these fascinate Wordsworth, even as, overflowing temporal and psychological categories, they escape him. These impel his poetry, although, he already knows in 1799 that "our puny boundaries are things / Which we perceive, and not which we have made" (1799, 2.253–54), that "each most obvious and particular thought— / . . . Hath no beginning" (1799, 2.264, 267), that we must not "point as with a wand, and say / 'This portion of the river of my mind / Came from yon fountain'" (1799, 2.247–49).

Mapping nothing—least of all sources—Wordsworth multiplies verbal approximations, discovering early in poetic doublings and variations the freedom of indecision. What is inner, what is outer in Wordsworth's youthful universe? It does not matter. The answer is in the question, in the possibilities, not certainties, not even probabilities, one more than the other, that asking—not answering—helps Wordsworth articulate. Whether

> To unorganic natures I transferred
> My own enjoyments, or, the power of truth
> Coming in revelation, I conversed
> With things that really are, I at this time
> Saw blessings spread around me like a sea.
>
> (1799, 2.440–44)

Their origin left in question, what, then, is the nature of these "blessings"? One response, Wordsworth's tempered and accepted version of 1799, is that "in all things / I saw one life and felt that it was joy" (1799, 2.459–60). Another response, that of the so-called pantheistic and excluded fragment, is "That what we see of forms and images / . . . and what we feel / Of active or recognizable thought" are "but accidents, / Relapses from that one interior life / That lives in all things" (*Peter Bell* MS. 2 (d), 2–4, 9–11).[3] Either way—his subjectivity dominating or nature's mysterious bounty, his seeing into the life of things or they alive in him—Wordsworth could hardly be further from charts and delineations, all the necessary preparation for voyages and prophecies. Intellectually, morally, autobiographically, why go anywhere? Joy is everywhere. Feel, and there is the imaginative energy, the impetus for writing poetry . . . but only lyric poetry.

In the envoi to his earliest *Prelude,* Wordsworth, ambivalent, begins to balance between poetic freedom and prophetic direction, between lyric and epic.[4] Lines of "joy" (1799, 2.446–64), originally the Pedlar's of *The*

Ruined Cottage, he appropriates and follows by lines spoken to Coleridge, "The most intense of Nature's worshippers, / . . . [his] brother" (1799, 2.507–8). Pedlar and poet, solitary and studious—these are Wordsworth's early alter egos until, exchanging third- and second-person otherness for the outrightness of "I," he asserts his poetic identity. Having "sought / The Truth in solitude" (1799, 2.505–6), Pedlar, brother, self— all merit the praise and promise he offers Coleridge:

> Fare thee well:
> Health and the quiet of a healthful mind
> Attend thee, seeking oft the haunts of men—
> But yet more often living with thyself,
> And for thyself—so haply shall thy days
> Be many, and a blessing to mankind.
>
> (1799, 2.509–14)

Noble and, unless generously glossed, nearly nonsensical words: thou shalt be social, but more often solitary; for thyself, but ultimately for others. And this not thirty lines from Wordsworth's (borrowed from Coleridge's) criticism of "selfishness, disguised in gentle names / Of peace and quiet and domestic love" (1799, 2.483–84). Although as a wholly unexplained afterthought Wordsworth appends the glimmerings of social purpose ("so haply shall thy days / Be many, and a blessing to mankind" (1799, 2.513–14), the "blessing" to be bestowed could hardly be more mysterious, seemingly effortless, vacuous. Promising little, Wordsworth ends his long and lofty lyric no more than implying the mission essential to the pilgrim and prophet of 1805 and beyond.

The solitary eventually finds his voice for prophecy, certainly by 1805, but when exactly he does so is less a historical date than a psychological state. Themes extolling the single and persistent laborer—as in "Resolution and Independence" (1802), "The Solitary Reaper" (1805), and portrayals of the ever-watchful poet performing "Evening Voluntaries" (1802–46)—are perennial in Wordsworth's poetry. And the scheme for communal good of the philosophical and instructional *Recluse* is finished early, sixteen years before the 1814 *Excursion* preface enshrines the unwritten whole in the echoing cathedral of Wordsworth's ambition. Between thematic extremes, Wordsworth's desire to make poetry becomes a desire to merit it, and his love of the lyric gives way to his search for the great subject. Book 1 of 1805 chronicles the earliest *Prelude* years, when Wordsworth, hesitating between historical epic, Spenserian romance, and Miltonic might, decides all the styles damned as he casts vainly about for a sufficiently valiant hero to vanquish the many doubts and denials of a poet without a program or a purpose, who, nevertheless, yearns to write "some philosophic song / Of truth that cherishes our daily life" (1805, 1.230–31). Yet even when Wordsworth writes this philosophic song, sung mostly in and of the present, 1800 in *Home at Grasmere,* he does not sufficiently express his essential self. A truism, certainly, but for Wordsworth more than for any other poet, Mnemosyne is the mother of the Muses. When the remembered is reimagined and magnified, when the years past sustain inspiration through the very hours of composition, then Wordsworth writes from the springs of his youthful imagination—at once his source and subject—his lyrical autobiography. But only when he strives to merit and share a vision more ample than personal—when he learns to read the autobiographical in terms of the historical; his evolution in his reaction to the French Revolution, and to read the psychological in the Christian spiritual tradition, his progress on a pilgrim's path and his calling in prophecy—only when he expresses the individual in the communal language of established symbols: then, as the five-book *Prelude* takes the full shape of 1805, and only then does Wordsworth realize in the personal the immense potential—and burden—of epic.[5]

By January 1804, Wordsworth clearly chooses "the story of [his] life" and, there and then, "the road lies plain before [him]" (1805, 1.667, 668), broadening by its very metaphor—for better and for worse—his individual way. The imagery of epic fantasy and history, of French, Scottish, and English heroes, he rejected early, uneasy that "the whole beauteous fabric seems to lack / Foundation, and withal appears throughout / Shadowy and unsubstantial" (1805, 1.226–28). Wordsworth's choice of a substantial metaphor, moral and weighty, is the pilgrim's way with his pack and his promises, a journey with its accompanying imagery. The imagery often twists from scenic expectations, as the "pilgrim [goes] / In quest of highest truth" (1805, 11.391–92), and even evades philosophic expectations: "A traveler I am / And all my tale is of myself" (1805, 3.196–97). Yet both Wordsworth's mapmaking metaphor of mental landscapes and his pathfinding figure of inner itineraries are originally borrowed. Certainly, Wordsworth builds with innovative brilliance on Bunyan, but where are the Slough of Despond and Vanity Fair if not in the mind?[6] And where is Wordsworth's Romantic freedom in Christian allegory?

Wordsworth's adventure is illusory. A pilgrim knows his goal, a dedicated spirit his vision of the grail, a revolutionary his dream of the millenium, and Wordsworth the end of his "tale": all seekers after preconceived answers, certainly after-the-fact autobiographers, undertake seemingly desultory but actually directed journeys. Beginning "As if on wings," Wordsworth "saw beneath him stretched / Vast prospect of the world which he had been, / And was" (1805, 13.378–80). Ending with his "world" sung, Wordsworth conventionally (if then only recently so) surveys the picturesqueness of the stilled and schematic landscape below. All is in prospect, for having "tracked the main essential power— / Imagination" (1805, 13.289–90), Wordsworth steadily eyes the "termination of [his] course" (1805, 13.372) as beyond beckons—"I have other tasks" (1805, 13.370)—his worthy *Recluse* goal.[7] Wordsworth, become the pilgrim, unquestionably must advance, but—his spiritual territory already past and in his poetic purview—where to?

By the end of 1805, the valleys are sketched in, the shadows illuminated, and in place of the lovely but suspect "beauteous fabric" of fantastic poesy is the close-woven Wordsworthian work "of fabric more divine," its concluding message radiant with Wordsworth's high expectations for mankind:

> Prophets of Nature, we to them will speak
> A lasting inspiration, sanctified
> By reason and by truth; what we have loved
> Others will love, and we may teach them how:
> Instruct them how the mind of man becomes
> A thousand times more beautiful than the earth
> On which he dwells, above this frame of things
> (Which, 'mid all revolutions in the hopes
> And fears of men, doth still remain unchanged)
> In beauty exalted, as it is itself
> Of substance and of fabric more divine.
>
> (1805, 13.442–52)

The very splendor of the lines disguises their disturbing stillness. The promises of "reason and truth" resonate in 1805; then 1850 ousts "truth" for the sanction of "faith." But a word change, yet thus "reason, blest by faith" (1850, 14.448) reveals heaven on the horizon of this world—this framed and static and inadequate world. Cherishing mutability yet chastened by his mortality, Wordsworth makes, with a word, a compromise. He makes "the mind of man" "more" and "exalted" and "above" a changeless earth; he composes emotion, mood, mutability in a munificent paradise, in which this time we live in is elevated to timelessness. So paradoxical and questionable a gesture is, unfortunately, no longer investigated by Wordsworth, who by the same gesture is elevated to sublimity. The apotheosis is apt, for thus speaking prophecy at his height, Wordsworth is silenced: poetically, philosophically, effectively.[8]

This, then, is Wordsworth's autobiographical path from originality to generosity, translated along the way by a Christian figural tradition that renders the individual communal, accessible to all morally and splendidly, but no longer to the poet poetically.[9] In 1799, the path is not yet a path; it is inner, viewless, has no beginning save in "days / Disowned by memory" (1799, 1.444–45) and no ending save the creative continuum of memory, reverie, and a wished-for futurity of successful poetry. By 1805, the poet-become-pilgrim roams the more complex and grand topography of epic poetry, beginning in medias res with a present poetic sally into the past, into regions youthful and free, then down the mid-epic descent into a hell of obscure and Romantic disappointment, to circle back and up to Mount Snowdon, the emblem of the imagination at work and the promise of future creations. The 1850 poem is the same journey, the road retaken and retold—and old. The 1850 is but 1805 mapped in more detail, as, over the years, Wordsworth draws in the lines and inscribes the names, marks the depths as hell and paradise here, but become otherworldly in very Christian imagery. And all the difference is in the emphasis as it shifts decisively from the seeker to his route: from the poet roaming spiritual countries to his terminus faithfully admired; from the traveler whose tale is all of himself to the pilgrimage whose Christian goal is for—and known to—all. Wordsworth's joy and splendid discovery are all early—of unclosing "spots of time" and unending routes back to their power—but we must have the map if we are to follow. Knowingly or not, inevitably or not, Wordsworth sacrifices his life of poetic adventure that we might venture, however hesitantly, down his well-marked, now how overgrown, path.

Wordsworth's ambition to "teach," to preach of "beauty exalted" is admirable; its realization as desirable for his readers as it is deplorable for Wordsworth. For making too manifest his message, Wordsworth stills his method in certitude. Speaking too intently the language of others to others, thus he silences a portion of his self, the youthful persona "capable of being in uncertainties, mysteries, doubts, without any irritable reaching after fact and reason."[10] Thus Wordsworth's inspiration, bright in images from his chosen poetic lexicon, ends snuffed in conventional poetic imagery, the light extinguished in the later poetry of personifications and moral excursions, the ember of the falling star, the crater after the meteor. And why? Here the guess and the limited story. Because

Wordsworth's method is his message; because, ultimately, becoming is all. And Wordsworth's error, his only error, was to arrive too swiftly and definitively at being (the "Prospectus" paradise which is on this earth) and beyond (the *Prelude* paradise which is "above this frame of things").[11] When a conclusion announces the end of discovery, it resounds too decisively. His conclusion resounding too knowingly with "reason and truth" as early as 1805, and too conventionally "reason" and "faith" assured by 1850, Wordsworth in the same last *Prelude* breath announces the end of his aspiration—and of his inspiration.

Nature spake to me / Rememberable things

Early—before prophecy—Wordsworth's autobiographical focus is more mnemonic than mimetic, with no one metaphor ruling; save perhaps the meandering river Derwent, which he more often pursues upstream, through "alder shades" and up "rocky falls" (1799, 1.4), than follows to the sea. Incessantly, Wordsworth harkens back to origins, but, in 1799, he does so less to locate his poetic source than to drink freely from its current. In 1799, Wordsworth does not chart sources, he explores them; he does not class sensations, he cultivates them. His endeavor is to recollect nature's earliest lessons: her images, seasons, and enduring relations; her language at its freshest become the conscious resource of his imagery and philosophy. In the carefully conned Book of Nature, Wordsworth seeks in his beginnings the perfect phrasing for his ending, that his poetry may record his memory, not his history, in the language of his spirit, not his study.

In the dark and depths of memory, Wordsworth discovers phenomenological "spots of time," which belie the convention of telling a lifetime on a narrative time line. "Spots of time" are emotional not chronological, changeable, not chartable, idiosyncratically mnemonic, not traditionally mimetic, metaphoric but only as feeling colors metaphor with "youth's golden gleam" (1805, 11.322) or the dark of "blasted tree" (1805, 11.377). Wordsworth's classic example is from early childhood: a five-year-old child, he is lost in horror before the gibbet, the "naked pool," the "beacon on the lonely eminence" (1799, 1.324, 325); but come again years later, the same scene is transformed by the light of youthful love, radiating all the brighter as it shines on the horror: for a reciprocity exists between the child solitary and now grown in company, between fear and beauty, his emotions early and mature. And a reciprocity exists between versions of *The Prelude;* 1799 offering the fearful child, 1805 his illumination by love, and 1850 his ongoing ability to "beguile" or "animate" "Down to this very time" (1850, 12.333, 335, 327). Temporal spaces or spatial pauses, "spots of time" link—rarely chronologically, often oddly—feeling to feeling, self to self, and scene to scene in time gone, here, and to come again. Far from a mere refinement on the time-line life story, they represent the reversion—read subversion—of the habitual chronological line that advances the autobiographer from birth to misled maturity to conversion.[12] Not literary, not logical, "spots of time" metaphorically and philosophically contradict path-and-progress imagery, competing, and from the start, for structural precedence in *The Prelude*.

Imaginatively revisiting his childhood scenes (first in memory from his residence in Germany [1799], then in reality home at Grasmere [for 1805]), Wordsworth writes autobiography to see each scene newly. For the 1799 *Prelude,* the example from far back in time is the rule, as scene loosely follows scene, each a sort of "spot of time" untethered to a narrative or explanatory line. For far back in time, early memories—often raw, fragmentary, and unconsciously chosen—are freest from past superadded meaning, freest for present imaginative transformation on the psychic continuum. Of many early memories, as a happily bathing, easily skating, trap-pilfering, and boat-stealing boy, Wordsworth writes songs of innocence and experience. Of these he makes a mosaic of—almost—a fall. But blessed, to be regained not repudiated, are Wordsworth's youthful experiences. Though the confessional similarity of his early "sins" to pear stealing and comb breaking is undeniable, Wordsworth orders his transgressions haphazardly, not at all causally, subsuming his stories under the contraries of "fear" and "pleasure" (1799, 1.433, 434), and thus the figure of the fall does not develop.[13] The Wordsworthian child, living almost solitary, emotionally and practically distant from people, can—at least poetically—hardly sin against humanity. And even violating nature—"a fell destroyer" (1799, 1.35) hunting and hurrying from snare to snare—he does no more than nature does; his power is no greater than her "danger or desire" (1799, 1.195), his destruction no worse than hers done in due season. Though he hear "Low breathings coming after [him], and sounds / Of undistinguishable motion, steps / Almost as silent as the turf they trod" (1799, 1.47–49); even so a golden age does not close, nor God appear in this northern garden. The child's "glad animal movements" ("Tintern Abbey," 74) are in nature's rhythm, and nature, according to Wordsworth, though not "red in tooth and claw," is certainly far from pastoral innocent or given over to the meek.

Not in the sylvan imagery of Pan a-playing or in the solemn and sonorous Christian imagery of fall and exile, Adam and Eve wandering, the Prodigal Son exploring—neither in paganism nor in crusading Christianity does this latter-day pilgrim's progress start. "Blessed the infant babe" (1799, 2.267), "No outcast he, bewildered and depressed" (1799, 2.291); no sinner he, marred by original sin. And until his last days, nature offers "lofty speculations," "A never failing principle of joy / And purest passion" (1799, 2.493, 495–96). Infant to adult, Wordsworth is "With God and Nature communing" (1799, 2.476). Indubitably, to his mind, nature is still golden, paradise is not lost. In the 1799 *Prelude,* there are allusions to a Miltonic Satan "Suspended by the blast which blew amain" (1799, 1.61) but he is young Wordsworth adventurous; allusions to "an act of stealth / And troubled pleasure" (1799, 1.90–91) but the skiff is only temporarily taken; to a "path" with its "broken windings" (1799, 2.317, 319) but it is difficult and to be overflown. In 1799, biblical and many Miltonic allusions abound, but no Christian conclusions.

The Book may be truth, but it does not teach the Wordsworthian child. To him "every hour brings palpable access / Of knowledge, when all knowledge is delight, / And sorrow is not there" (1799, 2.335–37). In the very moonlight extending over "three long leagues / Of shining water" (1799, 1.409–10), in the sheer, not mere, sensuality of such a scene is a generous gift of knowledge. And if the child forgets his lesson, it does not matter:

> Thus often in those fits of vulgar joy
> Which through all seasons on a child's pursuits
> Are prompt attendants, 'mid that giddy bliss
> Which like a tempest works along the blood
> And is forgotten, even then I felt
> Gleams like the flashing of a shield. The earth
> And common face of Nature spake to me
> Rememberable things—sometimes, 'tis true,
> By quaint associations, yet not vain
> Nor profitless, if haply they impressed
> Collateral objects and appearances,
> Albeit lifeless then, and doomed to sleep
> Until maturer seasons called them forth
> To impregnate and to elevate the mind.
>
> (1799, 1.413–26)

Knowledge does not corrupt; it "impregnates," "elevates," and not to the ironic or histrionic heights of Miltonic sin (Eve, hovering, dreaming over

paradise; Adam, superior, reasoning then falling). Nature does not despair, groaning at man's fall; she enters in innocent union with the
human, her "hues and forms" "Allied to the affections" (1799, 1.441–42).
Enough that her "hues and forms" remain; all the young boy's joy can go:

> And if the vulgar joy by its own weight
> Wearied itself out of the memory,
> The scenes which were a witness of that joy
> Remained, in their substantial lineaments
> Depicted on the brain, and to the eye
> Were visible, a daily sight.
>
> (1799, 1.427–32)

The mountain, stream, moon, shining sea—the early scenes must stay to
nurture the imagination. As for the usual autobiographical and educa-
tional details—the early influences of mother or father, the habitual
studies of the young boy, even the individuality of the "quaint associations," the "Collateral objects and appearances," the very lessons in
Wordsworth's early education—they are hardly essential. Never mind—
not directly, at least—the self; the "scenes" remain, all speaking "Rememberable things" (1799, 1.420), but theirs is a "ghostly language,"
heard dimly in distant winds:

> I would walk alone
> In storm and tempest, or in starlight nights
> Beneath the quiet heavens, and at that time
> Would feel what'er there is of power in sound
> To breathe an elevated mood, by form
> Or image unprofaned; and I would stand
> Beneath some rock, listening to sounds that are
> The ghostly language of the ancient earth,
> Or make their dim abode in distant winds.
> Thence did I drink the visionary power.
>
> (1799, 2.351–60)

These, then, are the varied sources of Wordsworth's "visionary power":
from cherished scenes "in their substantial lineaments / Depicted on the
brain," he hears "Remememberable things"; in tempest or starlight silence,
from sounds blustering or all but unheard, he drinks "visionary power";
and even from "the lines / Of curling mist," he "[drinks] in / A pure or-
ganic pleasure" (1799, 1.396–97, 395–96). In short, to the young poet, the
visual speaks, the auditory is seen, and either can quench a spiritual thirst.

Early visions, ghostly auditions, shadowy exaltations—all put to the rhythmn of emotion, not meter, introduce the universe of poetry. And all, resisting traditional biblical or philosophical meanings, awaiting "maturer seasons," resonate, becoming ever richer in memory than they were in reality. But richer is not necessarily clearer, nor deeper necessarily describable: early memories may offer poetic inspiration but no assurance of autobiographical comprehension or expression.[14] Indeed, forgetting what exactly of visionary power is spoken, seen, and drunk, Wordsworth praises most highly what he does not remember clearly:

> I deem not profitless these fleeting moods
> Of shadowy exaltation; not for this,
> That they are kindred to our purer mind
> And intellectual life, but that the soul—
> Remembering how she felt, but what she felt
> Remembering not—retains an obscure sense
> Of possible sublimity, to which
> With growing faculties she doth aspire,
> With faculties still growing, feeling still
> That whatsoever point they gain they still
> Have something to pursue.
>
> (1799, 2.361–71)

"Obscure," "possible," and "still growing"—Wordsworth's very lack of imagery for his creativity emphasizes the movement in his mood that is the veritable impetus to his poetry.

Assuredly, Wordsworth's mimetic work is not made easy by his material: viewless images, "unconscious intercourse / With . . . eternal beauty" (1799, 1.394–95), sounds unheard by the sensual ear, apocalypse seen "when the light of sense / Goes out" (1805, 6.534–35). In turn blind, deaf, dumb, and unconscious, thus the poet learns his craft. In turn giddy and forgetting, thus he develops his art. No wonder De Quincey stridently prided himself on being one of Wordsworth's very early, very few admirers.

Yet knowing *The Prelude*, and for that matter the poet, did not inordinately privilege De Quincey; for as early as 1798, contemporary readers, to whom all *Prelude* versions were unknown, could encounter Wordsworth's extreme synesthesia, creative amnesia, and novel poetic theories in the *Lyrical Ballads*. "Tintern Abbey," his earliest published personal history, is amply introductory to the Wordsworthian meshing of senses in vague imagery and profound ambiguity. To the young Wordsworth, rock, mountain, wood, "Their colors and their forms, were then to me / An appetite" (79–80); and years later, lightening "the burthen of the mystery" (38), "beauteous forms" give "sensations sweet, / Felt in the blood, and felt along the heart" (22, 27–28). Characteristically, barely staying, these stay strongly in memory; for "unremembered pleasure" (31) and "unremembered acts / Of kindness and love" (34–35) are essential to "that serene and blessed mood" (41) in which "We see into the life of things" (49). And in the "Tintern Abbey" "sense sublime / Of something far more deeply interfused" (95–96)—therein is the "obscure sense / Of possible sublimity," the "something" still "to pursue" in 1799 (2.366–67, 371), and the glimmering beginning of "something evermore about to be" in 1805 (6.542).[15] Before the later poetry and the last *Prelude* finally fixes Wordsworth's inspiration, "something" is never a definition, rather an invitation to further exploration.

All this fruitful incertitude is early, when Wordsworth's memory, not caring for effects "regularly classed" (1799, 1.256), readily contributes to his still fluid mnemonic theory, his "spots of time" that in 1799 are still structurally stronger than the "broken windings" of his incipient path. Early, Wordsworth records, less autobiographical stages, or even images, than poetic changes, sensual and intellectual exchanges, ringing in the process of creating. "Remembering how . . . but what . . . / Remembering not" (1799, 2.365–66), early, is the rule of his poetic autobiography. The story in each memory matters little, the particularity of its "bliss" less, and its narrative position least of all. Indeed, lines 352–71 in part 1 of 1799 were originally written in the third person, their "ghostly language" probably for the Pedlar; thus even a particular memory or manner of remembering has not a sole owner. Valuing his "visionary power" over his individuality, Wordsworth writes autobiography in which only the emotion and atmosphere of each memory—freest from extrinsic meaning and farthest from cultural falsity—are essential.

Whether his practice defines his principles or his principles dictate his practice, either way young Wordsworth writes his poetic autobiography in accord with his rules for lyric poetry. As in the *Lyrical Ballads,* so in the early *Prelude:* "the feeling gives importance to the action and situation and not the action and situation to the feeling" ("Preface," 735). In emotion is the start of everyman's imaginative movement; in its cultivation is the poet's apprenticeship, he being "a man speaking to men," only "endowed with more lively sensibility" than many ("Preface," 737). In the eye of creative becoming, Wordsworth centers his art and his life. As the youthful poet, he begins his creative existence with "the spontaneous overflow of powerful feelings" ("Preface," 740) and writes of his "emotion recollected in tranquillity" ("Preface," 740). As the youthful autobiographer, he privileges, not events in sequence nor theories in hierarchy, but emotion tempered by recollection in his early self-writing.

The river Derwent need only run softly while Wordsworth sings his song, thus far the lyrical informs the autobiographical in the two-part *Prelude,* thus far memory, not mimesis, is Wordsworth's early muse. Offering praise to the dim, the vague, the faint, the barely there, Wordsworth offers worse—for the poetically uninitiated of his generation, the impatient of all ages: his highest praise is given to the "unremembered," a peculiarity of Wordsworthian autobiography. Still unlit, hidden in the temporal shadows, are the sharply actual spiritual revisions in time of "spots of time." As lines appearing only in the 1799 *Prelude* attest (ironically, revised out in 1805 and after), emotional revision is the essence of Wordsworth's creative continuation:

> I might advert
> To numerous accidents in flood or field,
> Quarry or moor, or 'mid the winter snows,
> Distresses and disasters, tragic facts
> Of rural history, that impressed my mind
> With images to which in following years
> Far other feelings were attached—with forms
> That yet exist with independent life,
> And, like their archetypes, know no decay.
>
> (1799, I.279–87)

In 1799, Wordsworth "might advert" to more than earliest feelings allied to archetypical "forms," to "tragic facts" attaching to "Far other feelings," but he does not. Not until the 1805 *Prelude* does Wordsworth temper his penchant for shadowy psychic permanence to clearly see his "spots of time" in the personal continuum of perpetual change. He is "loth to quit / Those recollected hours that have the charm / Of visionary things" (1799, I.459–61), but turn he does, from inner vision to outer sight, from his obscure memory to his communicable history.

The days gone by / Come back upon me

In the very act of lengthening his written life story, from two parts to five then thirteen books, Wordsworth alters its figural form. As his interest shifts from the lyricism of his youthful spirit to the ambition of his later personal history, Wordsworth, focusing his "shadowy" meta-phors into narrative clarity, reshapes his poem of memory more into mimetic story. And thus, perhaps inevitably, he begins his negotiation between his own mnemonic theory and traditional mimetic chronology and his hesitation over how deeply to color his poem conventionally Christian. Manuscript evidence for the five-book *Prelude* shows "spots of time" still amply glossing early memories beginning and ending the poem.[16] But by March 1804, when the five-book *Prelude* gives way to more, Wordsworth begins his compromise between the random richness of "spots of time" and the Christian moral design of the time line, progress or no, reward or sin—goal. Maneuvering between the flexibility of personal symbology and the communality of the Christian figural tradition, Wordsworth, in the clash and flash of contrast, illuminates both: "spots of time" become sharper, the pilgrim's spiritual path clearer, but neither simpler. Striking his balance between complexity and com-municability, between his youthful solo creativity and "The still, sad mu-sic of humanity"; in the equilibrium, Wordsworth shows "loss," though he would believe "Abundant recompense" ("Tintern Abbey" 91, 87–88).

This classic Wordsworthian equation (of "Tintern Abbey" wisdom, of "Immortality" compensation) is writ large and long in the 1805 *Prelude,* which promises "in the end / All gratulant if rightfully understood" (1805, 13.384–85). Along his autobiographical way to Snowdon and prophecy, Wordsworth pursues desirable detours. Via memories, reveries, and youthful poetry, he succeeds in innovating from within the Christian autobiographical tradition, appropriating for individual lyricism the usual advancing, never regressing, progress plot of spiritual enlighten-ment. But the established figures of the progress—the good pilgrim, the wanderer converted to the way, the prophet come to the mountain—may hinder Wordsworth's imagination even as they help communicate his vision. For his plot demanding development, Wordsworth turns from his inner source to advance to his mountain wisdom, pressing forward, sometimes inspiredly, sometimes merely sequentially, whether with ar-dent historical instruction (France young and golden, then wizened and dangerous) or with dutiful satirical description (Cambridge and London, his moral mirrors of less-than-moral societies). Gradually, the interpretive concentration of "spots of time" becomes diluted by the sheer length of narrative extending Wordsworth's history from "spots of time" to sweep-ing life stages. Gradually, the very mystery of "spots of time" becomes too lighted by the widening of his autobiography from lyrical focus to narra-tive breadth. And, finally, the variability of the extraordinary—such as

Snowdon in reality and retrospect—is composed into orderly vision as Wordsworth declaims certainty from the summit of his conclusion.

But early in the 1805 *Prelude*—before prophecy, before finality—in the poetic exchanges as youth gives way to age, Wordsworth acknowledges new temporal complexity without succumbing to schematic theory. As the "rememberable" things of childhood come to life in adult consciousness, Wordsworth exceeds his highest praise for all the autobiographical past of early visions, ghostly auditions, and shadowy exaltations. By 1805, he clearly announces that it does not matter in his self-writing what is past, what present, what is "naked recollection" and what "after-meditation" (1805, 3.646, 648). Yet even as he announces his indifference to differentiating "The shadow from the substance" (1805, 4.255), he details mnemonic, mimetic, and metaphoric autobiographical layers more than before in his simile of self-searching as like peering from a slow-moving boat into still water:

> As one who hangs down-bending from the side
> Of a slow-moving boat upon the breast
> Of a still water, solacing himself
> With such discoveries as his eye can make
> Beneath him in the bottom of the deeps,
> Sees many beauteous sights—weeds, fishes, flowers,
> Grots, pebbles, roots of trees—and fancies more,
> Yet often is perplexed, and cannot part
> The shadow from the substance, rocks and sky,
> Mountains and clouds, from that which is indeed
> The region, and the things which there abide
> In their true dwelling; now is crossed by gleam
> Of his own image, by a sunbeam now,
> And motions that are sent he knows not whence,
> Impediments that make his task more sweet;
> Such pleasant office have we long pursued
> Incumbent o'er the surface of past time—
> With like success.

                          (1805, 4.247–64)

In the dim, the vague, the faint, the barely there, herein still is the fascination for Wordsworth of past time; but now—knowing the perplexity of his perspective, acknowledging seeing and fancying, remembering and interpreting—Wordsworth knows he does not know the precise angle of his vision, or opinion, or even comprehension.

From his "slow-moving boat," Wordsworth conveys change in un-compromising confusion. In context (1805, 4.222–360) his celebrated simile reveals his "congratulation and regret" (1805, 4.232) as he contemplates youthful extremity in memories spanning from sublime to trivial. Wordsworth writes of "A dawning, even as of another sense, / A human-heartedness" (1805, 4.224–25), "A new-born feeling" (1805, 4.233); "Yet" —with characteristic ambivalence—"in spite" of such apparent progress "an inner falling off" (1805, 4.268, 270) to "vanities" (1805, 4.288). "And yet"—again, he reconsiders—"in chastisement of these regrets, / [a] memory . . . / Doth here rise up" (1805, 4.314–16). The memory of what? What else but of "congratulation," his dedication to beauty, creativity, poetry. After these scrupulous measurements of varying attainments, this passage of profoundly untenable pronouncements, Wordsworth's summary, in keeping, refuses easy reconcilement between opposites:

> Strange rendezvous my mind was at that time,
> A party-coloured shew of grave and gay,
> Solid and light, short-sighted and profound,
> Of inconsiderate habits and sedate,
> Consorting in one mansion unreproved.
>
> (1805, 4.346–50)

Young, Wordsworth is sometimes the dandy, sometimes the "dedicated spirit" (1805, 4.344); older, he is the honest chronicler of his marked diversity.

Little wonder that Wordsworth as autobiographer chooses half perceiving and half creating as his preferred mode of being ("Tintern Abbey," 106–7). For seeing sharply, separately, and too analytically strips the past of its context and continuity, variety and mystery. "Incumbent o'er . . . past time," Wordsworth more profitably contemplates its images and its changes, as resolutely he refuses to pilfer the past for answers useless outside their historic element, like stones shining lovely in water, seen and coveted, but no sooner held, darkening dull in the drying air, then discarded, dropped back into their original region, their "true dwelling." Wordsworth knows that "Impediments"—his self ("crossed by gleam / Of his own image"), his circumstances ("by a sunbeam now"), and unidentifiable changes ("motions that are sent he knows not whence")—mediate, even distort, his "pleasant" pursuit of poetry in past time. But, no matter, even were he to tell shadow from substance, memory from imagination, the past in its "true dwelling" from his version in his current writing; inevitably, all would shimmer anew as "gleam" of self, circumstance, or strange motion set afloat the distinctions once again. And never will they settle decisively, as the boat will always drift, the weather darken or lighten, the poet decide and write, again, differently, his history.

Drifting easily in reverie like the solitary dreamer by the island of Saint-Pierre, Wordsworth makes many an autobiographical decision with emotion and imagination, to suit moral not factual truth, to suit inner not outer "reality." Fascinated by the metamorphoses of memory in time, Wordsworth effects most by creatively trespassing over the very boundaries marking fact from fiction that traditional autobiographers, zealous for order, create. All chronological birth-to-newborn-self autobiographers respect, whether diligently or grudgingly, some factual and verifiable measure of "truth." Even Augustine intoning for ultimate "truth," and Rousseau spinning with defiant sophistry his impassioned denial of factual truth's validity; even Montaigne ignoring history, identity, certainty, any "truth" higher than man's fallibility—not one entirely dismisses the distinction between outer and inner reality. Wordsworth, never so argumentative or exhaustive a writer, is merely heedless of what he feels are needless boundaries.[17] Fact and fiction, "truth" and interpretation, so-called objectivity and subjectivity (which Ruskin calls the most "useless" distinction in philosophy)—these, strictly separate, Wordsworth eschews as so many autobiographical versions of murder in the service of dissection, so many false and displeasing definitions into "absolute independent singleness" ("Essay," 748).[18] "In nature, everything is distinct," Wordsworth insists; in false writing, everything is "defined, insulated, dislocated, deadened—yet nothing distinct. It will always be so when words are substituted for things" ("Essay," 748–49). Inner and outer, subjective and objective are but words to one who "proclaims / How exquisitely the individual Mind . . ."

> to the external world
> Is fitted:—and how exquisitely, too—
> Theme this but little heard of among men—
> The external World is fitted to the Mind.
> And the creation (by no lower name
> Can it be called) which they with blended might
> Accomplish:—this is our high argument.
>
> ("Prospectus," 62–63, 65–71)

This is Wordsworth's at once creative and iconoclastic argument.[19]

Breaking rules of autobiographical veracity—concerning "naked recollection" and "after-meditation," fact and fiction—Wordsworth shatters traditional autobiographical time. "Spots of time"—ever capable of changing in memory and actuality as they shift in and out of emotional focus, and desirable in their very instability, their interpretive multiplicity—with these Wordsworth moves far from narrative history, far from the habitual orderly historical line. Fitting the external world to his mind, Wordsworth fits history to his memory. That is, he forms time to the contours of his mind—but the metaphor is misleading. The more telling image for Wordsworthian time is water, seen as depths from the slow-moving boat, as river surface for "a twig or any floating thing" pointing his poetic course (1805, 1.31). Lake, river, sea—therein the image of time is clear and opaque, flowing, changing. As a metaphor, water matches fully revisionary memory, which allows perpetual variability, which allows emotional continuity. As the autobiographical resource, revisionary memory allows Wordsworth to move his narrative by nuance or stall his narrative with emotion.

Wordsworth's autobiographical validity is acceptably temporary, if it but end in poetry. By 1805, in "spots of time," the scared child is illuminated by light, the drowned man is glossed by the fairy film of fantasy, and he, Dorothy, Mary, and Coleridge are together by that beacon, that lonely eminence, in the summer of their golden gleam of youthful love and promise of new poetry: "spots" have this interpretive variability. But they also have an ability to hold firmly to young emotion, to "enshrine the spirit of the past / For future restoration" (1805, 11.341–42), despite wan afteremotion, despite wise afterthought. Even knowing Coleridge to eat opium and the Revolution to devour its children, Wordsworth faithfully keeps his early emotional visions of poetry and liberty. In Wordsworth's textual explanation of "spots of time" (1805, 11.257–388), early scenes remain and emotions change. But in his textual demonstration of history contradicting memory, often scenes change and early emotions remain.

Knowing no conversion, Wordsworth repeatedly reverts to one memorable "spot of time" or another.[20] Even his so-called "Moment of Dedication" to poetry, Wordsworth doubles. Of an earlier moment, he recalls a sense of summons, a "blessedness, which even yet remains" (1805, 4.345). "Magnificent / The morning was, a memorable pomp, / More glorious than I ever had beheld," yet "with all the sweetness of a common dawn" (1805, 4.330–32, 337): the extraordinary is ordinary. And the dedication is without drama:

> I made no vows, but vows
> Were then made for me: bond unknown to me
> Was given, that I should be—else sinning greatly—
> A dedicated spirit.
>
> (1805, 4.341–44)

Perhaps face to the fields and the common dawn, Wordsworth gives his life to poetry. Yet perhaps coming into great London, in a later "divine" moment (1805, 8.710), he understands his calling. Writing book 4, lines 268–315, Wordsworth thinks his summons come in the country; writing book 8, lines 689–710, he thinks in the city: "Never shall I forget the hour, / The moment rather say . . ."

> When to myself it fairly might be said
> (The very moment that I seemed to know)
> "The threshold now is overpast," great God!
> That aught *external* to the living mind
> Should have such mighty sway, yet so it was:
> A weight of ages did at once descend
> Upon my heart—no thought embodied, no
> Distinct remembrances, but weight and power,
> Power growing with the weight. Alas, I feel
> That I am trifling. 'Twas a moment's pause:
> All that took place within me came and went
> As in a moment, and I only now
> Remember that it was a thing divine.
>
> (1805, 8.689–90, 698–710)

"'The threshold now is overpast'"—again. As Wordsworth describes "no thought embodied, no / Distinct remembrances," indeterminancy rules—again. And the wonder, that "aught *external* . . . / Should have such mighty sway," he emphasizes only to metamorphose external into internal, the city into the history of poetry, poetry into the power of humanity. Not a scene of dedication, but ongoing spiritual cultivation; not concepts, but "Capaciousness" (1805, 8.759): these are valid measures of Wordsworth's calling and creativity. In a crescendo of praise for power, Wordsworth insists:

> I sought not then
> Knowledge, but craved for power—and power I found
> In all things. Nothing had a circumscribed

And narrow influence; but all objects, being
In themselves capacious, also found in me
Capaciousness and amplitude of mind—
Such is the strength and glory of our youth.

(1805, 8.754–60)

Power and potential are the "strength and glory" of Wordsworth's youth: when he follows still his early autobiographical rule of "Remembering how . . . , but what . . . / Remembering not" (1799, 2.364–65); when, given his continual revision, he never fixes autobiographical pattern.

Usually Wordsworth's rewriting of personal history involves this imaginative freewheeling with memory; but also, and extensively, he zealously guards memory against temporal and hermeneutical transformation. On the continuum of emotionality, Wordsworth keeps his past, as it were, pure. He preserves his emotions from after-the-fact assessments determining their force, each memory being free to take on new feeling but also, if still sounding, to have its former force. He preserves his reflections from the judgments of hindsight interpretation and the domineering wisdom of proverbial pattern. By keeping emotion and reflection personally accurate—even in the face of patent external change—Wordsworth achieves his enduring consistency.

Wordsworth's rewriting changeable reality to accommodate his consistent spirituality is notable where Coleridge is concerned. In all the Lake "neighborhood"—those loved "spots" where together he, Dorothy, and Mary wandered—"was scattered love— / A spirit of pleasure, and youth's golden gleam" (1805, 6.240, 244–45). Identifying the love linking poet to poet, Wordsworth—ignoring the historically different before, during, and after—puts Coleridge in his past where he was not, his present where he is absent, and his future where he will refuse to be, on a loving continuum of spiritual, if idealistic, friendship:[21]

O friend, we had not seen thee at that time,
And yet a power is on me and a strong
Confusion, and I seem to plant thee there.
Far art thou wandered now in search of health,
And milder breezes—melancholy lot—
But thou art with us, with us in the past,
The present, with us in the times to come.
There is no grief, no sorrow, no despair,
No languor, no dejection, no dismay,

No absence scarcely can there be, for those
Who love as we do.

(1805, 6.246–56)

The boundaries down between past, present, and future, denial is possible of any history different from personal memory. The boundaries down between inner and outer, down too come the divisions between self and other. Coleridge, the very different poet, thus is "brother" not other to Wordsworth at the end of 1799; and through all his personal changes— opium, estrangement, residence in London, and, notably, his abandonment of poetry—Wordsworth keeps Coleridge with him, together "Prophets of Nature" (1805, 13.442) in 1805 and, still, in 1850. Poetry is the Wordsworthian preserve for the personal rescued from the perishable, released amidst the loosest of factual and temporal fences, free to roam.

Neither for his personal history nor for the amplitude of public history does Wordsworth force false definitions.[22] Napoleon himself cannot convert Wordsworth's remembered past Republicanism into a present cool assessment; his very empire cannot change the promise of the Revolution stirring into its known and lamentable excess. The tenacity of Wordsworth's memory is equalled by his will to witness his age. For example, Wordsworth faithfully remembers his early idealism in an ideological "spot of time" centered on Robespierre. Aptly, his metaphoric introduction is to "those bright spots, those fair examples given / Of fortitude, and energy, and love, / And human nature faithful to itself. . . ."

[For these] . . . was I impelled to think
Of the glad time when first I traversed France,
A youthful pilgrim; above all remembered
That day when through an arch that spanned the street,
A rainbow made of garish ornaments
(Triumphal pomp for Liberty confirmed)
We walked, a pair of weary travellers,
Along the town of Arras—place from which
Issued that Robespierre, who afterwards
Wielded the sceptre of the atheist crew.
When the calamity spread far and wide,
And this same city, which had even appeared
To outrun the rest in exultation, groaned
Under the vengeance of her cruel son,
As Lear reproached the winds, I could almost

> Have quarrelled with that blameless spectacle
> For being yet an image in my mind
> To mock me under such a strange reverse.
>
> (1805, 10.445–65)

The "strange reverse" is only in history, not in memory. Ineluctably, the prejudice of knowledge gained over time comes to gloss the hope of the Revolution with the blood of its outcome. But—until post-1805 revision—Wordsworth resists the reinterpretation of past golden expectation. Even when Wordsworth rejoices at Robespierre's death, his is the joy of the ardent youth, quick to feel "glee" in "vengeance" and free with "eternal justice," not the measured judgment of the mature poet or the prudent Victorian sage:

> Great was my glee of spirit, great my joy
> In vengeance, and eternal justice, thus
> Made manifest. "Come now, ye golden times,"
> Said I, forth-breathing on those open sands
> A hymn of triumph
>
> . . . . .
>
> Thus, interrupted by uneasy bursts
> Of exultation, I pursued my way
> Along that very shore which I had skimmed
> In former times, when spurring from the Vale
>
> . . . . .
>
> We beat with thundering hoofs the level sand.
>
> (1805, 10.539–43, 10.557–60, 10.66)

Wordsworthian honesty is in the very layering of his autobiography. Behind the political lurks the personal, and behind the personal the textual poetic: "that very shore," that "spot of time," saw, before Wordsworth's political innocence, his childhood innocence; and those written words, "We beat with thundering hoofs the level sand," the same line verbatim sounds book 2's conclusion.[23]

Encouraging endless reassessment and reexpression, such "spots of time" refuse definition. After all, revisionism is the innovation in "spots of time"—indeed, in Wordsworthian Romanticism. But as nebulous images of limitless change, "spots of time" ultimately lose to the clarity of chartable conviction written in orderly narration. Yet they lose late, for as late as Spring 1804, the "spots of time" sequence (1805, 11.257–388) comes after—hence their predominance is assured over—the ascent of Snowdon.[24] Closing *The Prelude,* "spots of time" as mnemonic theory can encompass Snowdon as mimetic experience. But the ascent of Snowdon as imaginative explanation cannot encompass the psychological complexity of "spots of time"—nor even encompass the changing significance of the very vision seen from the mountain, a metamorphosing, increasingly momentous memory with a long history.[25]

As lived and written history, the ascent of Snowdon is revisionary: at age twenty-one, Wordsworth climbs Mount Snowdon to contemplate "Joys only given to uncorrupted hearts" in creative communion with nature (*Descriptive Sketches,* 491); at age thirty-three, he essays diverse "living pictures, to embody / This pleasing argument" (MS. W, 32–33); and at age thirty-five, he composes his "meditation" to consolidate his vision, to appropriate the commanding view from on high (1805, 13.66–76).[26] As a "spot of time," Snowdon represents—intertextually—this autobiographical mutability. For the remarkable day varies—the scene remaining, the emotions in time metamorphosing, even the weather changing, mist where there was sunlight before—in the versions of early verse, rejected drafts, and evolving *Prelude* teaching. But become a composed vision and full-fledged meditation, Snowdon belies changing memory by imposing synchrony on history—thus fixing interpretive stability where all was flux before. By 1805, Snowdon represents the poet, stunned by roaring waters and hills heaving in the mist, stilling his confusion and settling his perspective (he above, the wonders below, all in his purview) as he composes the scene into instructive (by 1850, allegorical) vision. The scene, thus patterned and past, fosters concrete, convincing, and conclusive verse. Discovering therein "The perfect image of a mighty mind," and "above all, / One function of such mind" (1805, 13.69, 73–74), Wordsworth (as confidently as Augustine explicating scriptural figures and earthly correspondences) elaborates his certitude. Discerning "the express / Resemblance—in the fullness of its strength," the "genuine counterpart" of the "glorious faculty" for "Like transformation" and "like existence" that is the imagination (1805, 13.86–89, 94–95), he deduces no less than "religion, faith," "sovereignty within and peace at will," "Emotion," "chearfulness," "truth in moral judgements," "delight," "and genuine liberty" (1805, 13.111, 114, 115, 117, 118, 122).

So many noble equivalents and such a rational sequence, but what of Wordsworth's habitual and fruitful ambivalence? What of his disdaining "thought embodied" and "Distinct remembrances," his preferring "weight and power, / Power growing with the weight" (1805, 8.705–6)? And his "Remembering how . . . , but what . . . / Remembering not"

(1799, 2.365–66)? All, previously, were promising for his poetry. But in the light of theory Wordsworth dissipates the very mutability and ambiguity from which he writes poetry, brightly lighting the "dark deep thoroughfare . . . / The soul, the imagination of the whole" (1805, 13.64–65). Denying his own memory, he turns from metamorphosis to the "perfect image," from uncertainty to "express ressemblance." Denying his mnemonic theory of limitless revision and "renovating" (1805, 11.259) imagery promising future poetry, he attains clarity and finality. Yet Snowdon, admirable as mystical experience and as magnificent verse, is less exemplary as clear explanatory theory, which reduces "spots" to synchrony, which trades potentiality for polished poetry. If further splendid verse followed from "undiminished powers" (1805, 13.127), if his ending became a new beginning, Wordsworth's very finality would enshrine "renovating virtue." But as brilliantly as he analyzes his imagination, Wordsworth leaves unwritten his later great poetry. Fog lifts, and in the light of day even Snowdon gives up its mystery.

Closing his youth and his written life, Wordsworth comes to find the clarity necessary, perhaps for spiritual consolation, or autobiographical justification, or aesthetic reasons such as rounding out his conclusion. Possibly the death of Wordsworth's brother in February 1805 necessitates the design of his own life, from birth to here to hereafter. Possibly his evaluating and readying himself for *Recluse* writing tempts him to resonant authorial pronouncement. Or the demands of aesthetic closure impel him to pattern polishing and form finalizing. Impossible to say for Wordsworth personally, but in his last books of Spring 1805, Wordsworth textually moves from questions to answers, from poetic ambiguity to religious conformity. Choosing a higher than personal vision, a more universal than individual culmination—choosing early-written Snowdon to be late-read—Wordsworth achieves (as much by reordering early verse, as by writing new) his autobiographical conclusion.[27]

Wordsworth's closing his poetic progress with an ascent is no symbolic accident, for many are the recurrent metaphors—breeze falling and lifting, "spot" darkening and lightening, and river running—to which he could have given the structural course and climax of *The Prelude*.[28] Ignoring genre decorum, he could have achieved for his autobiography, perhaps not epic, but great ode status without schematic imagery, moralistic machinery, purposeful prophecy. Wordsworth did not need the Christian figural tradition (more or less learned in *Confessions* conversion or *Pilgrim's Progress*),[29] not to write autobiography, but perhaps he did need it to write epic poetry. His own "spots of time" have all the structure necessary for autobiographical honesty, but perhaps not for autobiographical morality. The sensual, the uncertain, and the changeable are unpromising subjects for prophecy. True, much mystery (pagan signs and portents, Christian types and symbols) accompanies prophecy, but even so a certain clarity, "thou shalt or shalt not," is finally necessary. As is ultimately, an answer to the question, "after this life, whither?" Already by 1805, Snowdon is a reverie become a meditation, a "spot of time" become an emblem, and many more such solutions will be charted as the 1805 becomes the 1850 *Prelude*. Come down from the mountain, Wordsworth earnestly predicts in poetry the course of flux and fixity, which is the course of his own and his century's search stilled in safety.

An apt type / This label seemed

Having drawn from the tradition of Christian progress to extend 1799 to 1805, Wordsworth draws further—from vocabulary to values—for the 1850 *Prelude*. Preparing for posthumous publication (principally in 1816/19, 1832, and 1838/39), he further tempers his youthful exuberance (his deviant reveries, pantheistic fancies, and unruly memories) by revising his 1805 *Prelude* into even stricter line with—deepening needs, deepening values—the spiritual tradition of purpose, the pilgrim persevering, the prophet come to our salvation at the price of his own inspiration. To merit his message from the mountain, Wordsworth retraces his erratic path from idiosyncrasy to theology, from flux to fixity, retrenching deeper into rigidity as his Romanticism leads (via a latter-day Augustinism—secular, but still inspired) to his Victorianism. By recharting his changeableness, Wordsworth transforms his early poem of memory into his public poem of identity. By revising his reveries into meditations then soothing consolations, by ferreting out from his early poetry basic principles then orthodox precepts, he valorizes his intimate poem to Coleridge as his moral poem to the world.[30] But in charting and Christianizing— increasingly and inevitably—Wordsworth betrays his own mnemonic theory.

How do "spots"—in their very essence locally fixed and emotionally fluid—become emblems, true and traditional and taught with a prophet's vigor? How does the originality, the very idiosyncrasy of the mnemonic continuum—mimetic and metaphoric varyingly, as need be— how does this marvelous and newly explored territory of memory and imagination get irrevocably pinned down to instruction, however noble? How does this poetic philosophy get appended to a latter-day pilgrim's progress? Sometimes with a momentous change of word: "faith" (1850, 14.448) replacing "truth" (1805, 13.444), "Providence" (1850, 14.298) newly in evidence, and "Holy Writ" (1850, 14.125) in paraphrase; or merely with the capitalization of early simplicity, "Love," "Imagination," "Reason," "Being, Eternity, and God" (1850, 14.188–206). Sometimes with a sweeping change from 1805 to 1850 of the lesson gleaned from musing or the moral setting for vision. With lesser and greater variations in later manuscripts, Wordsworth—completely in keeping with the practice—implicitly writes against the theory of his revisionary method. He preaches his method as a message: thus his early inspiration, "emotion recollected in tranquillity," becomes his mature reconsideration, sanctioned by conventional morality and careful theology. His idiosyncratic memory and singular imagination become consciously exemplary: thus the Romantic poet-pilgrim becomes the Victorian prophet; thus his reverie in the present becomes meditation for the future.

From the start, the 1805 beside the 1850 *Prelude* contrasts the early poet persona in reverie and the later persona deliberate in his musing.[31] Though but a supposed and staged impetus to the poem, the "Glad Preamble" reveals young Wordsworth characteristically—luxuriously (1805) or ambitiously (1850)—at liberty: early, he is figuratively free "To drink wild water, and to pluck green herbs, / And gather fruits fresh from their native boughs" (1805, 1.37–38); later, he briefly apostrophizes, "Dear Liberty!" to hurriedly add, "Yet what would it avail / But for a gift that consecrates the joy?" (1850, 1.31–32). The 1850 poem but begun, Wordsworth—"Free as a bird" to follow "a wandering cloud" (1850, 1.9, 17)—is already well-advanced in earnest progress. A few lines later, in character, the early and late personae pause. Thus in 1805:

> On the ground I lay
> Passing through many thoughts, yet mainly such
> As to myself pertained. I made a choice
> Of one sweet vale whither my steps should turn,
> And saw, methought, the very house and fields
> Present before my eyes; nor did I fail
> To add meanwhile assurance of some work
> Of glory there forthwith to be begun—
> Perhaps too there performed. Thus long I lay
> Cheared by the genial pillow of the earth
> Beneath my head, soothed by a sense of touch
> From the warm ground, that balanced me, else lost

Entirely, seeing nought, nought hearing, save
When here and there about the grove of oaks
Where was my bed, an acorn from the trees
Fell audibly, and with a startling sound.

(1805, 1.79—94)

Thus in 1850:

Many were the thoughts
Encouraged and dismissed, till choice was made
Of a known Vale, whither my feet should turn,
Nor rest till they had reached the very door
Of the one cottage which methought I saw.
No picture of mere memory ever looked
So fair; and while upon the fancied scene
I gazed with growing love, a higher power
Than Fancy gave assurance of some work
Of glory there forthwith to be begun,
Perhaps too there performed. Thus long I mused,
Nor e'er lost sight of what I mused upon,
Save when, amid the stately grove of oaks,
Now here, now there, an acorn, from its cup
Dislodged, through sere leaves rustled, or at once
To the bare earth dropped with a startling sound.

(1850, 1.70—85)

In 1805, Wordsworth "lay," "couched" (1.78), and "long [he] lay," indubitably, if inelegantly, flat on the ground. By 1850, "down [he] sate" (1850, 1.62), with dignity, to intently contemplate his promised poetry. Early, he enjoys the passivity of daydreaming, "Cheared," "soothed," and "balanced" by a vivid nature of earthy sensuality. Later, his poetic purpose prescribes useful activity, "thoughts / Encouraged and dismissed," and his ambition cuts intellectual divisions, his mind into "mere memory," low fancy, and higher power. The acorn falling with "startling sound" either falls into "nought," the poet genially "lost," or disturbs the most dutifully observant musing. Same acorn, very different interruption—even this nuance tells reverie from meditation.

In such simple details weighted with decided significance, emblems have their origin. Years decide their moral weight as Wordsworth stills his explorations and settles his autobiographical judgments, making of a detail a definition, of an image an emblem. For to impress well an image with moral and immovable meaning, Wordsworth must see it clear of change, as past without the potential for reinterpretation. His persona too, the youth of reverie given to endless reconsiderations, must also pass from questioning to certainty to become, on paper as in person, the pensive prophet. The "self-presence in [his] mind" of days gone by, such that when he thinks of them, he seems "Two consciousnesses—conscious of [himself], / And of some other being" (1805, 2.30–33); such double consciousness (which is multiple for "spots of time") serves Wordsworth's writing of autobiographical memory and metaphor, but not his forging of moral and communal emblems. "Two consciousnesses" may debate; many may in varying moments transform "spots of time"; one, the mature Wordsworth of 1850, he with the last word, dictates *Prelude* purpose. Such certainty, lost in reverie, learned in meditation, is not conducive to self-exploration, but is, of course, the better for moral instruction.

A flash of "fancy" (1805) / "Fancy" (1850) may serve as an example of Wordsworth's personal past become a lesson, of an image become an emblem. Returning from Cambridge sophistication to home simplicity, Wordsworth finds there "The froward brook," garden-tamed, flowing in "A channel paved by the hand of man" (1805, 4.40, 45):

> "Ha," quoth I, "pretty prisoner, are you there!"
> —And now, reviewing soberly that hour,
> I marvel that a fancy did not flash
> Upon me, and a strong desire, straitway,
> At sight of such an emblem that shewed forth
> So aptly my late course of even days
> And all their smooth enthralment, to pen down
> A satire on myself.
>
> (1805, 4.48–55)

In 1850, the same "pretty prisoner" greets the poet, but a more ponderous voice, adult and cited, chastises him:

> Well might sarcastic Fancy then have whispered,
> "An emblem here behold of thy own life;
> In its late course of even days with all
> Their smooth enthralment"
>
> (1850, 4.60–63)

For his view in 1805, Wordsworth, as so often, does not quite fix his vantage point. He certainly begins "now," but he ends back there, the potential youthful writer of satire. He reviews "soberly that hour" "now," and now is his flash of fancy, yet by "marvel[ing]" that he did not then see the lesson in the emblem, Wordsworth implicitly questions what he did then understand. He straddles the time between past and present; one moment he puts more weight to one side, one moment more to the other, as the "froward brook"—an image of time—runs from the hill to the garden, the mountain child to the Cambridge student. But the brook also runs far further—as an image of the mnemonic continuum—to the youth become the autobiographer. To change the image from continuity to surface uncertainty (in this book of the "slow-moving boat"), Wordsworth peers into past time to discern his youthful self and his reflected writing self as superimposed images, catching light more from the past, then from the present, uncertainly shimmering in his double consciousness of feeling from the past and judging in the present. But by 1850, the double consciousness of youth then and autobiographer now is dead. A fancy no longer fails to flash wisdom to the youth, the autobiographer no longer marvels, and neither, figuratively person to person, negotiates an understanding. "Well might sarcastic Fancy . . ."—as verse, pompous, literary, and totally present—represent a smug older man commenting surely on youthful folly. But the youth is abstracted and the autobiographer overshadowed. Fancy, capitalized, presumptuously obscures Wordsworth, naive and critical, young and old. Fancy, personified, is a sarcastic other whispering worldly-wise remarks of the genre *tempus fugit*. The fine marveling and feeling of 1805 falls flat for 1850; though, late, the image is more concise, the emblem more convincing, the verse more elegant, where, in 1850, is Wordsworth?

Reviewing early memories during *Prelude* revisions and reproaching youthful frivolity with the morality of maturity, Wordsworth is, more and more, given to corrective changes. As he identifies the negligible or notable merits of his youthful self, Wordsworth persistently transforms the wandering dreamer of 1805 into the worthy receiver of 1850 wisdom. No more wild water, or fresh fruit, or reverie for the 1850 pilgrim and future prophet of—irony clamoring—nature and imagination. Nowhere is the incongruity of Wordsworth's Victorian extremity—the late metaphoric mismatch of preaching pilgrim to poetic program—more evident than in Wordsworth's meeting with the discharged soldier. In 1805, Wordsworth offers the story almost casually, as a "[remembrance] not lifeless" retained "From many wanderings" (1805, 4.361–62). By 1850, he promises a lesson, sharp with contrast and social purpose, for "When from our better selves we have too long / Been parted by the hurrying world" (1850, 4.353–54).

Early—before overt instruction—Wordsworth is a "Solitary Walker," for to "walk alone / Along the public way" he avows is "A favorite pleasure" (1805, 4.364–66), which he describes in a long and effusive passage of praise (1805, 4.375–99; omitted by 1850). Sensuous, strangely incantatory phrases attest to his ease: "On I went / Tranquil, receiving in my own despite / Amusement" (1805, 4.375–77); feeling "Quiescent and disposed to sympathy, / With an exhausted mind worn out by toil / And all unworthy of the deeper joy" (1805, 4.380–82). The reward for such inner idleness? "A restoration like the calm of sleep, / But sweeter far" (1805, 4.387–88); "peace and solitude . . . O happy state" (1805, 4.389, 392); "beauteous pictures . . . / [Rising] in harmonious imagery" (1805, 4.392–93); "A consciousness of animal delight" (1805, 4.397); "A self-possession felt in every pause / And every gentle movement of [his] frame" (1805, 4.398–99). In this very bliss, this imaginative excess, Wordsworth "wandered" and "chanced" (1805, 4.400, 401) on the discharged soldier, a solitary and ghostly person, an eminently gratuitous vision. On the public way the "Walker" meets the English and the exotic, the soldier telling his tale. His poet's walk is a circle leading out to humanity and back home, an experiential foray with known shelter.

By 1850, Wordsworth is stripped of his reverie and his discovery. Far from his "better [self]" (1850, 4.353), caught up in the "hurrying world" (1850, 4.354) and exhausted by "strenuous idleness" (1850, 4.377), he climbs "a long ascent" that arduously brings him to revelation (1850, 4.378). His vision is of "Solitude . . . embodied," "an appropriate human center . . . of that great Power" (1850, 4.356, 366, 359, 365); which, in 1805, was an encounter with a soldier, human, weary, and hungry. Assiduously, Wordsworth presses his message: society is shallow and solitude is full of meaningful encounters with simple people, poverty, poetry. The 1850 *Prelude* parades the better story with its literary contrast of frivolity and dignity, social superficiality and poor simplicity; but lost is the oddity, the seeming fortuity of a poet in beauteous reverie coming on a person in poverty, helping a "comrade" (1805, 4.488) not a "traveller" (1850, 4.452), a "poor, unhappy man" (1805, 4.501) not a "patient" poor man (1850, 4.465), feelingly, yet without anchoring dogmatically into social consciousness. By 1850, Wordsworth pontificates: "This passed, and he who deigns to mark with care / By what rules governed, with what end in view, / This Work proceeds, he will not wish for more" (1850, 4.469–71). With "rules" and "end in view," Wordsworth approaches the extremity and the abstraction of allegory. He, not the soldier, tells his tale with a seeming "strange half-absence, as of one / Knowing too well the importance of his theme, / But feeling it no longer" (1850, 4.442–44). By 1850, Wordsworth's vision is an admonishment, and even the human has become emblem.

Black and white morality never sparks the same interest as the grey hues of ambiguity, else we would all read allegory, not lyric poetry. Yet myriad are the autobiographical occasions—religious, political, social, literary—that Wordsworth, late, shades allegorical; departing from past facts, even feelings, if they but serve the present lesson of his revising. Thus Wordsworth's belated call to "spare / These courts of mystery" (1850, 6.450–51), the Convent of Chartreuse, which he did not see subject to "Arms flashing, and a military glare / Of riotous men" (1850, 6.424–25) in reality, but which he recreates worthy of late, literary, and laureatelike defense in poetry. Thus his extravagant praise of Edmund Burke (1850, 7.512–43), he who popularized the view of the Revolution as abomination, ridiculing emotions that keep Robespierre's village gay in Wordsworth's memory though he is satanic in French history; he who denounced events that Wordsworth two books later recreates with his youthful fervor and five books later mourns in his "moral crisis," when— not stridently and personally anachronistic—he is accurately autobiographical. At the expense of narrative fact (Chartreuse), at the expense of narrative order ("Genius of Burke"), Wordsworth, late, sanctions established religion, established law—and justice, government, society, most anything English "Endeared by Custom" (1850, 7.528). Manifestly, by 1850, Wordsworth's lesson is in his detail, which is often highlighted "As the black storm upon the mountaintop / Sets off the sunbeam in the valley" (1850, 7.619–20). Thus Wordsworth strips from the blind beggar his sudden specter quality by setting him "off by foil" to "[appear] more touching" (1850, 7.601–2), by lending him "more than inherent liveliness and power" (1850, 7.625). Thus Wordsworth's London of 1805, which is "remembered idly" and "The work of fancy" (1805, 7.147, 148), a half-inhabited and half-imagined London—this reverie too is reduced to instructive reality. Wordsworth's London of 1850 is summoned by clanging imperatives: "Rise up, thou monstrous ant-hill on the plain / Of a too busy world!" (1850, 7.149–50). This horror come, sharp is the satire, instructive is the emblem, but where is the London of the young man? Framing a detail (the blind beggar), framing a description (London), Wordsworth sharpens his metaphor and his lesson, but framing thus, he stylizes mimesis and stifles memory. The falling acorn, froward brook, destitute soldier, the Revolution of hope, and now the great city—all are no longer animate as "spots of time": all have become lessons. In the 1850

Prelude, mnemonic flux is fully stilled in emblem and unruly imagination is channeled to metaphors serving the morality of vision.

To thee the work shall justify itself

Warning against the "dead letter" and wishing only for "the spirit of things" (1805, 8.432) (a decidedly biblical and Augustinian figure), does Wordsworth lose his own truth, its "motion and shape / Instinct with vital functions" (1805, 8.433–34), to a pious vision of eternal stillness? Does his "first creative sensibility" become "by the regular action of the world" subdued (1805, 2.379–80)? And his youthful imagination tempered, does he learn "to live / In reconcilement with . . . stinted powers, / To endure this state of meagre vassalage" (1805, 5.540–42)? The warning is Wordsworth's own, and the worry, and the harsh words. Answering indirectly his anxious queries, Wordsworth offers a simile of creativity and reality, his own allegory of the cave:

> As when a traveller hath from open day
> With torches passed into some vault of earth,
> The grotto of Antiparos, or the den
> Of Yordas among Craven's mountain tracts,
> He looks and sees the cavern spread and grow,
> Widening itself on all sides, sees, or thinks
> He sees, erelong, the roof above his head,
> Which instantly unsettles and recedes—
> Substance and shadow, light and darkness, all
> Commingled, making up a canopy
> Of shapes, and forms, and tendencies to shape,
> That shift and vanish, change and interchange
> Like spectres—ferment quiet and sublime,
> Which, after a short space, works less and less
> Till, every effort, every motion gone,
> The scene before him lies in perfect view
> Exposed, and lifeless as a written book.
> But let him pause awhile and look again,
> And a new quickening shall succeed, at first
> Beginning timidly, then creeping fast
> Through all which he beholds: the senseless mass,
> In its projections, wrinkles, cavities,
> Through all its surface, with all colours streaming,

Like a magician's airy pageant, parts,
Unites, embodying everywhere some pressure
Or image, recognised or new, some type
Or picture of the world—forests and lakes,
Ships, rivers, towers, the warrior clad in mail,
The prancing steed, the pilgrim with his staff,
The mitred bishop and the thronèd king—
A spectacle to which there is no end.

(1805, 8.711–41)

Visually, in these scenes of creativity, Wordsworth shadows forth a few moments of wonder and power; metaphorically, he figures forth changes that span years. Such is the flexibility of the Wordsworthian rhythm of flux and fixity: in the moment, the pulse of "genius . . . exists by interchange / Of peace and excitation" (1805, 12.8–9); over time, the periodicity or the perpetuity of the "first / Poetic spirit" is

By uniform controul of after years
In most abated and suppressed, in some
Through every change of growth or of decay
Preeminent till death.

(1805, 2.275–80)

For Wordsworth—the poet of extremity and duty—which fate awaits? For his person, none can say. On paper, he and his modern reader assess differently his "spots of time" become emblems, his progress come to the mountain, his vision subject to revisions.

In the cavern of his imagination, when the "ferment quiet and sublime," working "less and less," finally settles, does the new spectacle of second sight afford Wordsworth "Abundant recompense"? To images and echoes Wordsworth entrusts his response. In first vision, Wordsworth wanders amidst vague mysterious imagery as in his youthful fervent autobiography: "Substance and shadow, light and darkness," which evoke "shadowy exaltation" (1799, 2.362), which echo "ghostly" audition (1799, 2.358), which foreshadow darkening and new seeing "when the light of sense / Goes out" (1805, 6.534–35). Looking with second sight, he is enthralled by the ship, steed, warrior, bishop, king, the magician's airy pageantry—hardly habitual Wordsworthian imagery. And all are defined as "image," "type," or "picture" "into absolute independent singleness" ("Essay," 748)—hardly habitual Wordsworthian practice. To first vision, Wordsworth gives imagination's power; to second sight, fancy's worldliness. Thus in moments of creativity; thus also in a life of poetry. Early, Wordsworth wistfully wishes that he might give "to duty and to truth / The eagerness of infantine desire" (1799, 2.23–24); then, subdued, he acknowledges his "deep enthusiastic joy" "chastened, stemmed, / And balanced, by a reason which indeed / Is reason, duty, and pathetic truth" (1805, 13.261, 263–65); finally, pious, he stills the swing of vital opposites, "of sense and soul, / Of life and death, time and eternity" (1850, 14.286–87), by "leaning on the stay / Of Providence" (1850, 14.297–98). Identifying his "unruly times" and his "meditative mind" (1805, 1.146, 150), his "glad animal movements" of boyhood and his "still, sad music" of maturity ("Tintern Abbey" 74, 91), Wordsworth in the "dark deep throughfare" (1805, 13.64) of his imagination—the dim of his metaphoric cavern—loses the mystery of his first vision to the perfection of his second sight.[32]

Wordsworth's cavern is resplendent with values far from transcendental, but his hierarchy is as strict as any: imagination is high, fancy lower, and their absence the "dead letter." His hierarchy heeded, his age weighed, is, then, Wordsworth's loss of vision sufficiently bedecked by the aftershow; are the lines of disappointment convincingly redrawn in new interest? Rarely. But richly when the same scene offers new emotion, the same autobiographical juncture offers a new poetical venture; then every passage is, potentially, a literary "spot of time." Richly, when the sublime example of revision offering a new vision is this very simile of the cave reshifted (from 1805, 6.525, to 8.711–41), then replaced and reinvented as the famous passage of the Simplon Pass (1805, 6.525–72). Begun as the archetypical epic descent, the Simplon verse is repeatedly broken and begun again as the present impinges on the past, the poet's inspiration repeatedly interrupting his autobiographical explanation.[33] Revising the passage, Wordsworth revisits the pass—imaginatively descending into "Substance and shadow, light and darkness," creatively deciphering the "shapes, and forms, and tendencies to shape, / That shift and vanish, change and interchange"—discovering in the Simplon passage, over the years, the "ferment quiet and sublime": the archetypical literary "spot of time." Beside such changing vitality and complexity, the pilgrim, the bishop, even the magician seem the work of second sight—if not the fruit of fancy, at least the afterthought of fading imaginative individuality. The versatility of "spots of time," no moment wholly lost to creativity if it but come again, mnemonically, mimetically, metaphorically, however imaginatively—beside such originality, the apprentice, pilgrim, and prophet seem autobiographical stages hackneyed in their progress. Beside the discovery of Simplon, even Snowdon—the "spot" become emblem, the personal past fixed as lesson, the aftershow splendid in aery pageantry—seems, indeed, "some type / Or picture of the world," awesome but immobile in the universe of ideas.

The Prelude stilled—lying "in perfect view / Exposed, and lifeless as a written book"—does Wordsworth's reader look again, let it quicken, to recreate from the printed verse the first vision of "Substance and shadow, light and darkness," the second sight of "some type / Or picture of the world"? Only when he undertakes Wordsworth's method, which, relentlessly, Wordsworth preaches as process. As for the autobiographer, so for the reader: new quickening is in reimagining and rethinking, is in reading any one *Prelude* but, further, in stitching and unstitching the changes between versions. "Dead letter[s]" on the page reveal their "motion and shape / Instinct with vital functions," their vigor and their spirit in Wordsworth's visions and revisions, which are well documented in critical editions. In the changes, often so slight and so significant, that Wordsworth effects—which alter, be it by a nuance, for a moment, his message—there Wordsworth's reader best quickens his mind to find "the motions of winds / Embodied in the mystery of words" (1805, 5.620–21), the glory in "the turnings intricate of verse" (1805, 5.627), the flash of Wordsworth's profundity generously lighting his seeking.

Revision, written and read, then, is "Abundant recompense" for first vision? Amply, if autobiographer and reader continue the activity of going back in imaginative memory to quicken the literary "spot of time." Hardly, if one or the other passively accepts the lesson, the emblem, the pilgrim enlightened, the prophet down from the mountain, the last word as last. Indubitably, poetry is "A spectacle to which there is no end," but, indefatigably, Wordsworth insists that its force derives from creative origins, metamorphosing memories, and autobiographical revisions. Writing autobiography as palimpsest, Wordsworth best betrays his imaginative movement by his very compositional method, which modern scholarship—studying through the manuscript layers—finds so much more interesting than his manifest message. He spends his life monumentalizing versions of *Prelude* prophecy only to have his admirers discover and display—word by word—his brilliant beginnings, varying turnings, and ongoing revisions, lamentable and less so. The irony is not without rewards. For "the discerning intellect" ("Prospectus," 52) is an ever-active intellect, true to the Wordsworthian principles of memory and new creativity. First vision fled, second sight fixed, so be it—if writer and reader, remembering, know the feelings within; rereading, know the schism between; and rewriting, know to question again. The essential is not literary value, but keeping all "vital" (1805, 8.434), in the countless manuscripts, in the achronological publication of *The Preludes,* 1850, 1805, 1799—all so many literary "spots of time" to revisit for poetical and personal renovation.

AFTERWORD

Whether truth is tracked and taken or ahead still teasing, each age, autobiographer, reader decides. Whether recollection is better in general constructs or accurate fragments, each decides. In autobiography, order —Christian, Augustinian, even Bunyanesque—tends to be early, later in history, we admit our disarray. Pilgrims belong to Christians, paradise to those believing in innocence, conversions to those sure of no further reversion or revision. Harmony and unity are decidedly uncontemporary, so why persist in ascribing them to autobiography? Ours is the century for study of the unconscious in dreams, of reveries in fragments, the written and rewritten in notebooks, journals, letters, drafts, manuscripts, editions—the unruly psyche in all the unruliness of words. Ours is the century rapidly closing of the past potent in memory, the *bricoleur* in societies, the *mise en abyme* in texts. These are historically determined forms, recent fashionable figures, not absolutes or right judgments, but they identify—they define—our era of revision, of radical temporality in self-fascination.

Whence I hazard a guess at why the critical interest in autobiography now: precisely because it is a ragged, unreasonable genre. Obsessed with memory ever since the last century, we compulsively go back in time, seeking, not the straight and narrow way, not secular progress, but sensations stronger than conversions, yearnings after the former child, fissures in the forward narrative. Yet, strangely, we keep reading order into autobiography, tidying unruly metaphors into figures and forms in autobiographical tradition. We keep writing heritage into literary history, construing lines of generic descent and influence. Knowing ours to be a vantage point as historical and variable as any other, we nonetheless fix ours as progressive. Yet just as metaphors for mimesis are at odds with metaphors for memory, so too are the critical rulers imposed on the mnemonic detours, the historical order on the generic diversity.

Perhaps old methodologies serve where new seem impracticable, humanist philosophies stand where revisionary theories seem untenable— evaluative criticism necessarily opposing rampant eclecticism. Perhaps, more simply, old critical habits obscure and suppress new critical interests. And, stubbornly, subconsciously—according to our philosophies and psychologies—we reject what escapes our explanatory rigor only to see it return with mysterious vigor. We repeat what we cannot understand. Our canonical repetitions are without reason, our generic resolutions without power. Stronger than the systems—even those explaining our need for systems—are the nostalgia and nightmares leading back to childhood and early imaginative power. Beauty and terror: these are the source of the Romantic cult of memory and freedom, which is the veritable seed since Rousseau, since Wordsworth, for the flowering of autobiography—and the contemporary critical cult of its study.

Ignoble or not, nostalgia and nightmares are central: the origin of autobiography is loss—the loss of passion or of power. During writing, the passivity of loss becomes the power of longing to animate past time again, to replace the absent or fearful past with a new—merely verbal, methodically transitional, manifestly ephemeral—presence. Writing again means living the loss again, differently, filling the absence or fearful presence with another verbal, transitional, ephemeral presence. Whatever the writing—philosophical, autobiographical, critical—simply lingual, it is active, it is communicative. Writing, we change powerlessness to power, our unsettling individuality to comforting communality. In others, we write, we read, ourselves, and we are soothed into sense. In writing, in reading, less than in chosen texts, is our steadying.

Form consoles, and yet constrains. Formlessness in life is fearful, in art is incommunicable, and everywhere offers the freedom to change. We may accept ready understanding or we may dare rash questioning, but choose we must. Comprehension or courage: mercifully, autobiographers suggest, we may choose once and again. For in seeking, not in any one system, is the solidarity of all. Caught between time past and time passing, every seeker creates an identity rebounding between fixity and flux, surety and the intellectual slip, understanding and the extremity of writing. Every autobiographer writes between mimesis and memory, between seemly, wise tradition and ragged, unreasonable transgression, essaying the starkest choice of all.

NOTES

BIBLIOGRAPHY

INDEX

NOTES

Introduction

1. Paul Ricoeur, analyzing Aristotle, offers a definition of *mimesis* as "creative imitation," to which I oppose my notion of memory as inner and erratic revision: "There is *mimesis* only where there is 'doing' or 'activity'; and poetic 'activity' consists precisely in the construction of plots. Moreover, what *mimesis* imitates is not the effectivity of events but their logical structure, their meaning. . . . *Mimesis,* in this sense, is a kind of metaphor of reality" ("The Narrative Function," in his *Hermeneutics and the Human Sciences,* p. 292).

2. As Paul Ricoeur understands metaphor "to redescribe a reality inaccessible to direct description" and "the mimetic function of plots" to "re-configure our confused, unformed, and at the limit mute temporal experience," so I understand living to become metamorphosed—read "metaphorized"—in language (*Time and Narrative,* 1:xi; for Ricoeur's original French, see *Temps et récit,* 1:13).

3. History explicitly determines autobiographical theory from the earliest criticism, Georg Misch's *A History of Autobiography in Antiquity,* to more recent genre studies, such as Karl Joachim Weintraub's *The Value of the Individual,* William C. Spengemann's *The Forms of Autobiography,* Avrom Fleishman's *Figures of Autobiography,* and Jerome Hamilton Buckley's *The Turning Key:* all are ordered chronologically, early influencing later autobiographies, the genre evolving over the years. Exceptions include James Olney's *Metaphors of Self,* in which Olney favors ahistorical patterns in the "philosophy and psychology of autobiography" (p. viii), and Susanna Egan's *Patterns of Experience in Autobiography,* in which Egan derives narrative patterns from "psychological imperatives that determine man's perception of himself and of his world" (p. 5).

4. T. S. Eliot's sense of tradition, "a perception, not only of the pastness of the past, but of its presence," "a sense of the timeless as well as the temporal," is pertinent ("Tradition and the Individual Talent," in his *Selected Essays,* p. 4). And Robert Scholes and Robert Kellog, revising Eliot's theory, provide an instructive counterpoint: "the raw material of human existence remains ever the same, the molds by which it is given significance and recognizable shape are forever being re-created" (*The Nature of Narrative,* p. 156). Revering impersonality in great poetry, Eliot perhaps would allow idiosyncrasy in autobiography; arguing for "originality of vision" and "new types of actuality," Scholes and Kellog certainly stress the individual (*Nature of Narrative,* p. 156).

5. Bunyan's celebrated allegory, *The Pilgrim's Progress,* "reproduces the plot" of his spiritual autobiography, *Grace Abounding to the Chief of Sinners;* thus W. R. Owens argues in the introduction to his edition of the latter (p. xxiii). Abstracting further, Linda H. Peterson alludes to *The Pilgrim's Progress* as "what might be called a prospectus for anyman's autobiography" in *Victorian Autobiography,* her study of biblical typology in English autobiography (p. 103).

6. On Newman's theological-become-autobiographical models, see Linda H. Peterson's "Newman's *Apologia pro vita sua* and the Traditions of the English Spiritual Autobiography."

7. Having annotated thousands of *British Autobiographies* for his bibliography of that title, William Matthews offers a well-won say on conformity: "The autobiography offers itself as an individual receptacle for every individual man, and, offhand, one might expect

that every autobiography would be as different from every other one as every man is different from every other man. As a matter of fact, however, few autobiographers put into their books very much of that private, intimate knowledge of themselves only they can have. Oftener than not, they shun their own inner peculiarities and fit themselves into patterns of behavior and character suggested by the ideas and ideals of their period and by the fashions in autobiography with which they associate themselves" (p. viii).

8. Both Paul Ricoeur and Erich Auerbach, while stressing contrast, emphasize the explanatory in Christian and classical conceptions of history. Ricoeur asserts, "Christianity made a violent entry into the Hellenic world by introducing a concept of time containing events, crises, and decisions. . . . In light of these exceptional [Christian] events, man was made aware of those aspects of his own experience which he did not know how to interpret" ("Christianity and the Meaning of History," in his *History and Truth,* p. 84). Auerbach argues, "Wherever the two conceptions met, there was of necessity a conflict and an attempt to compromise—between, on the one hand, a [classical] presentation which carefully interrelated the elements of history, which respected temporal and causal sequence, remained within the domain of the earthly foreground and, on the other hand, a [Christian] fragmentary, discrete presentation, constantly seeking an interpretation from above" (*Mimesis,* p. 74).

9. An unchanging autobiographical overview qualifies these autobiographers as traditional, even though various drafts and editorial versions make up their fragmented texts. On, for example, just how dispassionately "Mr. Darwin Collects Himself," see John D. Rosenberg's essay of that title. On the complicated editorial history of each autobiography, see the informative introductions to Betty Radice's edition of Edward Gibbon's *Memoirs of My Life,* Jack Stillinger's edition of John Stuart Mill's *Autobiography,* and Francis Darwin's edition of *The Autobiography of Charles Darwin.*

10. Few critics today restrict the genre of autobiography as strictly as Philippe Lejeune once did: "DEFINITION: Retrospective prose narrative written by a real person concerning his own existence, where the focus is his individual life, in particular the story of his personality" ("The Autobiographical Pact," in his *On Autobiography,* p. 4). (On the "divided Lejeune, who asserts on the one hand an ideal of autobiography as 'a story without a narrative,' and on the other a definition of the genre as a 'retrospective narrative,' 'the story of a personality'" [p. xii], see Paul John Eakin's Foreword to Lejeune's *Autobiography,* pp. xii–xv.) Yet even as critics open the genre to varying forms (poetry, fiction, drama) and varying groups (established white males and arriving minorities) and varying (indeed, all) national literatures—as Eugene Stelzig summarizes and analyzes well in his "Is There a Canon of Autobiography?"—even so the desire for autobiographical structures, patterns, figures, myths, archetypes rules autobiography studies.

11. For example, Jean Starobinski is unequivocal: "One would hardly have sufficient motive to write an autobiography had not some radical change occurred in his life— conversion, entry into a new life, the operation of Grace" ("The Style of Autobiography," p. 78). And Roy Pascal asserts that the "realization of a meaningful standpoint, the emergence from shadows into daylight, is a condition of autobiography altogether. It is the reason why the autobiographies of younger men are rarely satisfactory" (*Design and Truth in Autobiography,* p. 10).

12. Even James Olney, given to generous metaphors of self, insists on the form of life: "If *bios* in the sense of 'lifetime'" is "a process, then it possesses a certain shape, and we might say that memory is the forever hidden thread describing this shape. The thread necessarily remains hidden, unconscious, unknown to the individual until the time when it rises to consciousness *after the fact* to present itself to him as recollections that he can trace back—a kind of Ariadne's thread—to discover the shape that was all the time gradually and unconsciously forming itself" ("Some Versions of Memory / Some Versions of *Bios*: The Ontology of Autobiography," pp. 240–41).

13. On "new model" autobiographers who resist chronological narrative and figural tradition, see Paul John Eakin's incisive survey in his "Narrative and Chronology as Structures of Reference and the New Model Autobiographer." "Making a case for narrative and chronology as structures of reference in autobiography," Eakin, nonetheless, "would like to align [himself] in this respect with Barthes' commitment to *le pluriel*" (p. 38). Yet, for all his critical largess, Eakin's emphasis is on "structures of reference," "forms that a life, a *bios,* may take," and the "irreversibility of individual experience" (pp. 38–39). My emphasis is on changes: true, individual experience is irreversible, but writing of it autobiographically is not.

14. On Apocalypse as "type and source" (p. 6) for literary and life fictions, see Frank Kermode's *The Sense of an Ending.*

15. "When this reverie of remembering becomes the germ of a poetic work, the complex of memory and imagination becomes more tightly meshed; it has multiple and reciprocal actions which deceive the sincerity of the poet" (p. 20)—or, I argue, the autobiographer; see Gaston Bachelard's *The Poetics of Reverie,* especially pp. 104–12.

16. Indeed, "the original sin of autobiography is first one of logical coherence and rationalization," writes Georges Gusdorf in "Conditions and Limits of Autobiography" (p. 41).

17. "L'autoportrait se distingue de l'autobiographie par l'absence d'un récit suivi" ("Self-portrait differs from autobiography by its lack of sustained narrative"): thus argues Michel Beaujour in his *Miroirs d'encre: Rhétorique de l'autoportrait* (p. 9). The argument is clear for Montaigne's *Essays* and Rousseau's *Reveries;* and Susan K. Jackson, citing and developing Beaujour's distinction, takes it further to speak of *Rousseau's Occasional Autobiographies* (p. 21).

18. On the duality of persona and person in autobiography, see Louis A. Renza's "The Veto of the Imagination: A Theory of Autobiography."

19. "Thou hast the keys of Paradise, oh, just, subtle, and mighty opium," De Quincey writes of the "Pleasures of Opium" (p. 83). And "when looking back from afar," he closes the "Pains of Opium," he echoes Milton's close to *Paradise Lost* (p. 116). See Alethea Hayter's edition of the *Confessions of an English Opium Eater* for the 1821 text cited here and for two useful appendices: one containing De Quincey's comments on his first version of the *Confessions,* the other offering passages from his 1856 revision.

20. For an insightful analysis of the relation between Stendhal's personal history and his two autobiographies, *Souvenirs d'égotisme* and *Vie de Henry Brulard,* see Béatrice Didier's introduction to the former.

21. For the side of the doubters, Paul de Man writes: "To the extent that language is figure (or metaphor, or prosopopeia) it is indeed not the thing itself but the representation, the picture of the thing and, as such, it is silent, mute as pictures are mute. Language, as trope, is always privative" ("Autobiography as De-facement," p. 930).

22. Parallel and persuasive theories may be found in Roy Schafer's "Narration in the Psychoanalytic Dialogue," which focuses on "free association as neither free nor associative" (p. 39) and on "narrative structures that . . . control the telling of events" (p. 49), and in Hayden White's "The Value of Narrativity in the Representation of Reality," which stresses the inescapable morality of narrativity.

23. The tautness between sequence and sense in narrative may be sounded in different keys: as "surfacing and . . . depth" by Roland Barthes ("Introduction to the Structural Analysis of Narratives," in his *Image, Music, Text,* p. 122); as "sequence" and "[secrets]" by Frank Kermode ("Secrets and Narrative Sequence," p. 83); as "story" and "study" by Nelson Goodman ("Twisted Tales; or, Story, Study, and Symphony," p. 115). In autobiography, the exuberance of sense in memory is certainly given to depths, secrets, and subtle twists, but, more extremely, to metamorphosing meaning.

24. Thus I disagree with those who argue for the "essential narrativity of human

Notes

experience." The handy phrase is Eakin's (in the Foreword to his edition of Lejeune's *On Autobiography,* p. xii), whose ready examples include (p. 245, n. 20): Paul Ricoeur, "Narrative Time," pp. 169–90; Fleishman, *Figures of Autobiography,* pp. 475–78; and Janet Varner Gunn, "Autobiography and The Narrative Experience of Temporality as Depth," pp. 194–209. Arguing (as I too believe) that "our knowledge of past events is usually not narrative in structure or given in storylike sequences" but is "organized, integrated, and apprehended as a specific 'set' of events only in and through the very act by which we narrate them as such," Barbara Herrnstein Smith rallies an opposing camp ("Narrative Versions, Narrative Theories," p. 225): Roy Schafer at the symposium "Narrative: The Illusion of Sequence" (Univ. of Chicago, 26–28 October 1979); Hayden White in "The Historical Text as Literary Artifact"; Jonathan Culler in "Fabula and Sjuzhet in the Analysis of Narrative"; and Nelson Goodman in *Ways of Worldmaking,* p. x.

25. Barrett J. Mandel's idea of the autobiographical present choosing and "ratifying the past" in the "ongoing activity of writing" (pp. 64–65), if extended—as time, as theory—ends in what I call "revisionary memory"; see his "Full of Life Now."

26. On several of these issues, *Approaches to Victorian Autobiography,* edited by George P. Landow, offers essays; see especially Elizabeth K. Helsinger's analysis of changing attitudes toward the self in "Ulysses to Penelope: Victorian Experiments in Autobiography." On reality and relativity in modern autobiography, Paul John Eakin is illuminating, particularly when advocating a wise compromise in post-Romantic language: "Instead of debating the old either / or proposition—whether the self is a transcendental category preceding language in the order of being, or else a construct of language brought into being by it—it is preferable to conceptualize the relation between the self and language as a mutually constituting interdependency" (*Fictions in Autobiography,* p. 8).

Chapter 1

1. "The view that Augustine is the inventor of autobiography is so squarely placed among our cultural presuppositions that it would take a Nietzsche to dispel it entirely": such is the witty assessment of Fleishman in *Figures of Autobiography,* p. 53. For the numerous precursors of Augustine's *Confessions,* see Pierre Courcelle's *Les Confessions de Saint Augustin dans la tradition littéraire.*

2. All references to Augustine's *Confessions* will be to book and chapter, rather than to the page number of a specific edition that, there being so many editions of the *Confessions,* many may not possess. The English translation quoted throughout will be that of R. S. Pine-Coffin.

3. Often Augustine specifies that he speaks to his "brothers" (9.13, 10.4), "those who have the gifts of [the] Holy Spirit" (5.10), "readers with love of [God]" (11.1). Sometimes he envisions a more numerous, anonymous public: "[his] own kind" (2.3), "any man" (9.12), "the many who will read [his *Confessions*]" (10.1). Once he desires—appropriately, just following his conversion—to be heard by the Manichees, those who set their "hearts on shadows," "those deaf corpses of whom [he himself] had been one" (9.4).

4. For an overview of Augustine's changing—pagan to Christian—language theory, see Marcia L. Colish's chapter on "Augustine: The Expression of the Word," in *The Mirror of Language.*

5. Certain critics have found the key to the relationship between the narrative and the theoretical books in the *Confessions* in Augustine's *De catechizandis rudibus,* written some five years after the *Confessions.* There Augustine explains that a catechumen should first be taught to see God's guidance in his past life (the parallel to Augustine's narrative books), then be instructed in the Scriptures, starting with Genesis (the subject of Augustine's theoretical books). The theory is Max Wundt's (see his "Augustins Konfessionen," p. 185 and following), and is cited with approval by Pierre Courcelle (in *Recherches sur les*

Notes

Confessions de Saint Augustin, pp. 21–22), with an important qualification: "Mais Augustin, dans les *Confessions,* joue moins le role du catéchumène que celui du catéchiste: montrer, d'après l'exposé d'une vie, que Dieu prend toujours soin des hommes" ("But Augustine, in the *Confessions,* plays less the role of catechumen than that of catechist: showing, by means of a life story, that God always takes care of men") (p. 22, n. 2). The theory is convincing, but all the more so when Augustine, as catechist, is understood to teach in his theoretical books not only the Scriptures but self-interpretation in terms of the Scriptures, the method that allows every man his own discovery of God's guidance in his life and, after, his own study of the Scriptures.

6. Indeed, Augustine's contemporaries already showed a preference for his narrative over his theory. As Courcelle (in *Recherches sur les Confessions de Saint Augustin,* pp. 25–26), citing Eduard Williger ("Der Aufbau der Konfessionen Augustins," pp. 103–6), demonstrates, book 10 is a late addition to the *Confessions,* written at the request of Augustine's first readers, who were more curious to know of Augustine's life after his conversion than of his scriptural theories, already written, in books 11–12. But these first readers may well have been disappointed by book 10, for there Augustine studies the sins of each of his senses without the hint of an anecdote to appease the "inquisitive race."

7. See Augustine's *On Christian Doctrine,* and the helpful introduction by D. W. Robertson, Jr., to his translation of this work, especially pp. x–xii.

8. On Augustine in the tradition of "Patristic Exegesis," see Tzvetan Todorov's chapter thus titled in his *Symbolism and Interpretation.*

9. Compare Hans-Georg Gadamer, drawing on Augustine and the Scriptures, for his hermeneutical theory: "When [a text] does begin to speak . . . it does not simply speak its word, always the same, in lifeless rigidity, but gives ever new answers to the person who questions it and poses ever new questions to him who answers it. To understand a text is to come to understand oneself in a kind of dialogue" ("On the Problem of Self-Understanding," in his *Philosophical Hermeneutics,* p. 57).

10. Augustine will, in 10.14, claim that "the mind and the memory are one and the same. We even call the memory the mind, for when we tell another person to remember something, we say 'See that you bear this in mind,' and when we forget something, we say 'It was not in my mind' or 'It slipped out of my mind.'" But the argument is purely linguistic, and it directly precedes Augustine's once again dividing the functions of memory and mind in his simile of memory as "a sort of stomach for the mind."

11. Augustine insists, repeatedly, that God guards him from the "snare" of his past (1.16, 2.7, 4.6) and that his bitter memories are now a "sacrifice of joy" (2.1, 4.1). But Augustine's memory alone, according to his theory, protects him, for its power to emotionally divorce him from his former sins is complete.

12. For a detailed study of "phantasiae," "ostensiones," and the moral questions posed by each sort of dream, see chapters 5, 6, and 7 of Martine Dulaey's *Le Rêve dans la vie et la pensée de Saint Augustin,* to which I am indebted. In particular, see p. 93, where Dulaey, drawing on Augustine's *De Genesi ad litteram,* 12.20, identifies the distinguishing traits of "phantasiae" and "ostensiones."

13. See Georges Poulet's brilliant analysis of eighteenth-, nineteenth-, and twentieth-century thinking on time in his *Etudes sur le temps humain,* 1:24–47, especially pp. 31–32 and 44–45 on memory's power and limits in contributing to an individual's sense of self.

14. Even Augustine's doctrine of predestination does not deny a man's choice in determining his life. On this point, Jean Guitton and Peter Brown are unequivocal: "Les élus . . . sont doués de liberté. Dieu ne peut pas les sauver s'ils ne se sauvent eux-mêmes" ("The chosen . . . are endowed with liberty. God cannot save them if they do not save themselves") (Guitton, *Le Temps et l'éternité chez Plotin et Saint Augustin,* p. 278); "A doctrine of predestination divorced from action was inconceivable to [Augustine]. He had never written to deny freedom" (Brown, *Augustine of Hippo,* p. 406). Guitton's analysis of

Notes

the relation of free will to predestination focuses on the *Confessions* (pp. 277–82); Brown's, on Augustine's later works (pp. 398–407): both are illuminating.

15. In Augustine's rich paragraph of analogies, Ricoeur finds ample matter for his *Time and Narrative* in three volumes: "The entire province of narrative is laid out here in its potentiality, from the simple poem, to the story of an entire life, to universal history. It is with these extrapolations, which are simply suggested here, that the present work is concerned" (*Time and Narrative*, 1:22; for Ricoeur's original French, see *Temps et récit*, 1:41).

16. See Ricoeur's close reading of 11.29 in the Latin, which arrives at a similar conclusion: "While the *distentio* becomes synonymous with the dispersal into the many and with the wandering of the old Adam, the *intentio* tends to be identified with the fusion of the inner man. . . . So the *intentio* is no longer the anticipation of the entire poem before its recitation which makes it move from the future toward the past, but the hope of last things" (*Time and Narrative*, 1:27; *Temps et récit*, 1:50). For the many levels on which Ricoeur reads Augustine's "*distentio-intentio*" contrast, follow his argument in *Time and Narrative*, 1:16–30 or in *Temps et récit*, 1:34–53.

17. Augustine explicitly interprets "the intellectual heaven" in terms of 1 Corinthians 13:12 in 12.13.

18. On the "simultaneous proclamation and concealment" (p. 47) in the parables and the differing Gospels, see Frank Kermode's *The Genesis of Secrecy*, especially p. 25, where Kermode situates a "parable" between the "extreme points [of] the maxim and the short story," "a word . . . [covering] so many things, from proverbial wisdom to dark sayings."

19. For the verbal echoes in Augustine's Latin of 2 Corinthians 12:3 and a typological reading of Augustine's conversion (from theft in the garden to grace in the garden, "from Eden to Eden, from pear tree to fig tree, from Adam and the fall from grace to Christ, the second Adam, who comes to redeem the sins of man on the cross"), see Warren Ginsberg's *The Cast of Character*, pp. 87–88.

20. In *Le Temps et l'éternité*, Guitton identifies some of the lives Augustine describes as parallel to his (p. 273), but without a sense of the religious principle Augustine would have them demonstrate, or of how it determines the design of the *Confessions*. Later critics study the literary nature of Augustine's conversion; for instance, John Freccaro in "The Fig Tree and the Laurel," who is cited by Geoffrey Galt Harpham in "Conversion and the Language of Autobiography"; and Harpham himself takes a "stacking of [conversion] models" (p. 43) far—beyond Christianity to speak of all autobiography.

21. The passage that Augustine reads—"Not in revelling and drunkeness, not in lust and wantonness, not in quarrels and rivalries. Rather, arm yourselves with the Lord Jesus Christ; spend no more thought on nature and nature's appetites" (Romans 13:13–14)—is another mirror of words that reveals Augustine to himself in the very act of renunciation and resolution. Perhaps the start of the passage—"Let us pass our time honourably, as by the light of day"—is not retained by Augustine precisely in order to mirror the sequence, not the consequence, of his passage from willful sin to serving God.

22. Analyzing 1 Corinthians, particularly "Paul's separation between 'man's wisdom,' which demands concrete proof, and wisdom of the 'spirit,' which 'believeth all things spoken in its name'" (p. 108), Brooke Hopkins traces and transforms the Paulian distinction—I believe, inadvisably far—from Augustinian to Rousseauian to Wordsworthian autobiography in his "Reading, and Believing In, Autobiography."

23. Augustine's image of God as helmsman of his life illustrates well the bifurcation in his narrative between God's providence and Augustine's former ignorance: "You were guiding me as a helmsman steers a ship, but the course you steered was beyond my understanding" (4.14). With faith, Augustine understands that the Scriptures are the God-given chart of his course in life and reveal God's will to him, but he does not pretend to understand all the mysteries of His will. With this caveat in mind, see Spengemann on how

Notes

Augustine adopts a "God-like" point of view in his narrative to explain, definitively, his past life (*The Forms of Autobiography*, pp. 6–16).

Chapter 2

1. Quotations from Montaigne's *Essays* will be in English from Donald M. Frame's admirable translation (which has often helped me with idioms and oddities in Montaigne's sixteenth-century French) and will henceforth be identified in the text by page number in parentheses. Montaigne's original French will rarely be given. But following each quotation from Frame's translation, a reference by page number in square brackets will be given to the Pléiade edition of the *Essais* for those wishing to consult the French. As in both the English and the French editions, quotations will identify the (*a*) 1580, (*b*) 1588, and (*c*) 1595 strata in Montaigne's palimpsest of a text. Here the opening (*a*) quotation is from (243) [320].

2. Many critics who derive order from Montaigne's contradictions work in a dialectical framework. Tzvetan Todorov, one of the most interesting, contends that "since man is infinitely changeable, it is natural that he contradicts himself" is "merely . . . one of the theses in question" (p. 142); the other, of course, being man's stability hence consistency. Believing that Montaigne's "position emerges from the copresence of both theses, neither one of which really represents his 'truth'" (p. 143), that Montaigne's "position depends on their interaction" (p. 143), Todorov argues that to conclude for diversity in Montaigne, in man, "would be to play Montaigne's own game which he wants to impose on us" (p. 142). The complexities of Todorov's argument cannot be justly summarized; see his essay, "L'Etre et L'Autre: Montaigne." My questions, which his argument provokes, can be summarized: When reading Montaigne, why not play his "game" of contradictions winning against conclusions, of theses without syntheses? When reading Montaigne, why play a Hegelian "game"?

3. Donald M. Frame's complex version of this early diversity / late universality pattern is scrupulously documented and splendidly argued in his *Montaigne: A Biography*, a work of such amplitude that, although I often disagree with it, I am all the same indebted to it.

4. For example, Montaigne closes his *Essays* with his paean to the (*b*) "most beautiful lives . . . [which] are those that conform to the common (*c*) human (*b*) pattern (*c*) with order, but (*b*) without miracle and without eccentricity" (857) [1096]. Yet in another example, a later (*c*) addition, Montaigne scorns conformity and complacency: "I have a singular desire that we should each be judged in ourselves apart, and that I may not be measured in conformity with the common patterns" (169) [225]. The question arises: which should one honor, textual or revisionary order, what Montaigne reserved for last or what Montaigne wrote last? What I argue Montaigne prefers is neither the one more than the other.

5. The most exhaustive study of evolution in Montaigne's written thought remains Pierre Villey's *Les Sources et l'évolution des Essais de Montaigne*. But numerous critics trace Montaigne's development in terms of what Gérard Defaux calls "the grand and inevitable trilogy of Stoicism, Skepticism, and Naturalism" ("Readings of Montaigne," p. 92).

6. Does Montaigne write to efface Etienne de La Boétie or to preserve him? Most critics argue the latter, as does, particularly insightfully, Jean Starobinski in *Montaigne en mouvement*, chapter 1. A quite other explanation, as textual as it is psychological and of considerable interest, is François Rigolot's "Montaigne's Purloined Letters."

7. Addressed are Madame Diane de Foix (106) [144], Madame de Grammont (145) [194], Madame d'Estissac (278) [364], Marguerite de Valois (418) [540], and Madame de Duras (595) [763]. Alluded to three times is Marie de Gournay, Montaigne's "fille d'alliance" and literary executrix. Frame identifies the allusions to her—(41) [60], (502) [645–46], (752) [961]—and discusses their dubious, perhaps posthumous, origin in *Montaigne: A Biography*, pp. 277–80.

Notes

8. Frame identifies the reader Montaigne sought as "the rounded, preferably wellborn man of experience and judgment" (*Montaigne: A Biography*, p. 315). On Montaigne's contribution to the seventeenth-century ideal of the "honnête homme," see Villey's *Les Sources et l'évolution des Essais de Montaigne*, pp. 452–90; see also Weintraub's *The Value of the Individual*, pp. 192–94.

9. See Rigolot's "Montaigne's Purloined Letters," pp. 156–60.

10. Gérard Defaux, citing, as I do, Montaigne's insistence on "the form" not "the substance," "the manner" not "the matter," makes a case for

> two singularly modern, and complementary, characteristics of Montaigne's writing: namely, on the one hand, a studied devalorization of all that has to do, within this writing, with the "message," with the "ideological content," i.e. with the *signified;* parallel to this, on the other hand, the indubitable valorization, the promotion of all that has to do, within writing, not with the subject itself, the argument, the theme that is treated, but with the *act* of judgment, with the intellectual performance for which this subject, transformed into an object, becomes the pretext: and this performance, which is transcribed by its author and thus made readable, visible on the page, ineluctably brings us to the level of the *signifier.* ("Readings of Montaigne," p. 90).

11. For the stoical texts that inspire Montaigne's critique of memory and learning, see F. Joukovsky's *Montaigne et le problème du temps*, p. 85 n. 20.

12. See Starobinski's section on "Le refus des livres, les emprunts, l'appropriation" in *Montaigne en mouvement*, pp. 132–48.

13. Montaigne's is hardly a dispassionate view of antiquity, and there may be something to Starobinski's suggestion that Montaigne's nostalgia is deeper still, for his own lost world rooted in Latin, his "langue 'maternelle'" ("mother tongue"), which he learned so early owing to "l'arbitraire et . . . la bienveillance paternels" ("the arbitrary and . . . [his] father's kindness") (*Montaigne en mouvement*, pp. 144, 148).

14. For the influence of Stoic and Epicurean thought on Montaigne's appreciation of the present, see Joukovsky's *Montaigne et le problème du temps*, chapter 1.

15. See Hiram Haydn's *The Counter-Renaissance*, pp. 468–97, cited by Frame in *Montaigne: A Biography*, p. 368.

16. As Claude Blum notes, "le repentir briserait l'essai. . . . le repentir renie ce qui a été; il 'corrige,' il 'oste,' il exclut 'l'addition'" ("repentance would destroy the essay. . . . repentance denies what has been; it 'corrects,' it 'deletes,' it excludes the 'addition'") ("Ecrire le 'moi': 'J'adjoute mais je ne corrige pas,'" p. 46).

17. "A force de peindre le passage, voici que Montaigne obtient *communication a l'être;* car l'être véritable n'est point une entité métaphysique, mais l'action continue d'une pensée sur les choses et sur la durée" ("By continually painting passing, thus Montaigne attains *communication with being;* for true being is not a metaphysical entity, but rather a sustained attentiveness to things and to time passing"): thus Poulet concludes his analysis of time in Montaigne's thought (*Etudes sur le temps humain*, 1:49–62), an analysis to which I am indebted.

18. On the fallacy of isolating Montaigne's essence from chance, Auerbach is explicit: "Any such attempt to attain to the essence by isolating it from the momentary accidental contingencies would strike [Montaigne] as absurd because, to his mind, the essence is lost as soon as one detaches it from its momentary accidents. For this very reason he must renounce an ultimate definition of himself or of man, for such a definition would of necessity have to be abstract" (*Mimesis*, p. 299).

19. Many critics argue Montaigne's indebtedness to Plutarch for his essay form; for example, Guy Davenport, vigorously, in his Foreword to *Montaigne's Travel Journal*, p. x. Frame identifies Montaigne's "chief antecedents" as "Plutarch's *Moralia* . . . , Machiavelli's *Discourses on the First Ten Books of Livy,* Erasmus' *Colloquies,* and . . . various books of

'selected lessons'" (*Montaigne: A Biography*, p. 184), of which Frame gives an impressive list (*Montaigne: A Biography*, p. 144). But, as Frame emphasizes, none "of these works are as personal as Montaigne's; none of the authors have the brashness to take themselves as subject" (*Montaigne: A Biography*, p. 184).

20. On the close ties between the open form of the essay and the freedom of reverie, see Robert J. Morrissey's *La Rêverie jusqu'à Rousseau*, pp. 38–43.

21. In practice, Montaigne did correct his *Essays*, particularly after 1588. Comparing the 1588 to the 1595 edition, Villey counts more than three thousand corrections in the latter. Few are substantial; most are stylistic—the changing of a word, the tightening of a phrase, the suppression of a repetition (*Les Sources et l'évolution des Essais de Montaigne*, pp. 533–43). Given that Montaigne would "écrire la 'parole vive'" ("write the 'spoken word'") (p. 49), Blum argues that all corrections, in the logic of the *Essays*, are additions; see his "Ecrire le 'moi,'" pp. 49–50.

22. Montaigne never systematizes the changing editions of his *Essays* and the undated marginalia in his last "Bordeaux copy." The modern scholarly mind, not Montaigne's, practices the dissection of his text into (*a*), (*b*), and (*c*) strata to construe, typically and paradoxically, the development of Montaigne's mind.

23. The modern critical idea of an "unreliable narrator" is quite other than Montaigne's idea of an undependable narrator. Frank Kermode writes, "all narrators are unreliable, but some are more expressly so than others. . . . They break down the conventional relation ship between sequential narrative and history-likeness, with its arbitrary imposition of truth; they complicate the message" (*The Art of Telling*, p. 140). Montaigne's complaint about undependable narrators is the inverse: they build up "the conventional relationship between sequential narrative and history-likeness, with its arbitrary imposition of truth"; they simplify "the message."

Chapter 3

1. Citations from Rousseau's works will be (by page number noted in parentheses in the text) to J. M. Cohen's translation of *The Confessions* (for which a *C* will precede the page number) and to Peter France's translation of the *Reveries of the Solitary Walker* (for which an *R* will precede the page number), and when no English page reference is given in parentheses, my own translations of Rousseau's various autobiographical texts will serve. Following each quotation in English, a reference (by page number appearing in square brackets) will refer the interested reader to the French Pléiade edition of *Les Confessions et autres textes autobiographiques*.

2. How Rousseau's title was heard by his contemporaries, Lionel Gossman reveals: "In the plural, *Confessions* would invite comparison with the *Confessions* of St. Augustine, with Duclos' *Confessions du Comte de**** (1741), and with a number of narratives in the manner of the latter." Contemporary assumptions, Gossman continues, would accentuate Rousseau's looked-for contrast between literature and life: "In general, eighteenth-century readers thought of St. Augustine as a severe critic of literature, art, and science, and of his *Confessions* as an authentic account of a man's life, written for the moral edification of readers, rather than as a literary work of art" ("The Innocent Art of Confession and Reverie," p. 60).

3. Ironically, Rousseau argues against Montaigne—with Montaigne's argument. The portrait-painting metaphor is Montaigne's, and so is the theory that selectivity equals falsity in biographical and autobiographical writings; see his Preface to his *Essays*, p. 2, or *Essais*, p. 9. For Rousseau's few and far-from-flattering mentions of Montaigne as autobiographer, see Colette Fleuret's list and commentary in *Rousseau et Montaigne*, pp. 126–27.

4. Weintraub makes explicit the contrast: "while Augustine, befitting a God-centered

view, confesses his soul to God and only incidentally to his fellow men, Rousseau, as a measure of the degree to which the world had become secularized, has nothing to confess to God, but everything to his fellow men" (*The Value of the Individual*, pp. 299–300).

5. Montaigne's Preface (*a*), *Essays*, p. 2; *Essais*, p. 9.

6. For related and complicated analyses of Rousseau's assessment of speech and writing, see Jacques Derrida's *Of Grammatology*, pp. 97–316; Paul de Man's analysis thereof in "The Rhetoric of Blindness," in his *Blindness and Insight*, pp. 102–41; and the source of their mutual work, Rousseau's *On the Origin of Language*, wherein, as de Man writes, Rousseau opts for the "primacy of voice over the written word" only to have his "own texts provide the strongest evidence against his alleged doctrine" (p. 116).

7. Language differentiates between the private and public Rousseaus, I argue. More traditionally, and not entirely contradictorily, Marcel Raymond argues that a sort of behavioral psychology determines Rousseau's constancy of self in solitude and Rousseau's becoming "other" ["autre"] in response to others. Situations solicit his reactions (Rousseau as Vaussore de Villeneuve [147–50]) and people call out his inner resources (Rousseau as Mr. Dudding [249–55]); see Raymond's "J.-J. Rousseau: Deux aspects de sa vie intérieure (intermittences et permanence du moi)."

8. The antithesis of revealing and concealing is central to Jean Starobinski's groundbreaking work, *Jean-Jacques Rousseau: La Transparence et l'obstacle*.

9. For example, the ribbon incident and the Fourth "Walk" (as Rousseau calls sections in his *Reveries*) are classic passages of questionable sincerity in Rousseau. From just these two, Paul de Man spins, on a different axis of revealing and concealing than I choose, a theory for reading Rousseau. See his *Allegories of Reading*, pp. 278–301.

10. For the purposes of textual analysis, I supply here a literal translation of the *Confessions* passage wherein this important linkage of "to write" ["écrire"] and "to hide" ["se cacher"] occurs. Cohen offers, "The role I have chosen of writing and remaining in the background is precisely the one that suits me" (*C*116).

11. For picaresque and poetic parallels in Rousseau's written life and an analysis of the historical interdependency of autobiography and the "roman-mémoire et roman picaresque" (p. 245), see Gita May's "*Les Confessions* de Rousseau, roman picaresque?"; and (cited therein) Christie McDonald Vance's *The Extravagant Shepherd: A Study of the Pastoral Vision in Rousseau's* Nouvelle Héloïse.

12. Exploring far reaches of where the fictional and the autobiographical meet, Jean Starobinski charts the territory in Rousseau between "des images (toutes empruntées à des sources livresques) . . . [et] l'intensité muette de l'émotion primitive" ("the images [all borrowed from literary sources] . . . [and] the silent intensity of primitive emotion") ("Jean-Jacques Rousseau et les pouvoirs de l'imaginaire," p. 58). But he stops short of erasing frontiers, of allowing the fictional to *be* autobiographical.

13. As Weintraub pithily remarks, "Augustine's psalmodic *confessio laudis* became in Rousseau's version *apologia pro vita sua*" (*The Value of the Individual*, p. 300). Yet Rousseau is blind to the interpretation: "For I have no fear of my reader's forgetting that I am writing my confessions and supposing that I am making my apologia" (*C*262) [279].

14. See Mark Temmer's "Art and Love in the *Confessions* of Jean-Jacques Rousseau," p. 216.

15. Another instance of Rousseau's atoning with sorrow and suffering for his sins, for which he clearly claims his absolution, concerns his final renunciation of Maman (*C*364–65) [391–92].

16. Amidst many contradictions, which he even acknowledges, Rousseau maintains the innocence of his exile. For every transgression, he construes an explanation that excuses. Deservedly, Rousseau loses Les Charmettes, for his unfaithfulness to Maman leads him temporarily astray and his ambitions lead him irremediably into the world (*C*245–46) [259–60]. But undeservedly he loses paradise, for he was just then returning, all

devotion to Maman, all dedication to his pastoral life (C246) [260]. Dramatically, Rousseau returns to find his place taken by Wintzenried, Maman's chosen, who effectively expels him. But he lingers on at Les Charmettes, anticlimactically, undramatically, devotedly serving Maman (C250) [264], before going into voluntary exile (C252–53, 256–57)[266–67, 270–72], no flaming sword at his back barring his return.

17. Much given to personae, Rousseau is also other literary figures, before and after his ephemeral golden age ("Alas, my most lasting happiness was in a dream" (C108) [108]). Young, he is quite the troubador, singing under castle windows; older, he is the rejected and heartbroken lover: both are well within the courtly love tradition.

18. For example, Philippe Lejeune, drawing on the work of Starobinski, Raymond, and Michel Launay, envisions Rousseau as a "bricoleur en mythologie" (p. 88), who combines and transforms religious and classical archetypes. See his analysis of several Rousseauian complements and clashes between the traditions in *Le Pacte autobiographique*, pp. 87–99.

19. A notable exception to the general tendency to carve Rousseau's ages in stone—his innocence resolutely in a period prior to broken combs and his experience in Paris—is Starobinski, who so relentlessly and remarkably pursues the changeable Rousseau. Fleishman intriguingly observes, "The *Confessions* may be seen as a succession of Edenesque landscapes in each of which primal innocence and happiness are partially achieved, invariably to be followed by a fall—merited or unmerited—and expulsion," but with this Fleishman cuts short his "cursory overview" of Rousseau's *Confessions* in *Figures of Autobiography*, p. 95.

20. Thus argues Michel Foucault in his Introduction to *Rousseau, juge de Jean-Jacques: Dialogues*, p. viii.

21. Taking into account the ambiguity and contiguity of the states of reverie and thought, Arnaud Tripet nonetheless arrives at a more rigorous, tripartite classification of reveries, in his *La Rêverie littéraire*, pp. 92–130. Morrissey offers six distinct moments that identify the state of reverie; see his concise analysis in *La Rêverie jusqu'à Rousseau*, pp. 154–57.

22. "Recollected in tranquillity" is Wordsworth's famous phrase, and as trenchant as any in differentiating Wordsworth's composition of reveries from Rousseau's unremitting struggles.

23. On the psychology and the temporality of Rousseau's reveries, see Poulet's chapter on Rousseau in *Etudes sur le temps humain*, especially 1:214–19 on "le sentiment de l'existence actuelle" (1:214) and 1:225–27 on "le souvenir affectif" (1:227).

24. Compare Montaigne: (*a*) "I have no other marshal but fortune to arrange my bits. As my fancies present themselves, I pile them up; now they come pressing in a crowd, now dragging single file" ["Je n'ay point d'autre sergent de bande à ranger mes pieces, que la fortune. A mesme que mes resveries se presentent, je les entasse; tantost elles se pressent en foule, tantost elles se trainent à la file"] (*Essays*, p. 297; *Essais*, p. 388).

25. As Margery Sabin demonstrates, Rousseau loves the sweep of nature, but not its specificity. Sabin's observations in *English Romanticism and the French Tradition* are generally incisive (particularly on p. 114)—except that Rousseau's late and recurring passion for botany troubles their generality.

Chapter 4

1. Norton's *The Prelude: 1799, 1805, 1850*, edited by Jonathan Wordsworth, M. H. Abrams, and Stephen Gill, will be my *Prelude* text of reference, to which I owe all citations (which will be noted by date of version, part or book number, and line number) and several observations gleaned from its authoritative texts and extensive notes. Citations to two Wordsworth manuscripts will also be to texts as they appear in the Norton *Prelude:*

Notes

"Fragments from *Peter Bell* MS. 2" (d), p. 496; and "Draft Material from the Five-Book *Prelude* in MS. W," p. 497. Quotations from Wordsworth's other poetry and prose (which will be identified by brief title and line number for the verse, brief title and page number for the prose) will be to Ernest de Selincourt's revised edition of Wordsworth's *Poetical Works;* the last section of which contains Wordsworth's "Preface to the Second Edition of . . . 'Lyrical Ballads'" (hereafter referred to as "Preface") and Wordsworth's "Essay, Supplementary to the Preface" (hereafter referred to as "Essay").

2. For historical patterns in Wordsworthian criticism, see Karl Kroeber's chapter, "William Wordsworth," in *The English Romantic Poets,* especially pp. 271–84. For a selection of early reactions to *The Prelude,* see the Norton *Prelude,* pp. 541–64.

3. Jonathan Wordsworth offers a fuller discussion of "the One Life" (p. 574) in his "The Two-Part *Prelude* of 1799"; see particularly pp. 574–77.

4. For a textual study locating Wordsworth's ambivalence later and more pervasively in "autobiography's situation midway between the dialogical presence of 'discourse,' and the past, written, otherness of 'narrative'" (p. 34), between the genres of lyric and epic (pp. 34–35), see David P. Haney's "The Emergence of the Autobiographical Figure in *The Prelude,* Book I."

5. For a brief but detailed textual history of the two-part *Prelude* of 1799, the five-book *Prelude* of January–early March 1804, the changes of March 1804–May 1805 leading to the 1805 *Prelude,* and those contributing over the years to the 1850 *Prelude,* see the Norton *Prelude,* pp. 512–22. For a fuller analysis of earlier versions of the poem, Norton refers readers to Jonathan Wordsworth and Stephen Gill's "The Two-Part *Prelude* of 1798–99"; to Stephen Parrish's "*The Prelude,*" *1798–1799;* and to Jonathan Wordsworth's "The Five-Book *Prelude* of Early Spring 1804."

6. Wordsworth obviously does not follow the English Protestant tradition of explicitly spiritual autobiographies, such as those by John Bunyan, William Cowper, John Newton, and George Whitefield, which Peterson cites and characterizes as "all painfully introspective tales that dwell on a conviction of sin and despair of salvation" (p. 302). See Peterson's "Newman's *Apologia pro vita sua*"; and her cited resource, John N. Morris's *Versions of the Self.*

7. Wordsworth never finished *The Recluse,* which exists only as sizable fragments and his known intentions; yet from these, Kenneth R. Johnston argues that *The Recluse* "lives" (p. xiii), which he studies in detail in his *Wordsworth and* The Recluse.

8. On "The Poetics of Prophecy," see Geoffrey Hartman's essay of that title, in his *The Unremarkable Wordsworth,* which concludes: "A mighty scheme not of truth but of troth— of trusting the old language, its pathos, its animism, its fallacious figures—is what connects poet and prophet" (p. 179). Hartman believes that Wordsworth "still writes in the old language, yet how precariously" (p. 180), the language that I hear silenced finally in his strict scriptural allusion. But Hartman finds "[God-words] . . . in Wordsworth . . . rarely foregrounded" (p. 179), while I find them looming ever larger as Wordsworth—concluding, late revising—stills the animism of the spirit in the paraphrase of the letter.

9. The classic study of the Christian figural tradition in Romantic literature, which deals extensively with *The Prelude,* is M. H. Abram's *Natural Supernaturalism.*

10. John Keats to George and Thomas Keats, 21 December 1817, in *The Letters of John Keats, 1814–1821,* vol. I.

11. In Bloomian terms, Wordsworth, no longer "always in the process of becoming his own begetter" (p. 35), is no longer the "hero of internalized quest . . . the fulfillment [of which] is never the poem itself but the poem beyond" (p. 19); see Harold Bloom's "The Internalization of Quest Romance," in *The Ringers in the Tower,* pp. 13–35.

12. On "the paradoxical development-deterioration of the mind's mysterious power" (p. 12), see Karl Kroeber's "Spots of Time and *The Haywain,*" in his *Romantic Landscape Vision,* especially pp. 10–14.

Notes

13. Here I disagree with Brooke Hopkins, who analyzes Augustine's pear stealing, Rousseau's ribbon stealing, and Wordsworth's boat stealing, all in terms of "fault" and the figure of the fall, in "Pear-Stealing and Other Faults: An Essay on Confessional Autobiography."

14. On Wordsworth's "unconscious memory," see Robert Langbaum's *The Mysteries of Identity,* pp. 40–41.

15. Therein too is the beginning glow of "The light that never was, on sea or land" ("Peele Castle," 15).

16. See the Norton *Prelude,* p. 516.

17. That is, in his poetry he dismisses clear-cut distinctions, but in his critical prose, Wordsworth is often a rigorous anatomist; see, for example, his "Preface to the Edition of 1815," p. 752.

18. By 1856, Ruskin writes, "German dulness, and Engish affectation, have of late much multiplied among us the use of two of the most objectionable words that were ever coined by the troublesomeness of metaphysicians—namely, 'Objective' and 'Subjective.' No words can be more exquisitely, and in all points, useless" (from *Modern Painters,* vol. 3, pt. 4, chap. 12, quoted by M. H. Abrams in *The Mirror and the Lamp,* p. 242).

19. On iconoclasm and new representation, see Owen Barfield's "Symptoms of Iconoclasm," particularly his important distinction, pertinent to all Romantics, between subjectivity as man's "poor temporal personality" and the subjectivity of "Man" (pp. 45–46).

20. Strangely, Geoffrey Hartman claims in *Wordsworth's Poetry: 1787–1814* that Wordsworth's (lived and written) Simplon Pass "experience, like Petrarch's [on Mt. Ventoux] and Augustine's [in the garden] is a conversion" (p. 49), only to then claim—I think, more insightfully—that "Wordsworth generally avoids making epiphanies into epochs: into decisive turns of personal fate or history. . . . The reason for Wordsworth's avoidance of epochal structure is complex and linked probably to his avoidance of myth" (p. 54).

21. On the love between Wordsworth and Coleridge and its affinities with pastoral convention, see Sabin's *English Romanticism and the French Tradition,* pp. 43–44.

22. The "how" of Wordsworth's memory, not the "what" of his history, being my subject, I offer but a single example of the political Wordsworth. For an analysis of the "systematic dialectic between public and private affairs" (p. 88) in *The Prelude,* see Karl Kroeber's *Romantic Narrative Art,* pp. 88–103. See also Carl R. Woodring's chapter on Wordsworth in *Politics in English Romantic Poetry.*

23. Norton *Prelude,* p. 388 n. 3.

24. In their summary of *The Prelude*'s textual history, the Norton editors argue that "spots of time" by concluding the five-book *Prelude* "are a culmination of all that has gone before" (p. 517). See Jonathan Wordsworth's "The Five-Book *Prelude* of Early Spring 1804."

25. In her stimulating essay "The Spots of Time in Early Versions of *The Prelude,*" Sybil S. Eakin extensively reads "spots of time in the context of Snowdon" (p. 403), an interpretation with which, since I read Snowdon as one of many "spots of time," I extensively disagree. Eakin's tendency to spatialize the temporal, to favor the static "symbol" (p. 403) in Snowdon over the temporal and "simple austerity" (p. 394) in "spots," is representative of a literary yearning for transcendence to which many—not the least of whom is Wordsworth—succumb. A passage exemplary of this yearning reads thus: "The relationship with nature that Wordsworth, in the spots of time, presented as a progression—from early passivity and dependence to a mature self-consciousness—in fact operated instantaneously within each perceptive and creative moment. When the poet 'received' the 'universal spectacle' on Snowdon in all its striking contrasts and created from the scene a symbol of 'higher minds,' he exhibited in a single experience the entire range of responses to nature which, in sequence, had shaped his autobiography" (pp. 403–4). Thus "symbol"—"universal," of "higher minds," and "a single experience"—transcends

"self," "life," and "writing." In "auto-bio-graphy," is not such transcendence a dubious achievement?

26. See the Norton *Prelude,* p. 460 n. 5 and pp. 496–97.

27. The Snowdon passage being principally written (end of February 1804) before the "When, in blessèd season" (1805, 10.315; early March 1804) addition to "spots of time," Wordsworth in concluding the 1805 *Prelude* reverses compositional chronology to finish with communal symbology. See Eakin, "The Spots of Time in Early Versions of *The Prelude,*" pp. 398–401, again praising what I question.

28. As an example, antecedent to Wordsworth's "correspondent breeze," the climactic metaphor for Augustine's conversion is a tempest, when within him "there arose a mighty wind, bringing a mighty shower of tears" (*Confessions,* 8.12; quoted by M. H. Abrams in "The Correspondent Breeze: A Romantic Metaphor," p. 47).

29. Although Wordsworth's nature imagery may have Christian origins, as Abrams has shown (see preceding note), few would find Wordsworth's imagery necessarily derivative, less personal than communal, less sensual than schematic. Wordsworth's wind and water are mild and wet and—when metaphoric—evocative before they are symbolic of time and memory.

30. For the literal-linked-to-literary changes between the 1805 *Prelude* as "the poem to Coleridge" and the final revision after Coleridge's death—changes that turn the "addresses to the reader . . . to apostrophe," the "decorum . . . from epistolary to lyric, intimate to monumental," giving the poem "at once a dimension of fiction" (p. 37)—see Jonathan Arac's "Bounding Lines: *The Prelude* and Critical Revision," particularly its closing pages, which serve his "commitment to study literature not only heterocosmically but also historically" (p. 46 n. 18).

31. A starting point for my discussion of reverie and meditation is Jacques Voisine's remarking (citing Helen Darbishire) the trimming of reverie from the 1850 *Prelude* and his suggestive conclusion: "La rêverie n'a pas de place dans la philosophie poétique de Wordsworth, parce qu'elle n'a pas de place dans sa morale. Elle est remplacée par la meditation. En cela l'opposition est nette avec le Promeneur solitaire, qui avoue dans la 7e Promenade: 'La rêverie délasse et m'amuse, la réflexion me fatigue et m'attriste'" ("Reverie does not have a place in Wordsworth's poetic philosophy, because it does not have a place in his ethics. It is replaced by meditation. In this way the contrast is complete to the Solitary Walker, who confesses in the Seventh Walk: 'Reverie distracts and amuses me, reflection tires and depresses me'" (*J.-J. Rousseau en Angleterre à l'époque Romantique,* pp. 220–21).

32. Citing the cavern passage, Susan J. Wolfson skillfully opposes the mystery of living imagination to the deathlike mastery of literary artifact, without, however, differentiating between the vigor and value of the first and second "artifact" (p. 932); see her "The Illusion of Mastery: Wordsworth's Revisions of 'The Drowned Man of Esthwaite,' 1799, 1805, 1850," especially the last pages.

33. See Hartman's classic analysis in "The Via Naturaliter Negativa," in his *Wordsworth's Poetry: 1787–1814,* pp. 31–69.

BIBLIOGRAPHY

Abrams, M. H. "The Correspondent Breeze: A Romantic Metaphor." In *English Romantic Poets: Modern Essays in Criticism*, ed. M. H. Abrams, pp. 37–54. New York: Oxford Univ. Press, 1975.

———. *The Mirror and the Lamp: Romantic Theory and the Critical Tradition*. 1953. Reprint. New York: Oxford Univ. Press, 1971.

———. *Natural Supernaturalism: Tradition and Revolution in Romantic Literature*. New York: W. W. Norton, 1971.

Arac, Jonathan. "Bounding Lines: *The Prelude* and Critical Revision." *Boundary* 2, no. 7 (1979): 3–48.

Auerbach, Erich. *Mimesis: The Representation of Reality in Western Literature*. Translated by Willard R. Trask. Princeton, N.J.: Princeton Univ. Press, 1953.

Augustine, Saint. *Confessions*. Translated by R. S. Pine-Coffin. Harmondsworth, Middlesex: Penguin Books, 1961.

———. *On Christian Doctrine*. Translated by D. W. Robertson, Jr. Indianapolis: Bobbs-Merrill Company, Library of Liberal Arts, 1958.

Bachelard, Gaston. *The Poetics of Reverie: Childhood, Language, and the Cosmos*. Translated by Daniel Russel. Boston: Beacon Press, 1971.

Barfield, Owen. "Symptoms of Iconoclasm." In *Romanticism and Consciousness: Essays in Criticism*, ed. Harold Bloom, pp. 41–46. New York: W. W. Norton, 1970.

Barthes, Roland. *Image, Music, Text*. Translated by Stephen Heath. New York: Hill and Wang, 1977.

Beaujour, Michel. *Miroirs d'encre: Rhétorique de l'autoportrait*. Paris: Editions du Seuil, 1980.

Bloom, Harold. *The Ringers in the Tower: Studies in Romantic Tradition*. Chicago: Univ. of Chicago Press, 1971.

Blum, Claude. "Ecrire le 'moi': 'J'adjoute, mais je ne corrige pas.'" In *Montaigne (1580–1980): Actes du Colloque International*, ed. Marcel Tetel, pp. 36–53. Paris: Librairie A. G. Nizet, 1983.

Brown, Peter. *Augustine of Hippo*. Berkeley: Univ. of California Press, 1967.

Buckley, Jerome Hamilton. *The Turning Key: Autobiography and the Subjective Impulse since 1800*. Cambridge, Mass.: Harvard Univ. Press, 1984.

Bunyan, John. *Grace Abounding to the Chief of Sinners*. Edited by W. R. Owens. Harmondsworth, Middlesex: Penguin Books, 1987.

Colish, Marcia L. *The Mirror of Language: A Study in the Medieval Theory of Knowledge*. Rev. ed. Lincoln: Univ. of Nebraska Press, 1983.

Courcelle, Pierre. *Les Confessions de Saint Augustin dans la tradition littéraire: Antécédents et postérité*. Paris: Etudes Augustiniennes, 1963.

———. *Recherches sur les Confessions de Saint Augustin*. Paris: Editions de Boccard, 1950.

Bibliography

Culler, Jonathan. "Fabula and Sjuzhet in the Analysis of Narrative." *Poetics Today* 1, no. 3 (1980): 27–37.

Darwin, Charles. *The Autobiography of Charles Darwin and Selected Letters*. Edited by Francis Darwin. 1892. Reprint. New York: Dover Publications, 1958.

Davenport, Guy. Foreword to *Montaigne's Travel Journal*, by Michel de Montaigne. Translated by Donald M. Frame. San Francisco: North Point Press, 1983.

Defaux, Gérard. "Readings of Montaigne," trans. John A. Gallucci. In *Montaigne: Essays in Reading*, ed. Gérard Defaux, pp. 73–92. New Haven, Conn.: Yale Univ. Press, 1983.

de Man, Paul. *Allegories of Reading: Figural Language in Nietzsche, Rilke, and Proust*. New Haven, Conn.: Yale Univ. Press, 1979.

———. "Autobiography as De-facement." *Modern Language Notes* 94 (1979): 919–30.

———. *Blindness and Insight: Essays in the Rhetoric of Contemporary Criticism*. 2d ed., rev. Minneapolis: Univ. of Minnesota Press, 1983.

De Quincey, Thomas. *Confessions of an English Opium Eater*. Edited by Alethea Hayter. Harmondsworth, Middlesex: Penguin Books, 1971.

Derrida, Jacques. *Of Grammatology*. Translated by Gayatri Chakravorty Spivak. Baltimore: Johns Hopkins Univ. Press, 1976.

Dulaey, Martine. *Le Rêve dans la vie et la pensée de Saint Augustin*. Paris: Etudes Augustiniennes, 1973.

Eakin, Paul John. *Fictions in Autobiography: Studies in the Art of Self-Invention*. Princeton, N.J.: Princeton Univ. Press, 1985.

———. "Narrative and Chronology as Structures of Reference and the New Model Autobiographer." In *Studies in Autobiography*, ed. James Olney, pp. 32–41. New York: Oxford Univ. Press, 1988.

Eakin, Sybil S. "The Spots of Time in Early Versions of *The Prelude*." *Studies in Romanticism* 12 (1973): 389–405.

Egan, Susanna. *Patterns of Experience in Autobiography*. Chapel Hill: Univ. of North Carolina Press, 1984.

Eliot, T. S. *Selected Essays*. Rev. ed. New York: Harcourt, Brace & World, 1964.

Fleishman, Avrom. *Figures of Autobiography: The Language of Self-Writing in Victorian and Modern England*. Berkeley: Univ. of California Press, 1983.

Fleuret, Colette. *Rousseau et Montaigne*. Publications de la Sorbonne, Série Littérature II. Paris: Librairie A. G. Nizet, 1980.

Foucault, Michel. Introduction to *Rousseau, juge de Jean-Jacques: Dialogues*, by Jean-Jacques Rousseau. Paris: Bibliothèque de Cluny, 1962.

Frame, Donald M. *Montaigne: A Biography*. New York: Harcourt, Brace & World, 1965; San Francisco: North Point Press, 1984.

Freccero, John. "The Fig Tree and the Laurel: Petrarch's Poetics." *Diacritics* 5 (1975): 34–40.

Gadamer, Hans-Georg. *Philosophical Hermeneutics*. Edited and translated by David E. Linge. Berkeley: Univ. of California Press, 1976.

Gibbon, Edward. *Memoirs of My Life*. Edited by Betty Radice. Harmondsworth, Middlesex: Penguin Books, 1984.

Bibliography

Ginsberg, Warren. *The Cast of Character: The Representation of Personality in Ancient and Medieval Literature*. Toronto: Univ. of Toronto Press, 1983.

Goodman, Nelson. "Twisted Tales; or, Story, Study, and Symphony." In *On Narrative*, ed. W. J. T. Mitchell, pp. 99–115. Chicago: Univ. of Chicago Press, 1980.

———. *Ways of Worldmaking*. Indianapolis: Hackett Publishing Co., 1978.

Gossman, Lionel. "The Innocent Art of Confession and Reverie." *Daedalus* 107, no. 3 (1978): 59–77.

Guitton, Jean. *Le Temps et l'éternité chez Plotin et Saint Augustin*. Paris: Boivin, 1933.

Gunn, Janet Varner. "Autobiography and the Narrative Experience of Temporality as Depth." *Soundings* 60 (1977): 194–209.

Gusdorf, Georges. "Conditions and Limits of Autobiography," trans. James Olney. In *Autobiography: Essays Theoretical and Critical*, ed. James Olney, pp. 28–48. Princeton, N.J.: Princeton Univ. Press, 1980.

Haney, David P. "The Emergence of the Autobiographical Figure in *The Prelude*, Book I." *Studies in Romanticism* 20 (1981): 33–63.

Harpham, Geoffrey Galt. "Conversion and the Language of Autobiography." In *Studies in Autobiography*, ed. James Olney, pp. 42–50. New York: Oxford Univ. Press, 1988.

Hartman, Geoffrey. *The Unremarkable Wordsworth*. Theory and History of Literature 34. Minneapolis: Univ. of Minnesota Press, 1987

———. *Wordsworth's Poetry: 1787–1814*. New Haven, Conn.: Yale Univ. Press, 1964; Cambridge, Mass.: Harvard Univ. Press, 1987.

Haydn, Hiram. *The Counter-Renaissance*. New York: Scribners, 1950.

Helsinger, Elizabeth K. "Ulysses to Penelope: Victorian Experiments in Autobiography." In *Approaches to Victorian Autobiography*, ed. George P. Landow, pp. 3–25. Athens: Ohio Univ. Press, 1979.

Hopkins, Brooke. "Pear-Stealing and Other Faults: An Essay on Confessional Autobiography." *South Atlantic Quarterly* 80 (1981): 305–21.

———. "Reading, and Believing In, Autobiography." *Soundings* 64 (1981): 93–111.

Jackson, Susan K. *Rousseau's Occasional Autobiographies*. Columbus: Ohio State Univ. Press, 1992.

Johnston, Kenneth R. *Wordsworth and* The Recluse. New Haven, Conn.: Yale Univ. Press, 1984.

Joukovsky, F. *Montaigne et le problème du temps*. Paris: Librairie A. G. Nizet, 1972.

Keats, John. *The Letters of John Keats, 1814–1821*. Edited by Hyder Edward Rollins. 2 vols. Cambridge, Mass.: Harvard Univ. Press, 1958.

Kermode, Frank. *The Art of Telling: Essays on Fiction*. Cambridge, Mass.: Harvard Univ. Press, 1983.

———. *The Genesis of Secrecy: On the Interpretation of Narrative*. Cambridge, Mass.: Harvard Univ. Press, 1979.

———. "Secrets and Narrative Sequence." In *On Narrative*, ed. W. J. T. Mitchell, pp. 79–97. Chicago: Univ. of Chicago Press, 1980.

———. *The Sense of an Ending: Studies in the Theory of Fiction*. New York: Oxford Univ. Press, 1967.

Bibliography

Kroeber, Karl. *Romantic Landscape Vision: Constable and Wordsworth*. Madison: Univ. of Wisconsin Press, 1975.

———. *Romantic Narrative Art*. Madison: Univ. of Wisconsin Press, 1960.

———. "William Wordsworth." In *The English Romantic Poets: A Review of Research and Criticism*, ed. Frank Jordan, pp. 256–339. 4th rev. ed. New York: Modern Language Association of America, 1985.

Landow, George P., ed. *Approaches to Victorian Autobiography*. Athens: Ohio Univ. Press, 1979.

Langbaum, Robert. *The Mysteries of Identity: A Theme in Modern Literature*. New York: Oxford Univ. Press, 1977.

Lejeune, Philippe. *On Autobiography*. Edited by Paul John Eakin; translated by Katherine Leary. Theory and History of Literature 52. Minneapolis: Univ. of Minnesota Press, 1989.

———. *Le Pacte autobiographique*. Paris: Editions du Seuil, 1975.

Mandel, Barrett J. "Full of Life Now." In *Autobiography: Essays Theoretical and Critical,* ed. James Olney, pp. 49–72. Princeton, N.J.: Princeton Univ. Press, 1980.

Matthews, William. *British Autobiographies: An Annotated Bibliography of British Autobiographies Published or Written before 1951*. 1955. Reprint. Berkeley: Univ. of California Press, 1984.

May, Gita. "*Les Confessions* de Rousseau, roman picaresque?" In *Französische Litteratur im Zeitalter der Aufklärung,* ed. Wido Hempel, pp. 236–53. Frankfurt: Vittorio Klostermann, 1983.

Mill, John Stuart. *Autobiography*. Edited by Jack Stillinger. Boston: Houghton Mifflin, 1969.

Misch, Georg. *A History of Autobiography in Antiquity*. Translated by E. W. Dickes. 2 vols. London: Routledge & Kegan Paul, 1950.

Montaigne, Michel de. *The Complete Essays of Montaigne*. Translated by Donald M. Frame. Stanford, Calif.: Stanford Univ. Press, 1957.

———. *Oeuvres complètes*. Edited by Albert Thibaudet and Maurice Rat. Paris: Bibliothèque de la Pléiade, Gallimard, 1962.

Morris, John N. *Versions of the Self: Studies in English Autobiography from John Bunyan to John Stuart Mill*. New York: Basic Books, 1966.

Morrissey, Robert J. *La Rêverie jusqu'à Rousseau: Recherches sur un topos littéraire*. Lexington, Ky: French Forum, Publishers, 1984.

Olney, James. *Metaphors of Self: The Meaning of Autobiography*. Princeton, N.J.: Princeton Univ. Press, 1972.

———. "Some Versions of Memory / Some Versions of *Bios:* The Ontology of Autobiography." In *Autobiography: Essays Theoretical and Critical,* ed. James Olney, pp. 236–67. Princeton, N.J.: Princeton Univ. Press, 1980.

Pascal, Roy. *Design and Truth in Autobiography*. Cambridge, Mass.: Harvard Univ. Press, 1960.

Peterson, Linda H. "Newman's *Apologia pro vita sua* and the Traditions of the English Spiritual Autobiography." *PMLA* 100, no. 3 (1985): 300–314.

———. *Victorian Autobiography: The Tradition of Self-Interpretation*. New Haven, Conn.: Yale Univ. Press, 1986.

Bibliography

Poulet, Georges. *Etudes sur le temps humain.* Vol. 1. Paris: Librairie Plon, 1952; Paris: Editions du Rocher, 1976.

Raymond, Marcel. "J.-J. Rousseau: Deux aspects de sa vie intérieure (intermittences et permanence du moi)." *Annales de la Société Jean-Jacques Rousseau* 29 (1941–42): 5–57.

Renza, Louis A. "The Veto of the Imagination: A Theory of Autobiography." In *Autobiography: Essays Theoretical and Critical,* ed. James Olney, pp. 268–95. Princeton, N.J.: Princeton Univ. Press, 1980.

Ricoeur, Paul. *Hermeneutics and the Human Sciences: Essays on Language, Action, and Interpretation.* Edited and translated by John B. Thompson. Cambridge and Paris: Cambridge Univ. Press and Editions de la Maison des Sciences de l'Homme, 1981.

————. *History and Truth.* Translated by Charles A. Kelbley. Evanston, Ill.: Northwestern Univ. Press, 1965.

————. "Narrative Time." *Critical Inquiry* 7 (1980): 169–90.

————. *Temps et récit.* 3 vols. Paris: Editions du Seuil, 1983.

————. *Time and Narrative.* Vol. 1. Translated by Kathleen McLaughlin and David Pellauer. Chicago: Univ. of Chicago Press, 1984.

Rigolot, François. "Montaigne's Purloined Letters." In *Montaigne: Essays in Reading,* ed. Gérard Defaux, pp. 145–66. New Haven, Conn.: Yale Univ. Press, 1983.

Rosenberg, John D. "Mr. Darwin Collects Himself." In *Nineteenth Century Lives: Essays Presented to Jerome Hamilton Buckley,* ed. Laurence S. Lockridge, John Maynard, and Donald D. Stone, pp. 82–111. Cambridge: Cambridge Univ. Press, 1990.

Rousseau, Jean-Jacques. *Les Confessions et autres textes autobiographiques.* Edited by Bernard Gagnebin and Marcel Raymond. Paris: Bibliothèque de la Pléiade, Gallimard, 1959. Vol. 1 of *Oeuvres complètes.* 3 vols. 1959–64.

————. *The Confessions.* Translated by J. M. Cohen. 1953. Reprint. Harmondsworth, Middlesex: Penguin Books, 1988.

————. "Essay on the Origin of Language." In *On the Origin of Language,* trans. John H. Moran and Alexander Goode, pp. 1–74. New York: Frederick Unger Publishing Co., 1966.

————. *Reveries of the Solitary Walker.* Translated by Peter France. Harmondsworth, Middlesex: Penguin Books, 1979.

Sabin, Margery. *English Romanticism and the French Tradition.* Cambridge, Mass.: Harvard Univ. Press, 1976.

Schafer, Roy. "Narration in the Psychoanalytic Dialogue." In *On Narrative,* ed. W. J. T. Mitchell, pp. 25–49. Chicago: Univ. of Chicago Press, 1980.

Scholes, Robert, and Robert Kellog. *The Nature of Narrative.* New York: Oxford Univ. Press, 1966.

Smith, Barbara Herrnstein. "Narrative Versions, Narrative Theories." In *On Narrative,* ed. W. J. T. Mitchell, pp. 209–32. Chicago: Univ. of Chicago Press, 1980.

Spengemann, William C. *The Forms of Autobiography: Episodes in the History of a Literary Genre.* New Haven, Conn.: Yale Univ. Press, 1980.

Bibliography

Starobinski, Jean. "Jean-Jacques Rousseau et les pouvoirs de l'imaginaire." *Revue Internationale de Philosophie* 14.51 (1960): 43–67.

———. *Jean-Jacques Rousseau: La Transparence et l'obstacle.* Rev. ed. Paris: Editions Gallimard, 1971.

———. *Montaigne en mouvement.* Paris: Editions Gallimard, 1982.

———. "The Style of Autobiography," trans. Seymour Chatman. In *Autobiography: Essays Theoretical and Critical,* ed. James Olney, pp. 73–83. Princeton, N.J.: Princeton Univ. Press, 1980.

Stelzig, Eugene. "Is There a Canon of Autobiography?" *a/b: Auto/Biography Studies* 7, no. 1 (Spring 1992): 1–12.

Stendhal. *Souvenirs d'égotisme suivi de Projets d'autobiographie et de Les Privilèges.* Edited by Béatrice Didier. Paris: Gallimard, 1983.

Temmer, Mark J. "Art and Love in the *Confessions* of Jean-Jacques Rousseau." *PMLA* 73 (1958): 215–20.

Todorov, Tzvetan. "L'Etre et l'Autre: Montaigne," trans. Pierre Saint-Amand. In *Montaigne: Essays in Reading,* ed. Gérard Defaux, pp. 113–44. New Haven, Conn.: Yale Univ. Press, 1983.

———. *Symbolism and Interpretation.* Translated by Catherine Porter. Ithaca, N.Y.: Cornell Univ. Press, 1982.

Tripet, Arnaud. *La Rêverie littéraire: Essai sur Rousseau.* Genève: Librairie Droz, 1979.

Vance, Christie McDonald. *The Extravagant Shepherd: A Study of the Pastoral Vision in Rousseau's* Nouvelle Héloïse. In Studies in Voltaire and the Eighteenth Century, ed. Theodore Besterman. Banbury, Oxfordshire: Thorpe Mandeville House, 1973.

Villey, Pierre. *Les Sources et l'évolution des Essais de Montaigne.* 2d rev. ed. 2 vols. Paris: Librairie Hachette, 1933.

Voisine, Jacques. *J.-J. Rousseau en Angleterre à l'époque Romantique: Les Écrits autobiographiques et la légende.* Paris: Librairie Marcel Didier, 1956.

Weintraub, Karl Joachim. *The Value of the Individual: Self and Circumstance in Autobiography.* Chicago: Univ. of Chicago Press, 1978.

White, Hayden. "The Historical Text as Literary Artifact." In *Tropics of Discourse,* pp. 81–100. Baltimore: Johns Hopkins Univ. Press, 1978.

———. "The Value of Narrativity in the Representation of Reality." In *On Narrative,* ed. W. J. T. Mitchell, pp. 1–23. Chicago: Univ. of Chicago Press, 1980.

Williger, Eduard. "Der Aufbau der Konfessionen Augustins." *Zeitschrift für die Neutestementliche Wissenschaft* 28 (1929): 81–106.

Wolfson, Susan J. "The Illusion of Mastery: Wordsworth's Revisions of 'The Drowned Man of Esthwaite,' 1799, 1805, 1850." *PMLA* 99 (1984): 917–35.

Woodring, Carl R. *Politics in English Romantic Poetry.* Cambridge, Mass.: Harvard Univ. Press, 1970.

Wordsworth, Jonathan. "The Five-Book *Prelude* of Early Spring 1804." *Journal of English and Germanic Philology* 76 (1977): 1–25.

———. "The Two-Part *Prelude* of 1799." In *The Prelude: 1799, 1805, 1850,* ed. Jonathan Wordsworth, M. H. Abrams, and Stephen Gill, pp. 567–85. New York: W. W. Norton, 1979.

Bibliography

————, and Stephen Gill. "The Two-Part *Prelude* of 1798–99." *Journal of English and Germanic Philology* 72 (1973): 503–25.

Wordsworth, William. *Poetical Works.* Edited by Thomas Hutchinson. London: Oxford Univ. Press, 1904. Rev. ed., edited by Ernest de Selincourt. Oxford: Oxford Univ. Press, 1936.

————. *"The Prelude," 1798–1799.* Edited by Stephen Parrish. Ithaca, N.Y.: Cornell Univ. Press, 1977.

————. *The Prelude: 1799, 1805, 1850.* Edited by Jonathan Wordsworth, M. H. Abrams, and Stephen Gill. New York: W. W. Norton, 1979.

Wundt, Max. "Augustins Konfessionen." *Zeitschrift für die Neutestamentliche Wissenschaft* 22 (1923): 161–206.

INDEX

Index

Barthes, Roland, 159 nn. 13, 23
Beaujour, Michel, 159 n. 17
Beyle, Henri (Stendhal): as revisionary autobiographer, 6–7, 10, 11; *Souvenirs d'égotisme*, 7, 9, 10, 11, 159 n. 20; *Vie de Henry Brulard*, 10, 11, 159 n. 20
Bible: Augustine on, 17; Augustine's citations from, 31–32, 34–35, 38, 41–42, 43, 44–45; as Augustine's source, 13, 15, 37, 39, 44–45; Montaigne on, 48; Wordsworth on, 142
Biblical figures: Augustine's use of, 2, 37–39; Bunyan's use of, 2; critical readings of, 162 nn. 19, 22, 167 n. 19, 169 n. 13; Montaigne's avoidance of, 48; Rousseau's adaptation of, 78, 95–97, 98; Wordsworth's adaptation of, 115, 122, 124–25, 148. *See also names of individual figures*
Bloom, Harold, 169 n. 11
Blum, Claude, 164 n. 16, 165 n. 21
Brown, Peter, 161–62 n. 14
Buckley, Jerome Hamilton, 157 n. 3
Bunyan, John: influence on Wordsworth, 120; use of biblical figures, 2; *Grace Abounding*, 2, 157 n. 5; *Pilgrim's Progress*, 2, 157 n. 5, 168 n. 6

Carlyle, Thomas: *Sartor Resartus*, 2
Christ, 2
Cohen, J. M., 165 n. 1, 166 n. 10
Coleridge, Samuel Taylor, 119, 134, 141, 169 n. 21, 170 n. 30
Colish, Marcia L., 160 n. 4
Conversion: Augustine's, 39–43, 45, 162 n. 20, 170 n. 28; as autobiographical convention, 3–4, 11, 153, 162 n. 20; and free will, 24; Montaigne's lack of, 69; Romantic, 7; Rousseau's several, 96–97; Wordsworth's alternatives to, 115, 134–36, 169 n. 20
Courcelle, Pierre, 160 n. 1, 160–61 n. 5, 161 n. 6
Cowper, William, 168 n. 6
Culler, Jonathan, 160 n. 24

Darwin, Charles: *Autobiography*, 3, 158 n. 9
Darwin, Frances, 158 n. 9
Davenport, Guy, 164 n. 19

Death: Augustine on, 32–35; Montaigne on, 62; Rousseau's brush with, 108–9; Wordsworth's grief at brother's, 140
Defaux, Gérard, 163 n. 5, 164 n. 10
De Man, Paul, 159 n. 21, 166 nn. 6, 9
De Quincey, Thomas: as revisionary autobiographer, 6–7, 10, 11; as Wordsworth's admirer, 127
—WORKS
Confessions of an English Opium Eater: biblical figures in, 7, 159 n. 19; incongruities in, 8
Suspiria de Profundis, 10
Derrida, Jacques, 166 n. 6
Didier, Béatrice, 159 n. 20
Dreams: Augustine on, 22–24, 161 n. 12; of Montaigne, 57
Dulaey, Martine, 161 n. 12

Eakin, Paul John, 158 n. 10, 159 n. 13, 160 nn. 24, 26
Eakin, Sybil S., 169–70 n. 25, 170 n. 27
Egan, Susanna, 157 n. 3
Eliot, T. S., 157 n. 4
Eternity: Augustine on, 31–32; Montaigne on, 63; Rousseau's sense of, 108; Wordsworth's sense of, 121

Faith: Augustine on, 16, 31–32, 36–37, 45; Montaigne on, 49, 63; Rousseau's version of, 108; Wordsworth on, 121, 142, 150
Fall: as allusion in Wordsworth's *Prelude*, 124–25; as autobiographical convention, 169 n. 13; as trope in Rousseau's *Confessions*, 96–97, 166–67 n. 16
Fleishman, Avrom, 157 n. 3, 160 nn. 1, 24, 167 n. 19
Fleuret, Colette, 165 n. 3
Foucault, Michel, 167 n. 20
Frame, Donald M., 163 nn. 1, 3, 7, 164 n. 8, 164–65 n. 19
France, Peter, 165 n. 1
Franklin, Benjamin: *Autobiography*, 2
Freccaro, John, 162 n. 20

Gadamer, Hans-Georg, 161 n. 9
Gibbon, Edward: *Memoirs*, 3, 158 n. 9
Gill, Stephen, 167 n. 1, 168 n. 5

Index

Ginsberg, Warren, 162 n. 19
Goodman, Nelson, 159 n. 23, 160 n. 24
Gosse, Edmund: *Father and Son,* 2
Gossman, Lionel, 165 n. 2
Guitton, Jean, 161–62 n. 14, 162 n. 20
Gunn, Janet Varner, 160 n. 24
Gusdorf, Georges, 159 n. 16

Haney, David P., 168 n. 4
Harpham, Geoffrey Galt, 162 n. 20
Hartman, Geoffrey, 168 n. 8, 169 n. 20, 170
    n. 33
Haydn, Hiram, 164 n. 15
Hayter, Alethea, 159 n. 19
Helsinger, Elizabeth K., 160 n. 26
History: Christian conception of, 158 n. 8;
    classical conception of, 158 n. 8
Hopkins, Brooke, 162 n. 22, 169 n. 13

Interpretation: Augustine on, 16, 18, 19;
    Montaigne on, 75–77; as ongoing act,
    161 n. 9; Rousseau on, 85–87; Words-
    worth on, 148–49

Jackson, Susan K., 159 n. 17
Johnston, Kenneth R., 168 n. 7
Joukovsky, F., 164 nn. 11, 14
Joyce, James, 10–11

Keats, John: quoted on beauty, 7; quoted
    on individual, 1, 11; quoted on poetic
    character, 122
Kellog, Robert, 157 n. 4
Kermode, Frank, 159 nn. 14, 23, 162 n. 18,
    165 n. 23
Kroeber, Karl, 168 nn. 2, 12, 169 n. 22

Landow, George P., 160 n. 26
Langbaum, Robert, 169 n. 14
Language: Augustine on, 33, 36–37, 44,
    160 n. 4; figural, 11; and *jouissance,* 8;
    Montaigne on, 59–60, 70, 75; and ref-
    erence, 7–8, 159 n. 21, 164 n. 10; Rous-
    seau on, 82–83, 84, 104, 107, 108, 109–
    11; and self, 160 n. 26; Wordsworth's
    use of, 123
Lawrence, D. H., 10
Lejeune, Philippe, 158 n. 10, 167 n. 18
Life design: Augustine on, 30–36, 44–45;

Montaigne on, 46–48, 67, 68–69, 71–
    73; Rousseau on, 92, 99, 103; Words-
    worth on, 120–22, 140–41
Life writing: Augustine on, 37, 44–45;
    Montaigne on, 49–50, 54, 65, 67, 70–
    71; Rousseau on, 78–79, 81, 82, 85–87,
    102, 104, 109–11, 114; Wordsworth on,
    131–33

Man: Augustine on, 17, 22, 23–24, 30–31,
    44; Montaigne on, 47, 52–53, 57, 62–
    63, 71, 74–75; Rousseau on, 79, 93;
    Wordsworth on, 121
Mandel, Barret J., 160 n. 25
Matthews, William, 157–58 n. 7
May, Gita, 160 n. 11
Memory: Augustine on, 16, 20–30, 44, 161
    nn. 10, 11; Augustine's images for, 22;
    and Augustinian dreams, 22, 27; and
    Augustinian meaning, 24–25, 26; and
    Augustinian reason, 20, 23–24; in au-
    tobiographical act, 12; and imagina-
    tion, 4, 108, 159 n. 11; and mimesis, 1,
    4, 6–12, 153–54; modern, 10, 153; mod-
    ern theories of, 24; Montaigne on,
    54–62; nature of, 1, 157 nn. 1, 2; revi-
    sionary, 4, 9–10, 134, 151, 160 n. 25;
    Romantic, 6–7, 154; and Rousseauian
    sensation, 111; Rousseau on, 86, 92,
    99–100, 110, 114; Wordsworthian, 116,
    117, 120, 122, 123–24, 125, 127–29, 130,
    131–34, 136–40, 141–42, 147–48, 151,
    169 n. 14
Metaphor: in autobiographical act, 12; and
    memory, 4; nature of, 1, 157 n. 2; Ro-
    mantic, 6; self-realization in, 11–12;
    Wordsworthian, 116, 117, 122, 123–24
Mill, John Stuart: *Autobiography,* 3, 158
    n. 9
Mimesis: in autobiographical act, 12;
    Christian, 2–4; classical, 4; and mem-
    ory, 1, 4, 6–12, 153–54; modern, 10;
    and myth, 8; nature of, 1, 157 nn. 1, 2;
    Romantic, 6–7; Wordsworthian, 116,
    127
Misch, Georg, 157 n. 3
Moderns: autobiographical tendencies of,
    6, 10–11; and stream-of-consciousness,
    6

181

Index

Montaigne, Michel de: actions, 58–59; and ancients, 59–61, 62–63, 164 nn. 11, 13, 14; on art, 65–67, 68, 71–72; Augustine contrasted to, 46, 48, 53, 56, 63; on authors, 71–72, 76, 165 n. 23; avoidance of autobiographical tropes, 69; and Bible, 48, 63; borrowings, 48, 58, 60–62, 77; on chance, 64, 67, 68, 76; on change, 46, 47–48, 56–57, 64–65, 67–68, 71; as a Christian, 49, 63–64; contradicting himself, 47–48, 49, 55–56, 64, 67, 77, 163 nn. 2, 4; and death, 61, 62; on diversity, 47–48, 53, 57, 62, 64–65, 71, 72, 75, 77, 163 nn. 2, 3, 4; on eternity, 63; on friendship, 50–51; on his *Essays*, 47, 49–50, 52, 54, 55, 57, 58, 60–61, 65–66, 67, 68, 69, 70, 71, 72, 73–74, 76, 77; influence on Rousseau, 108–9, 165 n. 3, 167 n. 24; on interpretation, 75–77; on invention, 55–62; on judgment, 54–55, 65; and La Boétie, 50–51, 163 n. 6; on language, 59–60, 70, 75; on learning, 55, 58, 61–62, 63, 74–75, 77; on life design, 46–48, 67, 68–69, 71–73; on life writing, 49–50, 54, 65, 67, 70–71; on man, 47, 48, 52–53, 57, 62–63, 71, 74–75; and Marie de Gournay, 163 n. 7; on memory, 54–62; moods, 55–56, 57, 59; on narrative, 72; on nature, 65–67; as own reader, 76–77; on philosophy, 57; on questing, 46, 49, 69, 73, 74–75, 77; and readers, 50–52, 53, 65, 74, 76–77; reading, 53, 57–58, 60, 62; reveries, 57, 59, 60, 77, 108–9; as revisionary autobiographer, 5–6, 10, 11, 117; Rousseau compared to, 81; Rousseau's critique of, 79, 81; on the self, 5, 63, 67–68, 164 nn. 17, 18; on self-interpretation, 46, 49–50, 52, 71, 83; sense of his self, 58–59, 61–62, 68; on sincerity, 75; on solitude, 52; speaking, 51–52; thinking, 53–54, 55, 59, 74; in time, 46, 48, 62–63, 67–68, 69, 77, 164 n. 17; on truth, 49, 57, 73, 74–75, 133; on unity, 65, 163 n. 2; on universality, 163 nn. 3, 4; Wordsworth contrasted to, 115; writing, 51–52, 53, 55, 57–58, 60, 62, 69, 72, 74

—WORKS

Essays: (*a*) (*b*) (*c*) strata, 47, 69, 165 n. 22; additions to, 71; allusiveness in, 73–74; as autobiography, 5–6, 54, 62; disjointed style, 47, 69–70, 72, 77; drunkard metaphor, 71; editions, 10; form, 69, 70, 74, 164–65 n. 19; imagery, 73, 74; nonnarrative mode, 69, 72; personae, 5; portrait-painting metaphor, 65–68; reasons for writing, 49–52; revisions, 70, 164 n. 16, 165 n. 21; topics, 73–74, 75, 77; traveling metaphor, 69

Morris, John N., 168 n. 6

Morrissey, Robert J., 165 n. 20, 167 n. 21

Nabokov, Vladimir: *Speak, Memory,* 10, 11

Narrative: and human experience, 159–60 n. 24; morality of, 159 n. 22; potentiality of, 162 n. 15; structures, 159 nn. 22, 23

Nature: Rousseau on, 113–14; Wordsworth on, 121, 133

Newman, John Henry: *Apologia pro vita sua,* 2, 157 n. 6

Newton, John, 168 n. 6

Olney, James, 157 n. 3, 158 n. 12

Owens, W. R., 157 n. 5

Paradise: as autobiographical convention, 3–4, 153; as figure in Wordsworth's *Prelude,* 121, 123, 124–25; as trope in De Quincey's *Confessions,* 159 n. 19; as trope in Rousseau's *Confessions,* 95, 97, 166–67 n. 16, 167 n. 19

Parrish, Stephen, 168 n. 5

Pascal, Roy, 158 n. 11

Past: autobiographical nature of, 6; as seen from Augustine's present, 20–22, 27–28, 161 n. 11; as seen from Montaigne's present, 67, 71; as seen from Rousseau's present, 85–86, 104, 108, 109–11, 114; as seen from Wordsworth's present, 131–33, 136–38; as seen from writing present, 3, 69

Pater, Walter: "The Child in the House," 2

Paul, Saint, 2, 38–39

Peterson, Linda H., 157 nn. 5, 6, 168 n. 6

Index